SHAKESPEARE SURVEY

SHAKESPEARE SURVEY

AN ANNUAL SURVEY OF
SHAKESPEARIAN STUDY & PRODUCTION

14

EDITED BY

ALLARDYCE NICOLL

Issued under the Sponsorship of

THE UNIVERSITY OF BIRMINGHAM
THE UNIVERSITY OF MANCHESTER
THE SHAKESPEARE MEMORIAL THEATRE
THE SHAKESPEARE BIRTHPLACE TRUST

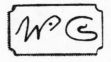

CAMBRIDGE
AT THE UNIVERSITY PRESS
1970

Published by the Syndics of the Cambridge University Press
Bentley House, 200 Euston Road, London N.W. 1
American Branch: 32 East 57th Street, New York, N.Y. 10022

ISBN 0 521 06427 9

First published 1961
Reprinted 1966 1970

Printed in Great Britain
at the University Printing House, Cambridge
(Brooke Crutchley, University Printer)

EDITOR'S NOTE

The present volume of *Shakespeare Survey* is largely concerned with Shakespeare and his contemporaries—the topic which formed the basis for discussion at the Shakespeare Conference, Stratford-upon-Avon, in September 1959. Of the articles printed here those by Marco Mincoff, I. A. Shapiro, Harold Jenkins and T. J. B. Spencer are based on lectures delivered on that occasion.

For the next, the fifteenth, volume, the central theme will be 'Shakespeare's Poems and Music'. The latest date for consideration of articles for Volume 16, the central theme of which will be 'Shakespeare in the Modern World', is 1 January 1962. Contributions offered for publication should be addressed to: The Editor, *Shakespeare Survey*, The Shakespeare Institute (University of Birmingham), Stratford-upon-Avon.

CONTENTS

[*Notes are placed at the end of each contribution. All line references are to the 'Globe' edition, and, unless for special reasons, quotations are from this text*]

LIST OF PLATES

STUDIES IN ELIZABETHAN AND JACOBEAN DRAMA SINCE 1900

BY

ARTHUR BROWN

Towards the end of his article, 'Studies in the Elizabethan Stage since 1900', in *Shakespeare Survey*, 1 (1948), Allardyce Nicoll considered future lines of research in this field and remarked, 'the already existent inquiries into particular, as opposed to general, problems have been seen to have yielded matter of prime interest. We need more of these, conducted with the most rigorous selectivity.' The same principle applies, I believe, to the material to be considered in this paper. A survey of the work produced on Elizabethan and Jacobean Drama (excluding Shakespeare for this purpose) over the last sixty years reveals fairly clearly a retreat from studies with the wide sweep of F. E. Schelling's *Elizabethan Drama 1558–1642* or W. Creizenach's *The English Drama in the Age of Shakespeare*; their place has been taken, in general, by more detailed examinations of the work of individual authors, of individual plays, of distinctive dramatic forms, and by specialized studies of theatres, companies, and acting technique. Bibliographical and textual studies have placed a salutary check on fanciful interpretation and emendation, and have shown how dangerously little is still known about the essential basis of all our work—the author's text and its transmission. The half-century has, in short, tended to be a period of stock-taking, old ideas being subjected to a more critical scrutiny in the light of, for example, more detailed knowledge arising from new documentary evidence, and new ideas tending to be based more firmly on evidence as opposed to conjecture and, as a result, tending to be more limited in scope. It is a stock-taking which no one will regret; it is by no means yet approaching its end.

A purely chronological approach to the period is perhaps not the most instructive way of viewing it, since many of the newer methods and disciplines mentioned briefly in the preceding paragraph grew up and developed in parallel. I intend, therefore, to work from general to more particular works, and to treat each section chronologically within itself. This will require a certain amount of cross-reference from section to section, but will show more clearly how fruitful has been a series of specialized methods, and how from time to time their intersection has been especially productive.

I. GENERAL WORKS

Fundamental to the period under survey and to research as far ahead as one can see are two works of astonishing scope and scholarship, E. K. Chambers' *Elizabethan Stage* (1923) and G. E. Bentley's *The Jacobean and Caroline Stage*, the first volume of which appeared in 1941 and the last in 1956. Nicoll referred to the former as 'a convenient and commodious halfway house on the road of research wherein we may rest and contemplate earlier accomplishments'. Both the former and the latter are more than this, for by their accumulation and arrangement of so much basic material they form inevitable starting-points for further investigations. Ironically they have been so successful in this respect that on a number of points they are already out of date; yet these shortcomings pale into insignificance against the steady light with which they have illuminated all aspects of Elizabethan and Jacobean drama.

Other more general studies which deserve notice are A. W. Reed's *Early Tudor Drama* (1926), which produced valuable documentary evidence from the early part of the sixteenth century for the importance of the 'More circle' in the history of drama; and U. M. Ellis-Fermor's *The Jacobean Drama* (first published in 1936, but still being reprinted), which, accepting T. S. Eliot's remark that the time had passed for estimates of the Elizabethan and Jacobean dramatists, nevertheless set out to consider 'the outstanding work of less than a dozen playwrights, chiefly in regard to certain dominant lines of thought and habits of dramatic technique'. Although at times highly individualistic and perhaps over-imaginative, this work is still stimulating, and capable of arousing that degree of either agreement or disagreement necessary for the further development of ideas. L. C. Knights' *Drama and Society in the Age of Jonson* (1937) is best explained by its sub-title, 'Economic and Social Background to Early 17th Century Drama', a field of research which is still being cropped to some profit. F. P. Wilson's all too brief *Elizabethan and Jacobean* (1945) succeeded in correcting an astonishing number of misconceptions with an equally astonishing conciseness. Alfred Harbage's works on theatres and audiences, especially his *Shakespeare and the Rival Traditions* (1952), may properly be mentioned here as being the source of much useful work which stretches beyond the apparent limits of his subject. Madeleine Doran's *Endeavors of Art: A Study of Form in Elizabethan Drama* (1954) is probably the most important of recent works in this section. She attempts a synthesis of the many studies which have been made of the various parts of the background against which the dramatists worked—critical theory, rhetorical theory and education, inherited literary forms, theatrical conventions, ideas about style, and so on. She gives an extremely detailed and valuable account of the context of ideas and assumptions about literature which resulted. Not an easy book to read, it is, nevertheless, one which must be consulted again and again by scholars of this period, and her remarks about Jonson are not the least important part of her work. These, then, are the most outstanding general contributions of the period. Considerations of space have made some omissions inevitable, but I do not believe that they affect the general picture; already in works of considerable scope it is possible to see a narrowing of the subject-matter to be treated, and the results have amply repaid this discipline.[1]

2. DRAMATIC FORMS

It seems possible also to see an increase in the number of studies devoted to distinctive dramatic forms during this century, although this tendency began quite early. The century opened with Schelling's *The English Chronicle Play* (1902), and was soon followed by Sir Walter Greg's *Pastoral Poetry and Pastoral Drama* (1906); Greg's name will appear many times in this article, and it is significant to note how his period of activity spans our period (his last published work appearing at the end of 1959), and how his fields of activity move from one section to another. It will be some time before his full influence on Elizabethan and Jacobean dramatic scholarship during the last sixty years can be properly assessed, but it may well be found that the tendency towards examination of particular as opposed to general problems, towards the establishment of solid body of evidence as opposed to conjecture, owes a very great deal to the rigid standards which he set for himself and which, as appears in his many reviews, he expected from others. F. H. Ristine published his *English Tragi-Comedy: Its Origin and History* in 1910, and it is perhaps fair to say that this particular genre is by no means exhausted in spite of a number of later excellent studies. The same may be said about the topics treated in the next two works, W. Smith's *The Commedia dell'Arte: A Study in Italian Popular Comedy* (1912), and F. S. Boas' *University Drama in the Tudor Age* (1914). Both topics are still capable of further development, and the former work was in fact largely superseded by Miss Kathleen M. Lea's *Italian Popular Comedy* (1934); yet both seem to require qualities oddly lacking in the present generation of young scholars. R. M. Smith's *Froissart and the English Chronicle Play* appeared in 1915, and R. Withington's still valuable *English Pageantry* in 1918–20, material from the latter being given a new lease of life in Glynne Wickham's *Early English Stages 1300–1660*, the first volume of which appeared in 1959. A. H. Thorndike's *English Comedy* (1929) was followed by the first of M. C. Bradbrook's important studies, *Themes and Conventions of Elizabethan Tragedy* (1935); the companion volume, *Growth and Structure of Elizabethan Comedy*, came twenty years later, in 1955, and was thus able to make use of the results of Harbage's and Doran's researches, though not, unfortunately, of Marvin T. Herrick's *Comic Theory in the Sixteenth Century*. Abandoning chronology for a moment, it is interesting to note how in 1955 Miss Bradbrook's Introduction reflects the agnosticism of present-day scholarship in this field: 'The development of Elizabethan and Jacobean drama cannot readily be plotted. Too many factors are involved. The older historians, such as F. E. Schelling, attempted some classification through the subject-matter of the plays, but only in the most general way.' She goes on to mention some recent studies of special forms, 'which depend on a new understanding of the poetic principles underlying dramatic composition', and shows how an awareness of rhetorical forms and popular traditions is, amongst other things, essential if we are to reach a better understanding of what our dramatists were attempting to do. It is also important to note her point that 'Comedy has received comparatively little attention from critics, perhaps because its ingredients are more varied and its lines of development less obvious than those of the well-marked forms of tragedy and history. Yet comedies outnumber tragedies on the Elizabethan stage by nearly three to one.' Here, surely, is a matter for serious consideration, although it is true that there are welcome signs of a growing interest in this genre.

Miss Bradbrook's statement may be exemplified by a brief mention of some of the important studies of special forms which appeared between her first and second books. Willard Farnham's *Medieval Heritage of Elizabethan Tragedy* was published in 1936, and happily reprinted in 1956; with a wealth of illustration and sound scholarship he made it clear beyond doubt that 'the English stage under Elizabeth was notable among the national stages of Europe in its time by being the particular, and on the whole unapologetic, heir of the medieval stage. It is only fitting that tragedy upon the Elizabethan stage should have accepted with the same particularity and in the same spirit a medieval heritage which was wider than the dramatic....' In 1940 Fredson Bowers, later to transfer his formidable energy to a different aspect of Elizabethan drama, produced his *Elizabethan Revenge Tragedy, 1587–1642*, and in 1943 came H. H. Adams' *English Domestic or Homiletic Tragedy, 1575–1642*. The earlier works on history and chronicle plays noted above were put in perspective by E. M. W. Tillyard's more specialized *Shakespeare's History Plays* (1944), but that the last word is still far from having been said on these plays is indicated by the position taken up by Irving Ribner in his *The English History Play in the Age of Shakespeare* (1957). This was the culmination of a long series of articles by Ribner, who, dissatisfied with many of the previous definitions of the genre, attempted to establish 'specific standards by which we may distinguish history plays from other plays of the Elizabethan era', a task not made any easier by the somewhat loose employment of the word 'history' at that time. For Ribner the essential feature involves an understanding of what the Elizabethans considered to be the purposes of history, and these he works out under two general headings: those which stemmed from classical and humanist philosophies of history, and those which stemmed from the medieval Christian philosophy of history. It will be noticed how often in this section important works have been concerned with getting back to the roots of Elizabethan drama; the tendency has been to look upon it less and less as a sudden and unpredictable outburst, and more and more to attempt to explain how and why it happened. Patient and detailed research into the sources of its inspiration is bearing fruit, and the picture now taking shape differs in many important respects from that in vogue at the beginning of the century. This section may, therefore, fittingly close with mention of another work which points to another body of material oddly neglected in the past, T. W. Craik's *The Tudor Interlude* (1958). Too often regarded as a rough and unworthy ancestor of the great drama to follow, the Interlude is now beginning to attract much more attention from critic and textual scholar alike, and may well repay this attention by providing the answers, or at least clues to them, to a great number of problems involving dramatic themes and their treatment, staging, and the transmission of texts.

It is convenient to mention at this point a few recent books of a more specialized nature than those included in the preceding paragraph, which may give some indication of the directions in which research may profitably be undertaken. Two volumes dealing with Comedy appeared in 1955, and suggest, however tentatively, that the warning sounded by Miss Bradbrook in that year of the neglect of this subject may have already occurred to other scholars. A collection of English Institute Essays, under the editorship of W. K. Wimsatt, Jr., entitled *English Stage Comedy*, included a study by R. L. Heffner, Jr. of 'Unifying Symbols in the Comedy of Ben Jonson'. Heffner attempted to define the 'unity of inspiration' which Eliot and others have found in Jonson's comedy, and to describe the dramatic devices by which it is expressed. Coming as it does in the company of essays devoted to Shakespeare, Restoration Comedy, Bernard Shaw, and T. S. Eliot, Heffner's takes on added importance in that it allows Jonson to be examined in a wider context than is usual, a method which may well be suitable for other dramatists of our period. The second work was J. V. Curry's *Deception in Elizabethan Comedy*, in which a great number of plays from the years 1553 to 1616 were examined from the point of view of their deliberate use of deception of one kind or another. Although this approach courts the risk of over-classification, it can throw new light upon dramatic methods which have been too much taken for granted. Baldwin Maxwell's *Studies in the Shakespeare Apocrypha* (1956) may be commended rather for its procedure than for its results, which tend to be largely negative; but his scrupulously fair and detailed examination of what can be discovered about the chequered history of four plays which have at various times been attributed to Shakespeare is a model of its kind. Similarly, C. L. Barber's *The Idea of Honour in the English Drama 1591–1700* (1957) gives some indication of the vast amount of material still waiting to be treated from a linguistic point of view; it may be noted that this matter has been raised more than once by Dr Alice Walker and others in their reviews of recent editions of Shakespeare and his fellows, and it is, of course, closely linked up with the bibliographer's approach to textual problems.

3. TEXTUAL STUDIES

It is desirable to survey textual, bibliographical, and palaeographical studies next, since these seem to me to occupy a central position in the sixty years under review, and an examination of editions and studies of individual authors cannot well proceed without taking them into account. Significantly Sir Walter Greg appears very early on the scene, with his *List of English Plays written before 1643 and printed before 1700* (1900), followed two years later by his *List of Masques, Pageants, &c.*, works which were later to develop into his great *A Bibliography of the English Printed Drama to the Restoration* (1939–59). It is no exaggeration to say that without this remarkable piece of scholarship any significant advance in the study of Elizabethan and Jacobean drama would be impossible. Between 1904 and 1908 Greg placed us still further in his debt with his edition of Henslowe's *Diary*, and in 1907 with his *Henslowe Papers*. The new disciplines were strengthened about the same time by R. B. McKerrow's five-volume edition of the *Works* of Thomas Nashe (1904–10), while a new source of information was being made available by A. Feuillerat's *Documents relating to the Office of the Revels in the Time of Queen Elizabeth* (1908), to be followed in 1914 by his *Documents relating to the Revels at Court in the Time of King Edward VI and Queen Mary*. A. W. Pollard's *Shakespeare Folios and Quartos* appeared in 1909, R. B. McKerrow's *Dictionary of Printers and Booksellers 1557–1640* in 1910, Percy Simpson's *Shakespearian Punctuation* in 1911, McKerrow's *Printers' and Publishers' Devices 1485–1640* in 1913, E. M. Thompson's *Shakespeare's Handwriting* in 1916, Pollard's *Shakespeare's Fight with the Pirates* in 1917, and J. Q. Adams' *Dramatic Records of Sir Henry Herbert* in 1917. It is worth pausing for a moment to contemplate the richness of the scholarship of this kind during the first twenty years of this century, and to ask where we should be now without it. In many respects some of it may be out of date, yet these pioneer works are still consulted with a frequency which many more modern authors may well envy, and even those which at first sight may seem remote from the study of drama have all had their contribution to make to our present state of knowledge. It may be added that McKerrow's *Introduction to Bibliography*, through which our present generation for the most part made its first acquaintance with the intricacies of textual problems, although not published until 1927, had already appeared in its earlier form in the *Transactions of the Bibliographical Society* in 1914. In all these the foundations of modern textual study were well and truly laid; exacting standards were established and methods of procedure were subject to close scrutiny. Manuscripts and early printed books were no longer objects of mere curiosity, but were being examined with a knowledge and a discipline which made them reveal their own stories to the great enrichment of our understanding of what their authors intended. The study of dramatic manuscripts in particular received a further impetus from Greg's two volumes, *Dramatic Documents from the Elizabethan Playhouses* (1931), and, as was mentioned above, the first volume of his *Bibliography* dealing with printed plays appeared in 1939.

Greg's recent death was a sad loss to scholarship. Yet the methods which he, with McKerrow, Pollard and others, did so much to establish are being adapted and developed by his successors, and if something of the original optimism of bibliographers has vanished—as it was sure to do when the complexity of the problems involved was more fully appreciated—the results so far attained have assured it of a respectable position among academic disciplines. A host of younger scholars has moved into the field, sometimes, one feels, with more enthusiasm than is strictly legitimate in the circumstances; new experiments are being tested in areas often untouched by the earlier workers, and provided that the original standards are not relaxed results in the future should be at least as significant as those we have now. Certainly under the guidance of Fredson Bowers there seems to be no reason to suspect that standards *will* be relaxed. In his *Principles of Bibliographical Description* (1949), his *On Editing Shakespeare and other Elizabethan Dramatists* (1955), his *Textual and Literary Criticism* (1959), and his many shorter articles in periodicals, he has shown himself no easy taskmaster, and his edition of the plays of Dekker (to be referred to more fully later) is a very prominent landmark in the provision of reliable texts of our dramatists. At the same time his encouragement of the research of others finds an outlet in his editorship of the annual *Studies in Bibliography* from the University of Virginia (which began in 1948), in which, to mention only one example, the Beaumont and Fletcher canon is receiving a much-needed overhaul in a series of articles by Cyrus Hoy. Nor is Charlton Hinman's work on the First Folio irrelevant here, for much of the information which he is making available about the printing of Shakespeare's plays will have to be taken into account by future editors of other Elizabethan dramatists. It seems reasonable to prophesy that for some considerable time to come we shall find this aspect of our studies much more prominent than others, and this is as it should be.

4. General Editions

For it cannot be said that the present state of editions of Elizabethan and Jacobean plays gives cause for satisfaction. At the beginning of the century it is true that most of the prominent dramatists were available in one form or another; but most of these old editions, whether of individual dramatists or of collections of plays, have long been out of print, and even when still accessible they are not of the quality that would allow a modern scholar to use them with confidence. This point has been made a number of times in recent years, not least by a group of scholars of the Modern Language Association of America who have considered the needs of Renaissance dramatic studies, and have emphasized the distressing fact that there is almost no important dramatist of the period whose works have been treated in the light of up-to-date textual knowledge. A few exceptions will be mentioned later. The picture is to some extent clouded by the disagreement of scholars over the kind of edition that is needed, and the claims of old-spelling enthusiasts, modernized-spelling enthusiasts, and facsimile enthusiasts will no doubt continue to be urged for a long time to come. Yet some progress has been made in the last sixty years. I shall mention first some of the more important series of plays which have been produced, and then pass to editions of individual authors.

The first volume of W. Bang's *Materialien zur Kunde des Älteren Englischen Dramas, The Blind Beggar of Bednall Green* (1659), appeared in 1902, and by 1914 forty-four volumes had appeared. From 1927 this series was continued as *Materials for the Study of the Old English Drama* under the editorship of Henry de Vocht. It is still happily in progress, although of late the volumes have not been appearing with their former regularity. In an obituary notice on Bang, de Vocht remarked of this series that 'it aimed at equipping scholars throughout all countries with absolutely necessary material, and especially at replacing the otherwise magnificent editions of the great English dramatists, highly desirable for literators and readers in general, by more objective texts: texts, namely, in which orthography and punctuation are *not* brought up to date; in which difficult and obscure passages are *not* replaced by what seems to be the most acceptable correction; in which even misprints and evident mistakes are *not* set right'. An austere programme, indeed, and one which would not altogether appeal to the most rigid of our present-day textual scholars! Yet at the time it was undoubtedly a healthy sign, and it is interesting to note that both Greg and McKerrow took part in the production of some of these volumes, and that Bang likewise contributed to the first volume of *Collections* of the Malone Society, of which he was an honorary member from 1906 to 1934.

The Malone Society was founded in 1906 at the suggestion of A. W. Pollard, who pointed out that 'every generation will need to make its own critical editions to suit its own critical taste, but that work of permanent utility can be done by placing in the hands of students at large such reproductions of the original textual authorities as may make constant and continuous reference to those originals themselves unnecessary'. Greg, Pollard, McKerrow, E. K. Chambers and F. S. Boas saw the new society off to a good start, and its first six volumes appeared in 1907. The story of its first fifty years has been well told by F. P. Wilson in its *Collections IV* (1956), and need not be repeated here. One or two points may, however, be noted. Up to 1959 the Society had published 110 volumes; of these seventy were reprints of early printed plays, thirty were editions of plays in manuscript, and ten were volumes or parts of *Collections*, the last being miscellaneous documents relating to the English drama. Complete texts have been provided of Greene, Peele, and Lodge, and two each of the plays of Lyly, Marlowe and Chapman have been included. The Society's principles and methods have been criticized from time to time, often, it may be suspected, by people who have simply misunderstood them; yet they have stood the test of time, the resulting volumes are generally regarded as possessing a very high degree of authority, and there seems to be little reason for any radical change in its habits for a long time to come.

It has been, and possibly still is, fashionable to speak slightingly of the work of J. S. Farmer, whose *Tudor Facsimile Texts* appeared between 1907 and 1913. It is true that the most up-to-date methods of photography were not available to him, and it is true that the volumes in the series vary greatly in quality. Yet there must be many hundreds of scholars who have uttered prayers of thanksgiving for the existence of what is still, after all, a most valuable basic tool of research. One might also add that the enthusiasts for photographic facsimiles of dramatic texts have a long way to go before they catch up with Farmer's achievement. On his edited texts it is charitable to be silent; but this should in no way detract from his merit in having seen what was required at the time and in settling down to fulfil this requirement.

It would be neither possible nor profitable to rehearse the names of all who, during the last sixty years, have produced anthologies of the plays of this period, whether they be collections of tragedies, or of comedies, or of pre- or post-Shakespearian plays. All of them have helped, it may be admitted, to circulate material widely; few, if any, of them would measure up to the standards of editing now required. Special mention may be made, however, of those works which stand apart from the general run of such collections: C. F. Tucker Brooke's *The Shakespeare Apocrypha* (1908), R. W. Bond's *Early Plays from the Italian* (1911), and J. W. Cunliffe's

Early English Classical Tragedies (1912). A much more recent venture which is bound to attract a great deal of attention is the launching of the series called 'The Revels Plays' under the general editorship of Clifford Leech. Two volumes have appeared, Middleton's *The Changeling*, edited by N. W. Bawcutt (1958), and Kyd's *The Spanish Tragedy*, edited by Philip Edwards (1959). These volumes are to be edited with the same critical standards and the same physical presentation as the well-known 'Arden Shakespeare'; they will have an editorial introduction, a text in modernized spelling, collations and notes on the same page, and a glossary. The General Editor, aware that editorial principles as far as these plays are concerned are only gradually becoming plain, has stated that there will be no hesitation in introducing modifications into the series should the necessity arise. It is also intended to keep in mind the special needs of actors and producers, especially in those sections of the volumes devoted to staging and stage history. The immediate danger that seems to arise is that of attempting too much in a single volume, but it is too early to pass judgement yet.[2]

5. EDITIONS OF INDIVIDUAL AUTHORS

In the next two sections, those dealing with editions of individual authors and with studies of individual authors, it will be convenient to abandon a strictly chronological account and present the material for each dramatist in turn. Kyd's plays were edited by F. S. Boas in 1901, and the edition was reprinted in 1955; apart from the edition of *The Spanish Tragedy* mentioned above nothing else has been done. The works of Marlowe were edited by Tucker Brooke in 1910. A series of separate volumes, *The Works and Life of Christopher Marlowe*, began to appear in 1930 under the general editorship of R. H. Case: *The Life of Marlowe and Dido Queen of Carthage*, edited by Tucker Brooke, appeared in 1930, as did *Tamburlaine*, edited by U. M. Ellis-Fermor; *The Jew of Malta and The Massacre at Paris*, edited by H. S. Bennett, appeared in 1931; in the same year the *Poems* were edited by L. C. Martin; *Dr Faustus* was edited by F. S. Boas in 1932, and *Edward II* by H. B. Charlton and R. D. Waller in 1933 (second edition, revised by F. N. Lees, in 1955). The editorial methods in these volumes were similar to those of the 'Arden Shakespeare'. A revised edition of the old 'Everyman's Library' *Marlowe's Plays and Poems* was produced with an excellent introduction by M. R. Ridley in 1955. *Dr Faustus* received individual attention from Greg in 1950 in his edition of the two texts of 1604 and 1616, which is likely to remain the standard work on the play.

Ben Jonson has fared better than most of his fellows with the eleven-volume edition of his *Works* by C. H. Herford and Percy Simpson (1925–52). A scholarly edition of his *Masque of Gipsies* was produced by Greg in 1952. Chapman seems to have remained untouched since T. M. Parrott's *The Tragedies of George Chapman* (1910) and *The Comedies of George Chapman* (1914). A. Glover and A. R. Waller edited *The Works of Francis Beaumont and John Fletcher* between 1905 and 1912, but it is unlikely that anyone will do anything more about them until the conclusions reached by Cyrus Hoy on problems of canon and collaboration have been tested and digested. F. L. Lucas' *The Complete Works of John Webster* has remained the standard edition since 1927 but is now out of print, and 'present costs of republication in full', we are told, 'are prohibitive'. In 1958, therefore, it was decided to re-issue, as two separate volumes, *The White Devil* and *The Duchess of Malfi*. Allardyce Nicoll edited *The Works of Cyril Tourneur* in 1929, and this remains the standard edition. There has been no complete edition of Middleton during the last sixty years, but *A Game at Chess* was edited by R. C. Bald in 1929, *Hengist King of Kent* by R. C. Bald in 1938, and *The Changeling* by N. W. Bawcutt in 'The Revels Plays' in 1958. *The Plays of John Marston* were edited by H. Harvey Wood, 1934–9. There has been no complete edition of Heywood, but his *The Rape of Lucrece* was edited by A. Holaday in 1950. One begins to realize what was in F. P. Wilson's mind when he wrote in the Malone Society's *Collections IV* (1956), 'How few are the editions of plays written before 1642 which satisfy the demands of modern scholarship!' One exception must be *The Dramatic Works of Thomas Dekker* edited by Fredson Bowers, the first volume of which appeared in 1953, the second in 1955, and the third in 1958; the fourth volume may well have appeared by the time these words are in print. Bowers has set out to provide a critical old-spelling text of the plays, and in his first volume gave some account of the principles upon which such a text had been constructed. In all cases the first editions, the only ones set from manuscript, provide the copy-text. As many copies of the first edition as possible have been examined to identify press-variants, and these have been considered on their own merits before being incorporated into the edited text. Finicky emendation has been avoided, but where, in the editor's opinion, the copy-text was corrupt, he has not hesitated to emend 'with due regard to bibliographical and palaeographical probabilities'. Certain silent alterations have been admitted in matters purely typographical or concerned with the formal presentation of the text, such as speech-headings and stage-directions, but not in matters which affect the text itself where attention is drawn to emendations. It will be seen from this very brief and incomplete account that Bowers' methods differ in almost every important respect from those of previous editors. He is quite deliberately putting into practice the accumulated theory of fifty years of textual scholarship in this field, and although he himself would be the first to admit that there is still room for improvement in a number of matters—punctuation, for example, about which we are still very much in the dark as far as the Elizabethans are concerned—his edition of Dekker will have to be taken into account very seriously by editors in the future. An editorial task is quite clearly one which can no longer be undertaken in an amateurish or light-hearted fashion.

6. STUDIES OF INDIVIDUAL AUTHORS

Marlowe has received a good deal of attention from critics and biographers, and the following works may be particularly noted. J. H. Ingram's *Christopher Marlowe and his Associates* was published in 1904, Leslie Hotson's *The Assassination of Christopher Marlowe* in 1925, and Ellis-Fermor's *Christopher Marlowe* in 1927. F. S. Boas' valuable and frequently neglected *Marlowe and His Circle* (1929) made available facsimiles of important documents which some later writers would have done well to study more closely before venturing into the realms of attractive but unfounded conjecture. Tucker Brooke's *Life of Marlowe* appeared in 1930, Mark Eccles' *Marlowe in London* in 1934, M. K. Mincoff's *Christopher Marlowe, A Study of His Development* in 1937, John Bakeless' *Christopher Marlowe* in 1938, and F. S. Boas' *Christopher Marlowe* in 1940. Once again it seems possible to notice a change of approach about this time; clearly nothing more could be done about Marlowe's life until the many problems had been solved by the discovery of new evidence, and there is a swing towards a closer examination of his plays. R. W. Battenhouse's *Marlowe's Tamburlaine: A Study in Renaissance Moral Philosophy* appeared in 1941, to be followed in 1946 by P. H. Kocher's *Christopher Marlowe: A Study of His Thought, Learning and Character*. F. P. Wilson's important *Marlowe and the Early Shakespeare* came in 1953, and reviewed afresh the three important problems of Marlowe's character, his text, and the chronology of the plays. He develops the thesis that Shakespeare and Marlowe 'first gave dignity and coherence to the historical play and raised it above the level of a chronicle'. Harry Levin's stimulating, if exasperating, *The Overreacher: A Study of Christopher Marlowe* was first published in this country in 1954, although it had appeared two years earlier in America. Some indication of the manner and scope of this book can be gained from the following passage: 'The "over-reacher" is Christopher Marlowe himself in his brief, passionate and tragic life. It is also in that age of ambitious and unscrupulous men, a typical Elizabethan symbol: the type portrayed by Marlowe himself in *Tamburlaine*, *Faustus* and the lesser figures of Gaveston and the Spencers. Finally the term belongs to Elizabethan rhetoric, signifying hyperbole and the heightened style of Marlowe himself.' Nor has Marlowe failed to attract undesirable attention to himself, and, for the sake of completeness only, mention may be made of Calvin Hoffman's *The Man who was Shakespeare* (1955), which put forward the odd theory that Marlowe not only wrote Shakespeare's plays but also *The Spanish Tragedy* and several anonymous plays, including *Edward III* and *Locrine*. It is satisfactory to be able to report that the book received the treatment it deserved at the hands of several reviewers.

A few out of many comparatively recent articles may be cited to show the general direction that Marlowe studies have taken. These include Ribner's 'Marlowe and Machiavelli' in *Comparative Literature* (1954), M. E. Rickey's 'Astronomical Imagery in *Tamburlaine*' (*Renaissance Papers*, Univ. of South Carolina, 1954), K. Lever's 'The Image of Man in *Tamburlaine I*' (*Philological Quarterly*, 1956), and J. T. McCullen's 'Dr Faustus and Renaissance Learning' (*Modern Language Review*, 1956). More detailed studies along these lines would be welcome.

Jonson, too, has not been neglected, although one suspects that Eliot's remark about the dramatist (*Elizabethan Essays*, 1934) is still holding good: 'The reputation of Jonson has been of the most deadly kind that can be compelled upon the memory of a great poet. To be universally accepted; to be damned by the praise that quenches all desire to read the book; to be afflicted by the imputation of the virtues which excite the least pleasure; and to be read only by historians and antiquaries—this is the most perfect conspiracy of approval.' Yet enough progress has perhaps been made to render it unnecessary, to quote Eliot again, 'to look back as far as Dryden before we find a living criticism of Jonson's work'. John Palmer's unassuming biography and criticism appeared in 1934. In 1945 G. E. Bentley published his *Shakespeare and Jonson: Their Reputations in the 17th Century Compared*. H. W. Baum's *The Satiric and the Didactic in Ben Jonson's Comedy* came out in 1947, to be followed by two important works in the following year, A. H. Gilbert's *The Symbolic Persons in the Masques of Ben Jonson*, and A. Sackton's *Rhetoric as a Dramatic Language in Ben Jonson*. It is worth noting that much of the more recent criticism of Jonson has been directed to precisely these two subjects, his masques and his dramatic language; I shall return to this point in a moment. J. J. Enck's *Jonson and the Comic Truth* (1957) to some extent supports Eliot's judgement, for the author, in spite of his commendable efforts to improve our understanding of Jonson's technique and development, protests too much against those who still think of him as 'correctly classical and regularly dull', and whose numbers he probably overestimates. This is surely not the best way to arouse interest in one's subject. E. B. Partridge in *The Broken Compass: A Study of the Major Comedies of Ben Jonson* (1958) approaches the plays through their imagery and metaphorical language, taking the trouble in his preface to explain to the reader exactly what he understands by these things, and showing his awareness of the shortcomings of the methods involved. This seems to be a more useful approach.

Again reference to a few recent articles will show which way the wind is blowing. Between 1943 and 1949 D. J. Gordon contributed a series of articles on the masques to the *Journal of the Warburg and Courtauld Institutes*. W. T. Furniss studied 'The Annotations of Ben Jonson's *The Masque of Queenes*' (*Review of English Studies*, 1954), and the same author contributed a long and valuable essay on the masques to *Three Studies in the Renaissance* (Yale Studies in English, 1958). D. Cunningham wrote on 'The Jonsonian Masque as a Literary Form' (*Journal of English Literary History*, 1955). R. I. C. Graziani wrote on *Chloridia* in *Review of English Studies* (1956), and in 1958 J. A. Barish contributed an extremely important article, 'Baroque Prose in the Theatre: Ben Jonson', to the *Publications of the Modern Language Association of America*. It seems fair to say that in linguistic studies alone, quite apart from anything else, there is still much to be done for Jonson.[3]

The other major dramatists may be dealt with more briefly, but it will be noticed that in a number of cases there is the same tendency to more detailed study of a narrower field. E. E. Stoll's *John Webster: The Periods of his Work as determined by his Relations to the Drama of his day* appeared in 1905. Other book-length studies are rare, but include Rupert Brooke's *John Webster and the Elizabethan Drama* (1916), Clifford Leech's *John Webster* (1951), and T. Bogard's *The Tragic Satire of John Webster* (1955). Other studies worth noting are those by W. A. Edwards in *Determinations* (edited by F. R. Leavis, 1934), Ian Jack in *Scrutiny*, xvi (1949), and David Cecil in *Poets and Story-Tellers* (1949). The almost universal concern with Webster's sources is well reflected in Gunnar Boklund's *The Sources of The White Devil* (1957). Tourneur remains a shadowy figure, though the problem of the authorship of *The Revenger's Tragedy* is still with us, Middleton being the chief contender for the honour; the two most recent studies of Middleton, Samuel Schoenbaum's *Middleton's Tragedies* (1955) and R. H. Barker's *Thomas Middleton* (1958), pressing the claims of their hero with more enthusiasm than many of us think legitimate under the circumstances. Marston was the subject of a detailed study by A. J. Axelrad in 1955, but a scrutiny of his bibliography shows that he stands more or less alone in the sixty years under survey, with many of the shorter articles cited being concerned with problems of date and authorship of the plays. The concern of students of Chapman reveals itself clearly in the titles of the following books and articles: Janet Spens, 'Chapman's Ethical Thought' (*Essays and Studies*, 1925); P. V. Kreider, *Elizabethan Comic Character Conventions in the Comedies of George Chapman* (1935); Hardin Craig, 'Ethics in the Jacobean Drama: The Case of George Chapman', and C. W. Kennedy, 'Political Theory in the Plays of George Chapman', both in *The Parrott Presentation Volume* (1935); R. H. Perkinson, 'Nature and the Tragic Hero in Chapman's Bussy Plays' (*Modern Language Quarterly*, 1942); Michael Higgins, 'Chapman's "Senecal Man": A Study in Jacobean Psychology' (*Review of English Studies*, 1945), and a similar article in the same journal two years later; J. W. Wieler, *George Chapman: the Effect of Stoicism upon his Tragedies* (1949). Only fairly recently do we find anything going much beyond ethics and politics, in

J. Jacquot's *George Chapman, sa vie, sa poésie, son théâtre, sa pensée* (1951), and the most recent work, Ennis Rees' *The Tragedies of George Chapman* (1954), reveals in its sub-title, 'Renaissance Ethics in Action', this almost unrelieved concern with Chapman's philosophy of life. This is not, of course, of necessity a bad thing; it is mentioned only to demonstrate the prevailing attitude towards Chapman's works.

Beaumont and Fletcher have been popular subjects in spite of the problems of the canon, to a great extent, one imagines, because of the interest in tragi-comedy and romance as it affects some of Shakespeare's plays. A. H. Thorndike produced his *Influence of Beaumont and Fletcher on Shakespeare* as early as 1901. O. L. Hatcher's *John Fletcher* came in 1905, Charles Gayley's *Beaumont the Dramatist* in 1914. Interest in the problem of collaboration appears in Maurice Chelli's *Étude sur la Collaboration de Massinger avec Fletcher et son Groupe* (1926), continues through R. C. Bald's *Bibliographical Studies in the Beaumont and Fletcher Folio of 1647* (1938) and Baldwin Maxwell's *Studies in Beaumont, Fletcher and Massinger* (1939), and is being continued through the series of articles by Cyrus Hoy already referred to. Two scholars have considered the influence of Beaumont and Fletcher on the Restoration Drama, A. C. Sprague in 1926, and J. H. Wilson in 1928. E. H. C. Oliphant's *The Plays of Beaumont and Fletcher* appeared in 1927, D. M. McKeithan's *The Debt to Shakespeare in Beaumont and Fletcher's Plays* in 1938, J. F. Danby's *Poets on Fortune's Hill* in 1952, E. M. Waith's important *The Pattern of Tragi-Comedy in Beaumont and Fletcher* in 1952, and W. W. Appleton's *Beaumont and Fletcher* in 1956.

Heywood has been generally neglected, only four major studies having been devoted to him since 1900: O. Cromwell's *Thomas Heywood, a study in the Elizabethan drama of everyday life* (1928), A. M. Clark's *Thomas Heywood* (1931), F. S. Boas' *Thomas Heywood* (1950), and Michel Grivelet's *Thomas Heywood et le drame domestique élizabéthain* (1957). Dekker's position is no better, except in so far as he has attracted the editorial attention of Fredson Bowers. F. E. Scheffler's *Thomas Dekker als Dramatiker* appeared in 1910, K. L. Gregg's *Thomas Dekker: A Study in Economic and Social Backgrounds* in 1924, and M. T. Jones-Davies' *Un Peintre de la Vie Londonienne: Thomas Dekker* in 1958, this being a most detailed study in two volumes. Dekker's non-dramatic activities have attracted a great deal of attention, and once again the problems of collaboration have tended to cloud the issues in his plays. T. M. Dunn's *Philip Massinger, The Man and the Playwright* (1957) was the first book on the subject since A. H. Cruickshank's *Philip Massinger* (1920) and Maurice Chelli's *Le Drame de Massinger* (1923). Studies in Ford are represented by M. J. Sargeaunt's *John Ford* (1935), S. B. Ewing's *Burtonian Melancholy in the Plays of John Ford* (1940), G. F. Sensabaugh's *The Tragic Muse of John Ford* (1944), Robert Davril's *Le Drame de John Ford* (1954), H. Oliver's *The Problem of John Ford* (1955), and Clifford Leech's *John Ford and the Drama of his Time* (1957).

7. THEATRE AND ACTING

Studies in the Elizabethan Stage since 1900 were admirably covered up to 1948 by Allardyce Nicoll in *Shakespeare Survey*, 1, but it is interesting to see what has been going on in the last eleven or twelve years. B. L. Joseph's *Elizabethan Acting* came in 1951, but the supporters of the 'formalized style' have been under heavy fire in a few articles which followed it. R. A. Foakes wrote on 'The Player's Passion. Some Notes on Elizabethan Psychology and Acting' (*Essays and Studies*, 1954), suggesting that the notion of a formal method of acting needs much closer examination, and that we need to know a good deal more about what the Elizabethans themselves had to say about acting. Marvin Rosenberg, in 'Elizabethan Actors: Men or Marionettes?' (*Publications of the Modern Language Association*, 1954) argued that the 'formalists' had placed too much emphasis on the supposed youth and lack of skill of the so-called 'boy actors', on passages from plays which are clearly attacking second-rate actors, on the assumption that a rigid time-limit for the performance demanded clockwork-like action, and on the theory that a clear relationship was felt to exist between actor and orator. In the same journal for 1956, David Klein followed up Rosenberg's points, and supported him with a number of remarks from the works of Chapman, Massinger, May, Randolph and others.

C. W. Hodges' *The Globe Restored* and R. Southern's *The Open Stage* both appeared in 1953, but already Leslie Hotson was thundering in the wings with 'Shakespeare's Arena' (*Sewanee Review*, 1953), a theme which he developed in *The First Night of Twelfth Night* (1954) and *Shakespeare's Wooden O* (1959). Most scholars are still prepared to be non-committal about his rather sweeping conclusions. More balanced studies of acting and the theatre appeared in F. P. Wilson's 'The Elizabethan Theatre' (*Neophilologus*, 1955), Alfred Harbage's *Theatre for Shakespeare* (1956), and W. A. Armstrong's *The Elizabethan Private Theatres: Facts and Problems* (1958). Only one volume has yet appeared of Glynne Wickham's *Early English Stages, 1300–1660* (1959), and comment may well be reserved until the second volume, of more direct interest to our period, is available. Mention should also be made of the Malone Society's Collections III, *A Calendar of Dramatic Records in the Books of the Livery Companies of London, 1485–1640* (1954), which made available a mass of material illustrative of the Lord Mayors' Shows and other pageants in the city with which a number of prominent dramatists were intimately involved.

8. DESIDERATA

Many of the needs of the future have already been suggested in the course of this article. First and foremost, it seems to me, we need a great many more critical editions of the major dramatists. A recent writer on Middleton remarked that he was taking quotations from Bullen's edition of his works, with a few exceptions, since 'the definitive edition remains to be issued'; there has been no edition of Massinger, apart from single plays, since Cunningham's in 1871, and this was a reprint of Gifford's second edition of 1813 with the addition of *Believe As You List*; for Heywood we must still rely on the Pearson reprint of 1874; other names could be added, for few of the dramatists edited since the beginning of this century have received the kind of treatment that modern scholarship ought to find acceptable. It is true that there is news of editions in progress, but the need is urgent. Secondly, we ought to have more editions of illustrative documents on the lines of the Malone Society's *Collections*; it is cheering to know that some of these are also in progress, including records of travelling companies and records from the Declared Accounts of the Treasurer of the Chamber, but the number of labourers dealing with this particular harvest is pathetically small. Thirdly, we should study again the needs listed by Allardyce Nicoll in *Shakespeare Survey*, 1, as they relate to the Elizabethan stage, for we can hardly be proud of the progress made in this direction since 1948. Fourthly, we need to bring up to date the information in *Elizabethan Stage* about the acting companies and the theatres. Fifthly, we need to know more about the Latin drama of the period, a great deal of which has not been edited at all. In general, to avoid too long a list, we ought to be aware that we are still in a period of stock-taking, almost, one might add, of stock-piling too; we should be prepared to continue to apply ourselves to fundamental material, to minutiae if necessary, until we are perfectly certain that the foundations for broader and more general studies are secure. To write about a man's work before being sure of what he wrote is a proceeding which in other disciplines would be regarded as bordering on lunacy; yet we have more than once come perilously close to regarding it as normal, and the attitude behind this kind of behaviour is apparent in other aspects of Elizabethan and Jacobean scholarship. There is plenty of room for imagination; but it needs something solid to work on. During the past sixty years the advances in our field of study have, in certain directions, been enormous, but there must be time allowed for them to be made use of in other directions. *Il faut reculer pour mieux sauter.*

NOTES

1. Alfred Harbage's *Annals of English Drama 975–1700* (1940) covers a much wider field than this paper, but has been of inestimable value. One welcomes the news that it is being revised for a new edition by Samuel Schoenbaum of Northwestern University.

2. Since this article went to press two more volumes have been added to 'The Revels Plays': Webster's *The White Devil*, edited by J. R. Brown, and Jonson's *Bartholomew Fair*, edited by E. A. Horsman.

3. J. A. Barish has since developed his subject considerably in his book *Ben Jonson and the Language of Comic Prose* (1960).

SHAKESPEARE AND LYLY[1]

BY

MARCO MINCOFF

Shakespeare's debt to Lyly has never been denied, and it might well seem that any attempt to resurvey the subject could be no more than the gleaning of an already well-harvested field. Yet in fact much more than the gleaning of a few stray ears of corn has been left for those who would apply themselves to the task of making a fresh study of the relationship between these two authors. In particular, it may be said at once that, in the earlier investigations of the theme, there has been a definite tendency to concentrate rather on concrete parallels than on fundamental principles, and thus to forget how far-reaching the effect of the Lylian formula was upon Shakespeare, how it dominated most of his comedies, overpowering even the Jonsonian humour of *Twelfth Night* and mingling with the Beaumontesque-D'Urfeian romanticism of *The Tempest*. Furthermore, it may be suggested that Lyly's example was of no less importance to Shakespeare for what it gave him positively than for its negative effect in raising in him a spirit of opposition.

Naturally, to speak of a Lylian formula or type of comedy is not altogether correct. If that particular sort of comedy should bear the name of any one man, it might rather have been that of Edwardes, who had given an excellent example of the type nearly twenty years before Lyly; and its roots reach back much further—to that extremely interesting, indeed almost seminal playlet *Fulgens and Lucrece*. But the fact is that Lyly represents for us a genre of which otherwise we should know extremely little; and though it is possible that much of what we may call the Lylian elements in Shakespeare derived either directly or through Lyly from other sources, we are justified in giving his name to English court comedy in general. And there is at least one feature of Lyly's comedies (perhaps the most important of all) that does not occur in *Damon and Pythias*—they are for the most part love-comedies, in which the mainspring of the comedy itself is love. And that was in those days something practically unique; nor has it been very frequent since then. A love interest had, of course, been a standing ingredient of comedy since Greek and Roman times; it had even provided the motive of the action. The scapegrace son of Roman comedy was generally in love with a courtesan, but there was nothing comic in that, it was part of the data. The comedy was provided by his attempts, or rather those of the wily slave, to hoodwink the father—it was essentially a comedy of intrigue. And if occasionally the infatuation of an old man who ought to know better, or of a boastful Thraso, comes up as a subject for satirical treatment, it is still only the inappropriateness of the passion, or the self-love of the character, that rouses laughter, and the nearest we get to the comic treatment of love itself is in a chance remark like Terence's, 'Heu, universum triduum', making fun of the lover's impatience. But with Lyly it is the way in which love cuts across our little plans and makes fools of us all that is the most constant theme—the mere fact of being in love almost is treated as a comic situation.[2]

The attitude of a given society to love depends on so many factors that it is extremely difficult, if not impossible, for another age to recapture it. And Lyly's concept of love is something to which one can only adjust oneself with difficulty, if at all. It was also little likely to appeal to Shakespeare, who had grown up among very different traditions. For Shakespeare's class, love was an easy and simple relation, the natural prelude to marriage, and marriage, as the later Puritans, rooted in the same tradition as Shakespeare, saw it, meant mutual solace and mutual support—a true companionship, in fact. But for Lyly love is above all the love of the courtier, and the main business of the courtier is, as he himself constantly proclaims, love—we should call it flirtation. In a very narrow society of men and women with a great deal of leisure on their hands, of waiting about in anterooms, and boring court functions, the game of flirtation is bound to develop, and it had developed, and had been elaborated into a complicated set of rules centuries before at the courts of Provence. Those rules had naturally undergone changes in the course of time: the rule, for instance, that love must and can only be adulterous was no longer insisted on in theory, although in practice it must still have been in force to a considerable extent, enough at least to put love and marriage into separate compartments. And the court of the Tudors had still enough of the Middle Ages clinging to it for the medieval love of strict symbolical ceremony, so fully described by Huizinga, to determine the behaviour of the lover. He had above all to be wondrous melancholy, to sigh and go without his meals, to affect a foppish slovenliness in his dress, to compose Petrarchistic love songs—in short, to cut every kind of caper and make it abundantly clear that he was in love so that his mistress could triumph in her conquest. And though Lyly still insists, like the trouvères, on secrecy, these flirtations must have been a very open secret. How many fingers were burnt in the game, in how far the convention that everything was strictly Platonic and Petrarchistic was maintained in practice, how far the emotions were engaged at all in the whole affair, we have no real means of knowing. Clearly, it would have been felt as bad taste for any third person to regard the matter in a serious light; but even so, admitted that the conventionality of the flirtation was itself a convention, one finds a difficulty in entering into the mood of Elizabeth's courtiers, or in understanding the public celebrations of *Astrophel* or *Endimion*, or in appreciating why Elizabeth should have wanted to see herself reflected in the love-sick Sapho.

Whatever the reality behind these conventions may have been, the whole concept was at once something highly serious and extremely frivolous. Love was the centre of existence, it was to be 'all made of sighs and tears, of faith and service', but also it was an elaborate game, not only between the protagonists, but one in which the whole court must have taken part, discussing who was paired with whom, and making fun of the lovers' antics. To some extent that is so all the world over: love is the subject of jokes of every kind, and the soft impeachment that Tom is in love with Sue will mostly be met with smiles, sniggers, or laughter, and most of all where there is a romantic tradition to give the joke a point. And the two aspects can seldom have been pushed to such extremes as in the atmosphere of a court when Petrarchism held sway. And it was this ambivalence, complicated by the Platonic doctrine that sexual love is after all the lowest in the scale, and by the necessity for compliments to the Virgin Queen, that provided the soil for a new comic idea.

Thus by introducing love and courtship not as a mere incident but as a theme of comedy, Lyly was opening up new and fruitful ground, and creating, as far as we can tell, an entirely new type. And his awareness of this is to be seen in his well-known assertion:

Our intent was at this time to moue inward delight, not outward lightnesse, and to breede (if it might bee) soft smiling, not loude laughing: knowing it to the wise to be as great pleasure to heare counsell mixed with witte, as to the foolish to haue sporte mingled with rudenesse.

The mingling of pleasure and counsel had, of course, been the expressed aim of Lyly's fore-runners too; but they had been content to mingle them. What Lyly did in this play was to run them together and to achieve what Sidney was, at about the same time, though his book was not published till much later, suggesting as a possibility—that 'the whole tract of a comedy should be full of delight'. For though, as Sidney explains, laughter and delight are almost opposed to one another in their sources, 'well may one thing breed both together', and he gives as an example:

in Hercules painted with his great beard and furious countenance, in a woman's attire, spinning at Omphale's commandment, it breeds both delight and laughter; for the representing of so strange a power in love procures delight, and the scornfulness of the action stirreth laughter.

That was certainly the sort of effect Lyly was striving after, and by poking gentle fun at love and its waywardness, by taking the sighs, the tears and the predicaments of lovers as fair game for smiles, while yet subscribing to the Petrarchistic doctrine, he was moving towards a deeper form of comedy, which, like Terence's, but in quite other ways, raises a sigh, half sympathetic, half acquiescent, over human nature itself. Not that he moved very far in that way—it remained for Shakespeare to achieve real depths, and even he did so, as we shall see, by invoking yet another principle; nor yet can one say that all Lyly's comedies are of this kind. Of his eight plays only five can lay any claim to be such comedies of courtship, and perhaps only two—*Sapho* and *Gallathea*—can really substantiate that claim. But he did make a very definite move in a new direction, and for that reason one may be justified in regarding those comedies in which that move is made to be most truly typical of him.

In what is probably his first play, *Campaspe*, there are already elements of this half-humorous, half-serious attitude of gentle laughter at love's foolishness, though the general effect of the main plot is, for us at least, romantic and serious, except for the reflected light it gets from the comic by-work. It is possible, however, that for an age unaffected by certain later romantic senti-mentalities, an age that distinguished very pointedly between *amor rationalis* and *amor sensualis*, there was less need to underline the humour inherent in the situation of Campaspe, with the world conqueror at her feet, falling in love with the mere painter Apelles, and of the all-powerful Alexander caught in the toils of a love that is no more rational than hers. And there is, even apart from that, some comedy in the treatment too—in the lovers' secretly pining for each other and too terribly unhappy and earnest over it to take in each other's hints and innuendos; or in Apelles trying to hide his love from Alexander and betraying it by the sighs and melancholy with which he regards Campaspe's portrait; and in the trick by which he is at last compelled to confess; or in the final summing-up, which in the same sentence both glorifies and belittles the power of love—that 'Alexander cannot subdue the affections of men, though he conquer their countries'.

Elements like these are, however, much more heavily underlined in the two succeeding comedies, which, as we said, represent the highest development of the comedy of courtship—chiefly because the introduction of the mischievous boy Cupid as an actual character in the play lends greater immediacy to the theme of love's waywardness. And Cupid, once having been introduced, needs more victims on whom to play his pranks, so that the theme is treated contrapuntally in a way already adumbrated by *Fulgens and Lucrece*. And that in its turn gives scope for the development of the love game in all its artificial conventionality, with its sighs and tears and the publishment of the obdurate beauties who refuse to play it. Here one might draw special attention to Sapho's love-sickness, her feverish tossings in bed, pretending that she is ill with a cold, the perversely coquettish hesitation with which she will and will not have Phao called in to bring simples, and the conversation of misunderstood innuendos in which the one complains that heart's ease grows too high to reach, the other that it grows too low, and both are too self-absorbed to grasp the other's meaning. That is all high comedy of a delicate and subtle kind. And in *Gallathea* there is the wooing by innuendo of two girls disguised as boys, each half divining the true meaning behind the other's words and partly suspecting that she is a girl like herself, and the scene in which Diana's nymphs one after the other confess their love for the disguised girls and their broken vows, a scene which Shakespeare was to take as the foundation of a whole play. But the fact that the two plays have essentially the same framework—the pranks of Cupid and, as a compliment to Elizabeth, his capture and punishment by the Virgin ruler or deity—probably shows why the vein was carried no further. Lyly seemed to have reached the utmost of which it was capable, and in the succeeding comedies that half-humorous treatment of love is pushed into the background—confined to the sub-plots or dropped altogether. In *Love's Metamorphoses* he introduced Cupid once more, no longer as a mischievous boy but as a supreme and ireful godhead punishing any infringement of his code, while in *The Woman in the Moon* the comedy of the shepherds devoting their Petrarchistic service to a woman incapable of valuing it at its worth pales before the satire on woman's capriciousness.

It was thus left to Shakespeare to carry on from the point reached in *Gallathea*. And this he was able to do not only because of his greater genius, but because he was *not* a court poet and was *not* drawn to the artificial code of love that ruled at court, a code which had been fruitful in creating the theme, but was powerless to carry it to any real heights. Indeed it must have taken Shakespeare some time to pierce through the artificialities of court comedy to the solid core of humanity that it did, after all, contain. At least there is something like definite hostility towards Lyly in his choice of models for his two earliest comedies *The Taming of the Shrew* and *The Comedy of Errors*—and that *The Taming of the Shrew* with its decorative classical imagery, the most Marlovian and at the same time the flattest in style of all his plays was his first attempt, I am firmly convinced. Lyly was, after all, the most prominent comic writer among his predecessors, and, given Shakespeare's obvious taste for romance, one would have expected him to turn to Lyly like the needle of the compass. But there is nothing of the Lylian mode in these plays, and if, as Warwick Bond suggests, Katharine's raillery and the Dromios' quibbles owe anything to Lyly, Shakespeare must have studied him for his wit, but not for his comedy. Italian and Roman comedy could not satisfy Shakespeare however; intrigue did not suffice him as a basis for comedy —it is characteristic, I think, that he took as his model the one Roman comedy in which misunderstandings are due to circumstances and not deliberate hoodwinking. Probably the fundamental reason was that they offered too little 'delight', or poetry, and too little variety of mood. And yet the work on these comedies was perhaps of immense importance, for though he did not actually work it out much in them, they already offered him what was to be the mainspring of his comedies—not actually courtship itself, though that was to be an important theme, but man's lack of knowledge of himself and others, the clash between appearance and reality, something that approaches the Terentian mood, without, however, reaching Terence's denial of the possibility of knowledge.

Then, with *Love's Labour's Lost*, Shakespeare submitted to the inevitable and turned at last to Lyly—and with a will. The very nucleus of the play, the scene in which the courtiers one by one come down the garden path and declare themselves foresworn, is taken from Lyly, as are the characters, and the contrapuntal structure, and the static scenes of wit. And yet it is Lyly with a difference. By comparison with Shakespeare's other comedies, *Love's Labour's Lost* may seem insubstantial and artificial, by the side of Lyly it is like a slice of life itself. Yet, even apart from the power and artistry of his language and character-drawing, Shakespeare introduced certain fundamental alterations in the Lylian formula, alterations so obvious that it is almost a truism to mention them, except that they probably show why it was he withstood Lyly's influence so long. In the first place he gave to Lyly's airy nothings a local habitation and anchored them firmly to the earth. No mythology, no nymphs and goddesses, no mischievous Cupid, but only men and women, though, like most of Lyly's characters, courtiers and sovereigns. And in the second, the love that he depicts is no flirtatious game, no Petrarchistic sentimentalizing, though, to its cost, it assumes the outer forms of both, but a normal, healthy, human love with marriage in view. Not that Lyly had altogether eschewed the treatment of such a love, but he had reserved it mostly for lesser mortals. What Shakespeare retains from Lyly and develops to the utmost, though with a certain satirical twist at the end, is the comedy of courtship—the capers of the men as they strut and preen themselves, the coquetry of the girls, who pretend they will not when they would and plague their lovers and tyrannize over them as hard-heartedly as any Petrarchistic beauty. There is in fact a sort of inversion of the Lylian formula, or a part of it. With Lyly the comedy of love's foolishness lies mainly in the desperate earnestness with which the lovers pursue what is mostly a very unsuitable affair. They are at bottom only playing a game, though compelled to it by Cupid, and they are as miserable over it as any tragic hero. Shakespeare's lovers are following their natural instincts, and in earnest, but their earnestness assumes the forms of a game. They enter into it with gusto, but they are more or less aware—even the men—that it is a game they are playing and that the natural thing would be to do their wooing as simply and directly as Costard; and it is because they have treated it as a game that they are punished in the end. And, furthermore, the very mechanism of the plot, the borrowing of Lyly's theatrical effect without its mythological machinery, almost imposes of itself another comic theme which Shakespeare is quick to seize on, and which he develops even more strongly than the first. In foreswearing love the young men have overestimated their strength of will; their position is very different from that of Diana's nymphs, they have set themselves through lack of self-knowledge in deliberate opposition to nature, and they continue up to the end to let their self-confidence lead them into failure after failure, till they are at last shown a glimpse of themselves as others see them. It is in fact an aspect of that clash between appearance and reality that Shakespeare had already treated in his earliest comedies, and was to treat again and again, subordinating to it as a rule the comedy of courtship and often fusing the two together.

But the final deflation of masculine complacence with the punishments it imposes brings a strangely harsh splash of colour into the Watteauesque picture. It is as if Shakespeare had suddenly lost patience with the very conventions he had been exploiting. Some new event, some sort of definite finish was needed to round the play off; the women could not just glide softly into their lovers' arms; the death of the king was prepared for, and no doubt intended from the first as a breath of stark reality against which to measure the artificiality of the courtly game of love. Actually the change of mood comes slightly earlier, before the arrival of Marcade, when Holofernes turns on his tormentors and shows them up for a set of conceited ruffians revenging themselves for the ill-success of their own masque on humble folk who cannot retaliate: 'This is not generous, not gentle, not humble.' It comes like a rebuke to the reader too, if he has been merely passively following the jokes, and puts him out of conceit with himself. The punishment of the courtiers is a sort of poetic justice—or so one feels it now—for their cruelty and obtuseness towards others, rather than for their 'taffeta phrases, silken terms precise' through which they had dragged honest love down to the level of courtly flirtation.

By comparison with *Love's Labour's Lost*, *The Two Gentlemen of Verona* seems like an attempt, and not a very successful one, to throw Lyly off once more—or possibly it is the earlier play, and represents a first half-hearted approach. It begins spiritedly enough with the comedy of love's foolishness—Julia's destruction of her lover's letter, which repeats the mood of Sapho's perverseness, the capitulation of the staunch infidel Valentine before the power of love, and Speed's diagnosis of his complaint or his blindness to Sylvia's hints. But these are, after all, only subsidiary touches; the groundwork of the play is pure sentimental romance, with only the by-work to provide the comedy as in *Endimion*—or *Mucedorus*, or *Sir Clyomon and Sir Clamydes*.

With *A Midsummer Night's Dream* comes a new advance towards Lyly, and further concessions. Shakespeare is now a fully matured dramatist, conscious of his powers and able to treat his material with an ease and freedom that seem to belie its origin. This play is, with the exception of *The Tempest*, his only comedy in which the supernatural plays a part, and with the exception of *The Comedy of Errors*, the only one with a classical background. Probably both these features are due to its having been planned as a wedding entertainment for an audience accustomed to Lylian comedy. And probably too the acceptance of these Lylian conventions again raised in Shakespeare a spirit of deliberate opposition, though mellower and less waspish than in the coda to *Love's Labour's Lost*. Instead of attacking and dealing out punishments he sets up a positive alternative to the Lylian viewpoint. Like Lyly he worked in his famous allegorical compliment to Elizabeth, but he refused to place her and her ideal of virginity and platonic flirtation in the centre. Of course in what seems to have been intended as a kind of prothalamion such a theme would have been out of place, but he not only avoids it, he rather pointedly disavows Lyly's contention that great minds stand superior to love by placing as a frame to the whole play and a standard by which love is to be measured, the mature, rational, unswerving love of Theseus and Hippolyta. Love is for Theseus the fitting crown of his achievements, not as for Alexander an aberration to be ashamed of. And, given the structural position of Theseus in the play, I think we must take his pronouncements on love as more than subjective, dramatic opinions. He is a chorus figure expounding objective values. Judged by the standard of Theseus' ideal love—a love, it must be stressed, in which mind and body are both given their full rights—that of the young people appears as heady, flighty, irrational; it is, in fact, *amor sensualis*; and as such Theseus cannot fully approve of it, though he understands human nature too well, and is too wise and magnanimous in his judgements, to condemn it altogether. He can even sympathize with

Hermia almost as obviously as Shakespeare himself, who while representing her love as un-reasonable, in defiance of all dramatic tradition, makes her father equally unreasonable in his preference for Demetrius, no better a match from a worldly point of view than Lysander; but he cannot set aside the natural rights of the parent and the laws of his country by openly favouring her. Love, the love of ordinary people at least, is like the wind, it bloweth as it listeth, it is often inconvenient in its waywardness, and so a fit subject for comic treatment, for a comedy that will rouse soft smiles and not rude laughter. And Shakespeare's ambivalent attitude is reflected in the comments of the immortals—in Oberon's ready sympathy with distress and Puck's contemp-tuous, 'What fools these mortals be!' and the humorous, homespun spell with which he solves the lovers' O so heart-rending problems and dismisses them:

> Jack shall have Jill,
> Nought shall go ill,
> The man shall have his mare again,
> And all shall be well.

As the love that Shakespeare treats is not Lyly's love, so also is he unable to use Lyly's mytho-logy of love. It is well known that Shakespeare's fairies are not the normal fairies of English folklore,[3] though his picture of tiny gossamer spirits has by now entirely replaced the true one. Generally, however, it is tacitly assumed that his invention of these new spirits was an act of creation needing no other explanation than the beauty of the result: Shakespeare, it is thought, was impelled only by sheer delight in creation. Naturally, this creative urge must have played a part, but I imagine that Shakespeare was fully aware of what he was doing in dethroning the mischievous Cupid and putting in his place a friendly, benevolent power that watches over lovers, and, although its performance does not always correspond to its intentions, leads, or tries to lead, them to happiness in spite of themselves and their foolishness. To a certain extent the fairies of folklore were capable of filling that role, for they were the guardians of hearth and home, punishing adultery and promiscuity, as they also punished sluttishness and laziness. But the good-folk were also feared for their love of mischief; they were, indeed more mischievous and unreliable than Cupid himself. Also their associations were too homely and countrified for the new role they were to perform. Shakespeare preserved those associations in his Puck, but he had to etherialize his fairies. And in introducing these new guardian spirits of love, and intro-ducing them too in classical Athens, the home of the classical Cupid, Shakespeare was, I am convinced, offering a deliberate challenge to Lyly and what Lyly stood for. Thus, in fact, his debt to Lyly was as great, or even greater, when he opposed him as when he followed him.

And did the events in the wood really take place? Theseus is convinced they did not, and Theseus' opinion cannot be dismissed out of hand; Shakespeare actually bears him out in the title of his play. And even if Theseus is wrong in this special case, he is right in the abstract; love is a very irrational, heady affair. And one thing is certain—in the moonlit woods the lovers have completely lost their bearings, and the actual comedy there rests on their inability to realize what is happening to themselves and to others: Lysander proclaims his love as the true *amor rationalis* when he has never been so fast in the grip of unreason before; Helena, like Campaspe or Sapho, is unable to realize her happiness when it is offered her, Hermia in her jealousy takes offence where none is meant—they are all at cross-purposes, floundering, like Terence's characters, in their own particular bog of misapprehensions. But unlike Terence's characters, they are in error as to emotions—including their own—not to facts; and they are watched over by a kindly power that will set them right. Moreover, they are contrasted with a pair of mortals who are above such errors. Error and incomprehension are not the inevitable lot of humanity, we may rise above them; but, after all, most of us are more like Lysander and Hermia than we are like Theseus and Hippolyta, and our laughter at the all-too-human pair is tinged with a realization that but for the grace of God there go we, and we despise them only at our peril. This particular effect, which lies I think at the bottom of the highest types of comedy, and which I believe breaks through in English comedy for the first time definitely here, might owe something to Terence, but it is almost bound to arise when we have a comedy based on inner misapprehensions and when we are in sympathy with the characters involved.

In the structure of his comedy Shakespeare continues to build on Lyly, no less than in his themes, but again he transmutes his material into something new. Counterpoint had, as we saw, long been an element in English comedy. Medwall had opposed the wooing of his heroes with that of the pages, Edwardes had contrasted the true friendship of Damon and Pythias with the selfish alliance of the philosophers; Lyly had employed a more fugal method in which whole groups of characters had been developed in parallel lines, their speeches and reactions chasing one another up and down the scale. In *Love's Labour's Lost* Shakespeare had taken over this method unaltered. Now in *A Midsummer Night's Dream* he has as many pairs of lovers as in *Love's Labour's Lost*, but they are not treated parallelly, there is no hint of a fugue (a form to which he reverted in a single scene of *As You Like It*), and the circumstances are all different for each pair. In the two pairs of young Athenians nearly all the possible permutations that Heywood had given in his *Play of Love* are represented. Pyramus and Thisbe, flying to the woods by night, re-echo the situation of Lysander and Hermia, and their love-making provides an ironic comment on the inflation of the lovers' speeches, just as Titania and Bottom give a farcical comment on the unreason of love, while Theseus and Hippolyta serve as a more serious, measured comment, and Oberon and Titania remind us that, after all, love's problems are not all solved with a Jack shall have Jill. The play is a veritable *tour de force* of construction with its interwoven strains of action and of theme producing a scintillating variety in which the colours blend and reflect on one another. Shakespeare never attempted quite so complex a structural pattern again—not even in *As You Like It*, which with its multiple pairs of lovers approaches it most closely, and where, besides the other permutations we even have Not-loved-nor-loving, but where the pairs are all kept strictly separate, not intercrossed as here. Still, a complexity of interwoven strains, contrasts of high romance, low comedy and scenes of verbal wit were to remain with him as a permanent legacy from Lyly in his formula for comedy.

In the themes of his later comedies, the Lylian strains die gradually away. Beatrice and Benedick still owe everything, if not to Lyly himself, at least to the direction indicated by him; and the comedy of courtship, of love's perversity and of the infidel caught, has never been treated with such gaiety, humour and depth as here. But contrasting with the lightheartedness of this plot is another, nearly tragic, strain. The two plots are brought together by the theme of appearance and reality, and even appearance here is imposed from outside. One pair of lovers is separated by inability to assess the truth, the other united; Dogberry's 'It is proved already you are false knaves, and it will go near to be thought so shortly' sums up the importance of opinion with unintentional irony. The Petrarchistic basis of Lylian comedy has been here overthrown. It is not darts from a beauty's eyes that engender love at first sight in Benedick, nor even in the more romantic Claudio; and the gradual love that grows up between the bickering pair promises a far better companionship than the more conventional pattern followed by the others. Placed before the Petrarchistic problem of love or friendship, Benedick (in contrast with Lyly's Eumenides) decides realistically for love.

In *As You Like It* the Petrarchistic love of the shepherd is openly ridiculed; Phoebe very neatly shows up the emptiness of his romantic imagery, and the utter selflessness of his moving appeal to Rosalind in Lodge, that she should have pity on Phoebe and love her, has been turned into an intrigue situation in which he is made the foolish and unwitting opponent of his own interests; while the sudden awakening of love in Phoebe has been transformed into a hilarious comedy of courtship in which love is awakened through round abuse and expressed in Phoebe's shilly-shallying discourse on the supposed boy's charms. In fact Lodge's Lylianism has been desentimentalized throughout. Orlando is still conventional enough to plaster the woods with despairing sonnets, but he is much too healthy and sensible an animal to forego a meal for love's sake. And while he is willing to play at Petrarchism in other respects too, both he and Rosalind, who has a lot of trouble to keep him up to the mark, are no longer playing it even half in earnest, as at the court of Navarre, but frankly with tongue in cheek, though Rosalind is woman enough to hanker after the privileges of the Petrarchistic beauty.

Even in *Twelfth Night* the ghost of Lyly continues to flicker in Viola's wooing of the Duke by innuendo. But the actual comedy again lies chiefly in Olivia's lack of self-knowledge and the mistaken estimates of the situation by nearly all the characters—the question of appearance and reality again. And indeed *Twelfth Night*, the swan song of Shakespearian comedy, as has often been pointed out, seems to sum up the situations of all the preceding comedies, and with them the comic principle behind them. At the same time a new principle appears—social satire.

Twelfth Night was to remain the last of Shakespeare's true comedies. The tide of fashion had set towards intrigue and satire, and he did not follow it. He had already, in response to Porter's success, tried his hand at intrigue once again in *The Merry Wives*, just as in *The Merchant of Venice* he had in response to a special demand departed, though less markedly, from his basic type, and again apparently it had not satisfied him. Now, since romantic comedy was no longer in demand, he turned instead to tragicomedy in the mode of *The Malcontent*, *The Dutch Courtesan* and *The Honest Whore*, producing his so-called problem plays, and the Lylian formula was shelved.

In this necessarily very summary survey of the field it will have been seen that the stress has been laid chiefly on the comic principle behind what one may call the main plot of the early comedies. This has of necessity involved a certain amount of what might be taken as interpretation of the comedies as a whole. It was not intended as such. The total meaning of a comedy, especially of so mixed a type as was practised on the Elizabethan stage, is not necessarily to be summed up in an analysis—even a very much fuller analysis than could be attempted here—of its comic situations and the sort of laughter they arouse; though I would suggest that the questions, 'by virtue of what is a given comedy truly comic', and 'what is the author laughing at and how', are essential to any interpretation of its meaning. And I think it is in this extremely important point, involving his very concept of comedy itself, that Shakespeare's greatest and most lasting debt to Lyly lies. In that and in the structural pattern, that peculiar blend of a romantic comedy of courtship with a strain of low-comedy genre scenes, and yet another strain of witty repartee: a blend which, repeated again and again in Shakespeare's comedies, had already been mixed to a nicety in *Gallathea*, and less perfectly in other comedies of Lyly's, but in no other of Shakespeare's forerunners. Shakespeare's comic principle cannot be summed up in the phrase 'comedy of courtship', it has been enriched with another principle, the discrepancy between appearance and reality. At least one aspect of that complex derives from Lyly. One may say, of course, that Shakespeare was perfectly capable of hitting on such points for himself, and so no doubt he was. But even a genius will not break down the wall to enter a room when there is an already open door waiting for him; and his impression of that room will not unnaturally be coloured thereafter by his first glimpse of it through the open door. It was Lyly who opened the door for Shakespeare, and when he was forced to abandon the Lylian view he abandoned comedy.

NOTES

1. A lecture delivered to the International Shakespeare Conference at Stratford-upon-Avon, 31 August 1959.

2. It is unfortunate that the one comedy of Lyly's which has been reprinted again and again in collections of pre-Shakespearian drama and which is commonly taken as representing the quintessence of court comedy, is *Endimion*. *Endimion* is, of course, of importance, not only for its own sake but also for its effect on Don Armado and Falstaff, and as an illustration of the Renaissance theme of friendship, but *Gallathea* or *Sapho* would better give the total effect of Lyly's comedy.

3. K. M. Briggs, *The Anatomy of Puck* (1959) gives reason to suppose that a genuine tradition of flower fairies did actually exist in some parts of the country, but it was not the normal one.

SHAKESPEARE AND MUNDY[1]

BY

I. A. SHAPIRO

If we may trust the scanty contemporary references to him, Anthony Mundy was one of the most prolific and successful of Elizabethan dramatists; in Francis Meres' opinion he was also one of the best. Yet very few of his plays are known to be extant, and even those have been identified as his only in modern times. Until Henslowe's theatrical account-book was discovered, no play by Mundy was known to have survived. Henslowe's records revealed that *The Downfall of Robert, Earl of Huntington*, printed anonymously in 1598, had been written by Mundy, that its sequel, *The Death of Robert, Earl of Huntington*, also printed anonymously in 1598, was partly Mundy's work too, and that he was one of the four authors of *Sir John Oldcastle*, printed (again anonymously) in 1600. Furthermore, Henslowe's accounts show that between 1597 and 1602, and for the Admiral's company alone, Mundy wrote or collaborated in twelve other plays, all now lost. Just over a hundred years ago knowledge of Mundy's original plays was greatly increased by the printing, for the first time, of the manuscript of his *John a Kent and John a Cumber*. In the present century *Fedele and Fortunio*, an adaptation of an Italian play by Luigi Pasqualigo, has been established as Mundy's beyond any doubt; it had been printed as early as 1585. Finally, but only as late as 1913, it was discovered that Mundy had a hand in another and more important play, *Sir Thomas More*.

Although historians of Elizabethan drama are now better equipped than ever before to judge for themselves the quality of Mundy's playwriting, they should, nevertheless, continue to keep in mind that most of his plays have been lost. We know that he wrote for other companies as well as for the Admiral's, but not for how many nor over what period. He was writing plays at least as early as 1584 and as late as December 1602, but there is no reason to suppose that those dates mark either the beginning or the end of his playwriting. Furthermore, there are no grounds for believing that his extant plays are his best, or that they are in any way necessarily representative. Except perhaps for the earliest, *Fedele and Fortunio*, the few that we possess have come down to us obviously by chance, and certainly not through any action taken by Mundy himself.

In trying to assess Mundy's achievement as a dramatist we must, therefore, still take into account the comments which his friends and enemies made about him and his writings, though fortunately we need no longer rely only on them. Contemporary references, when both few and brief, are always an unsafe basis for literary history, for comment that was in fact unsympathetic or even malicious may appear disinterested to later generations, whereas praise tends to be discounted as partial, or worse. Interpretation of contemporary references to Mundy has been influenced in this way, and biased further by a false picture of his career and public status. One can imagine the incredulous laughter that would have been evoked in, say, 1910, by a suggestion on grounds of style and content, that Mundy was the author of *Sir Thomas More*. It is therefore necessary, before we look for possible links with Shakespeare, to correct the traditional view of Mundy and his career.

Until very recently Mundy was thought to have been some dozen years older than Shakespeare, but to have started writing for the theatre only after Shakespeare's rise to eminence. Consequently, when Mundy's plays present incidents or characters resembling any in plays by Greene or Marlowe or Shakespeare, it has usually been taken for granted that Mundy must be the imitator, not the originator. We now know for certain that Mundy was only three and a half when Shakespeare was born and that he was acting in public before he was sixteen (that is, by 1576).[2] Moreover, he was writing for the theatre at least as early as 1584, and writing with a skill and maturity that explain why Francis Meres later singled him out as 'our best plotter'. Knowledge of his correct birth-date in itself dispels some of the Mundy mythology; for example, it is now impossible to suppose that Henry Chettle's reference to 'old Anthony Now-now' the ballad-singer in *Kind-Heart's Dream*, can be meant as an allusion to Mundy. But the Mundy mythology is too extensive to be discussed now. I can only review, very briefly, what is known for certain about Mundy's early career, so far as it concerns us on this occasion.

He was born in London, near St Paul's, in October 1560. Both his father, a freeman of the Stationers' and Drapers' companies, and his mother were dead by December 1570. Who then took charge of the boy, and how he was educated, we do not know. As there were several other Mundy families in the same parish he was probably cared for by relatives. The next datable event in his career is his apprenticing, in August 1576, when he was almost sixteen, to John Aldee, the well-known printer and stationer. Before that Mundy had been an actor, but for how long, and precisely when, is not known.[3] About a year after Mundy had been apprenticed to John Aldee he began to publish, at first mainly verse of a highly moral cast and reminiscent, in content and style, of the *Mirror for Magistrates*. In 1578 he was on the continent, ostensibly to learn languages but in all probability acting from the very first, as certainly later, as a spy on the English Catholic refugees in France and Italy. Under a false name he gained admission to the English College at Rome and studied there for a year, sufficient proof that he had received a good education and was fluent in Latin by the age of twenty. Mundy later published an account of his experiences at Rome in his pamphlet *The English Romayne Life*, printed about the middle of 1582. The veracity of this pamphlet was impugned immediately, and is still often doubted by literary historians, but quite without justification. Its accuracy on all important points can be demonstrated from contemporary writings by several eminent Catholics involved in the affairs described by Mundy.

By the middle of 1580, Mundy was apparently back in England, employed in countering the work of emissaries from the English College at Rome and other Catholic centres abroad. In 1581–2 he was active in tracking down and capturing Edmund Campion and other Jesuit emissaries, and in writing pamphlets to justify their execution as traitors. He was still engaged in such work in 1584. In that year he published *A Watchword to England* warning it 'to beware of traitors and treacherous practises which have been the overthrow of many famous Kingdoms and common-weals'. This he dedicated to the Queen. He had now been appointed to some minor post at court, but exactly what is uncertain.[4] By 1586, however, and quite possibly earlier, he was one of the 'Messengers of the Queen's Chamber', whose duties brought them into contact with a wide range of people both at Court and in the country, and occasionally took them abroad.[5] Messengers of the Chamber were, by Elizabethan standards, well remunerated, and seem to have been always of good education and upbringing. Appointment to the office, under Elizabeth as under James I, was evidently an indication of good social standing. It is necessary to dwell on these matters because Ben Jonson's gibe at 'Poet Nuntius' has been taken to mean that Mundy's status at court was that of a footman or flunkey; it was in fact much more nearly that of a diplomatic courier or Queen's Messenger of today. Mundy retained this court appointment, as far as we can tell, until the end of Elizabeth's reign. It was not a full-time post. Apparently a few Messengers of the Chamber were on duty for a limited period, while the others rested.

But rest was something Mundy rarely permitted himself, and certainly not during his first forty years. In the 1580's and 1590's his publications streamed from the press. As well as his own politico-theological pamphlets, he translated several others from French, all, like his own, of a distinctly anti-Catholic cast. Another of his interests at this time was the consideration of moral problems and dilemmas; he published a couple of original works of this nature (one disguised as a Euphuistic romance) and translated another from French. He also translated a dozen volumes of *Amadis de Gaule* and its various sequels, a task that in itself must have demanded years of work, even from so industrious and ready a writer as Mundy. Nevertheless, he found time to write also at least two volumes of poems, of which one or two possess sufficient charm to obtain a place in almost every anthology of Elizabethan lyrics. And on top of all this he was busy in the theatre. I say 'busy in the theatre' because he did some acting as well as playwriting.

Soon after his return to England in 1580 Mundy published a piece of topical journalism in which he described himself as a 'servant to the Earl of Oxford', a style he had first used in a book published in 1579. Since we know that he was acting again in 1580–1 it is tempting to conclude that he was then one of the Earl of Oxford's company of players, and that he had been a member of that company perhaps for some time. This is a conjecture that cannot be verified. What is certain, and much more interesting, is that after Mundy returned from Italy he attempted to 'play extempore'. According to the very hostile witness who reports this, Mundy failed, and was 'hissed from his stage'. 'Yet', the same witness continues, 'he now begins again to ruffle upon the stage.' That was written early in 1582; how much longer Mundy continued to act we do not know. Neither his court appointment of 1584 nor his Messengership of the Chamber need necessarily have put a stop to his acting. However, even if Mundy gave up acting soon after he began to write plays (in or before 1584) it is clear that he was by then an experienced actor and man of the theatre. In this respect he resembles Shakespeare. I suspect that such experience was no less important for Mundy than it was later for Shakespeare, and even more formative, for Mundy was a boy of only fifteen, or less, when he became a professional actor, whereas Shakespeare must have been at least twenty, possibly much more, when he first became connected with the London theatres.

The earliest evidence of Mundy's playwriting goes back to November 1584, when his adaptation of Pasqualigo's *Il Fedele* was entered in the Stationers' Register. This had been presented at Court with a special Prologue and Epilogue; the phrasing of the Prologue suggests that Mundy penned it for delivery by himself, presumably as one of the company presenting the play. *Fedele and Fortunio* is a very skilful adaptation of its Italian original. Mundy reorganized the plot, and reduced the number of characters to thirteen. He made the heroine, Victoria, an unmarried woman—so rendering the central intrigue more palatable to English taste—and he

27

anglicized the atmosphere of Pasqualigo's play in other ways also. He emphasized the comedy and greatly extended the part of Captain Crack-stone, making him utter malapropisms and 'derangements of epithets' which, years later, impressed even the critical Nashe. A great deal of Pasqualigo's prose Mundy turned into easy rhyme, in a variety of metres, and he also introduced, with very happy effect, songs and music.

Fedele and Fortunio was evidently a great success. It held the stage for years after it was first produced, as indeed it deserved to, for it is at least as amusing as any earlier or contemporary comedy of which we have the text. Its competence and finish make it difficult to suppose it was Mundy's first essay in playwriting, and also make us regret the loss of Mundy's subsequent plays. That he wrote plays regularly from 1584 onwards we cannot doubt; of this there is plentiful evidence in *Histriomastix* and in some of the 'Mar-prelate' pamphlets. If Mundy was as productive in writing plays as in other kinds of authorship, he must have been one of the most prolific of contemporary playwrights, quite possibly the most prolific in the 1580's. But the only other extant play-text by Mundy that can be dated in that decade is *John a Kent and John a Cumber*.

It has recently been shown that *John a Kent* cannot possibly be dated later than 1590, and that there are strong reasons for dating it before August 1589.[6] It may be even earlier, but it is a sufficiently remarkable achievement even if it is to be dated in 1589. Critics, especially academic critics, so often overestimate the achievement of writers they believe to be underrated or unfairly neglected, that I cannot expect readers to accept my judgement that *John a Kent* is as good a comedy, of its own kind, as has survived from the 1580's, and that it is much better than most. However, certain things may be said of it without suspicion of exaggeration. It has an extremely ingenious plot, full of surprises and turns which are always plausible, provided we accept the Elizabethans' belief in natural magic. Its unity of action and of time are quite remarkable, and could hardly be bettered; and it observes the unity of place almost as well. It is true that the interest is chiefly in plot and situation, but the characters are not mere puppets, and the two male lovers are nicely distinguished. In two respects *John a Kent* is quite unlike most other comedies of its period; it is still genuinely entertaining, and it is entirely free from smut and bawdy. This last characteristic is no accident, as other of Mundy's writings make clear. Its dialogue, whether prose, blank verse or rhyme, is always natural and easily spoken, and the verse is skilfully handled and flexible in rhythm. It is indeed a play that any aspiring dramatist in the late 1580's would have done well to study, and learn from.

One young dramatist who studied it, apparently to the extent of borrowing from it, was William Shakespeare. Certain resemblances between *John a Kent* and *A Midsummer Night's Dream* have often been noted. Both plays are concerned with the tribulations of two pairs of lovers whose union is first frustrated, and finally effected, by magical means. Turnop and his crew of rustics in *John a Kent* are so closely paralleled by Bottom and his fellows in *A Midsummer Night's Dream*, and Mundy's character Shrimp plays a part so similar to that of Puck in *A Midsummer Night's Dream*, that it seems almost certain one dramatist was here following the other. In the past, when *John a Kent* was dated 1595 or 1596, these resemblances could be held to prove that Mundy was imitating Shakespeare. Now, unless scholars are willing to date *A Midsummer Night's Dream* in 1589 or earlier, we must suppose that it was Shakespeare who was here the imitator.

Shakespeare might have learned much else from *John a Kent*. If he needed to be taught that conflict and suspense are the essence of drama, that the conflict should be presented at the beginning of a play and sustained thereafter until the very end, and that its climax should co-incide with its finale, here was a model for him to follow. In *John a Kent* the fight is on from the opening lines, and final victory is in doubt until the last. If Shakespeare needed a reminder that courtiers and characters of high degree are human, and feel and act and have their being accordingly, even when they are in love or crossed in love, here it was. And here also was an example of how such characters can be made to speak appropriately and with dignity in verse that is at the same time natural and easy. Finally, here was an example of magic being made credible because it is intermingled with the commonplace and made at home in a world we believe in because we all know it, the world of Turnop and his crew.

What other plays did Mundy write in the 1580's and early 1590's? Did Shakespeare pick up anything from them? Here indeed is a boundless sea for speculative exploration, which I should like to paddle about in for a while before going on to consider Mundy's next surviving play, *Sir Thomas More*.

Contemporary references to Mundy's plays report practically nothing about their subject-matter and themes. From a couple of hostile critics,[7] one of them Ben Jonson, we learn that Mundy was content to use 'Old England's mothers' words', to 'write plain' and 'keep the old decorum', and that he preferred to make his plays appeal through their subject-matter. He believed a good plot to be more important than the 'new tricks' and 'humours' that fascinated Jonson and other angry young men towards the end of Elizabeth's reign. By that time Mundy was comfortably off, and one of the 'best-selling' of Elizabethan professional authors. He had also become one of the best-known writers of comedies—that is, comedies in the wide Eliza-bethan sense. Francis Meres included Mundy in his catalogue of the 'best for comedy among us' in *Palladis Tamia* (1598), and singled him out as 'our best plotter'. He does not mention him in his list of 'our best for tragedy'. Meres does not distinguish the plays we now classify as chronicles or histories from comedies or tragedies. He lists *Henry IV* among Shakespeare's tragedies (together with *Richard II*, *Richard III*, and *King John*) but, to judge by his references to the work of Greene and Lodge, he considers their history plays as comedies. Is it possible that he classed Mundy's historical plays as comedies also?

In talking of 'Mundy's historical plays' I am hypothesizing. It seems to me almost certain that in the 1580's and early 1590's Mundy must have written a number of history plays now lost (or at least not now identified as his). There was at that time a vogue for such plays and Mundy was concerned, according to his enemies (but also according to what we know of his literary career) to supply what the general public called for. That would be a slender argument indeed if it stood alone, but there is much else to support it.

Mundy's surviving original plays are all partly historical, for we must remember that to most Elizabethans Randolph, Earl of Chester and other characters in Mundy's *John a Kent*, and Robin Hood and others in *The Downfall of Robert Earl of Huntington*, were figures just as historical as those in *Sir Thomas More*. This choice of historical settings and subjects is not accidental, but reflects a characteristic propensity. Mundy, in his very earliest publications, and increasingly throughout his long career, evinces a keen interest in history, and his writings disclose wide reading in it, in several languages. In 1611 he published a *Brief Chronicle of the Success of Times*, an epitome of universal history in 600 octavo pages, which is still a useful reference book.

A little earlier he had succeeded his old and intimate friend John Stow as Historiographer to the City of London, an appointment suggested by Stow himself when his health began to fail. The extent, and the value, of Mundy's work on *The Survey of London* is rarely recognized, partly no doubt because he left Stow's name on the title-pages of the greatly expanded editions he published in 1618 and later, but omitted his own.

At the beginning of his career Mundy's interest in history was political and ethical rather than antiquarian. A pamphlet mentioned earlier, *A Watchword to England*, 1584, illustrates very well both Mundy's use of history and his political outlook in the middle 1580's. Its immediate concern is the danger that threatens England, and Elizabeth in particular. It reviews the various treasons, rebellions and attempted assassinations of English sovereigns from the reign of Richard Cœur de Lion onwards to the 'miraculous preservation' of Elizabeth during Mary's reign, and follows up with a general discussion of the consequences of treason. Mundy does not argue that all English Catholics are necessarily potential traitors; he indicts only those who grant the Pope supremacy over Elizabeth and concede his claim to depose her and absolve her subjects from their vows of allegiance. This is the attitude Mundy takes in all his anti-papal and anti-Jesuit pamphlets. In his *Watchword* Mundy of course has always in mind the St Bartholomew massacre of twelve years earlier, and the very recent assassination of the Prince of Orange. He is concerned, like many other Englishmen at that time, lest Queen Elizabeth be similarly murdered. It may be difficult today to believe that any Catholic leaders, in this country or abroad, ever plotted, or even contemplated, the assassination of Elizabeth; and it may be that in fact none did. It certainly seemed otherwise, at the time, to many sober and responsible Englishmen. We have to remember that England was then involved in an ideological conflict, a 'cold war' far more intense and unremitting than anything we in this island have known in modern times, and that the odds seemed heavily on the side of her enemies. Mundy, moreover, had listened often to the most ardent of the English Catholics at Rome, and elsewhere abroad. It is not surprising that he returned strongly anti-papal and anti-Jesuit, for the surviving writings of some of the Catholic refugees with whom Mundy lived in 1579–80 show that the more fanatical consoled themselves with dreams, even if they realized they could be only dreams, of just the kind of purges and exterminations Mundy warns his countrymen against in his *Watchword*. No one reading that pamphlet could be blind to its sincerity or unimpressed by its sense of urgency, or imagine that its writer would lose any opportunity to communicate his fears and doubts to the public at large.

It seems to me highly probable, therefore, that during the 1580's and earlier 1590's some of the plays Mundy wrote would have been historical plays on patriotic and anti-papal themes, like that of the anonymous *Troublesome Reign of King John* and Shakespeare's *King John*. I hope I shall not be thought to be hinting that Mundy was probably the writer of *The Troublesome Reign*. I think that most improbable, but, I must add, only on stylistic grounds and because the diction and the rhythm of the verse seem unlike Mundy's. The plot, however, and most of the sentiments of *The Troublesome Reign* might well have come from Mundy, and it is at least conceivable that 'our best plotter' plotted it, leaving others to drape his outline with dialogue. This is admittedly speculation but it seems as plausible a theory about that play's genesis as some others that have been taken seriously.

At this point I should like to consider the implications of Meres' description of Mundy as 'our best plotter'. Does this describe only the quality of Mundy's own plays, or does it refer to his excellence, and eminence, as provider of what today we call scenarios?[8] I use the word scenario to avoid confusion with the Elizabethan prompter's 'plots'. We know from Henslowe's *Diary* that Elizabethan dramatists sometimes provided a scenario for others to work on. For example, in December 1597, Henslowe bought a 'plot', for twenty shillings, from Ben Jonson; Chapman later expanded it into a tragedy. Some of Henslowe's entries record that Mundy was associated with another two or three writers, sometimes even with four others, in the composition of a single play. Do any of these entries happen to conceal that Mundy composed the scenario for others to amplify? How should we interpret the payment to Mundy, on 2 December 1602, on behalf of the Admiral's company, of three pounds for *The Set at Tennis*? This was a 'payment in full', but Mundy is not likely to have sold the Admiral's men a complete play at such a bargain price, especially when he was at the height of his powers and reputation. It seems much more probable that this three pounds was the price exacted by 'our best plotter' for a promising scenario. On these grounds I believe we should interpret Meres' description of Mundy as 'our best plotter' as meaning that Mundy was known, not only as one of the best writers of comedies, or what Meres classified as comedies, but also as a provider of scenarios.

How far back might Mundy have been active in this capacity? As we noted earlier, Mundy was acting 'extempore' before the beginning of 1582. Even if it is true that he was unsuccessful then, it is quite clear that some seven years later, when he was caricatured as 'Posthaste' in *Histriomastix*, his reputation as an extemporist was well established. Indeed Posthaste's extemporizing is that character's most prominent trait. When he suggests to Incle:

> Let's make up a company of Players
> For we can all sing and say,
> And so (with practice) soon may learn to play

Incle replies 'True, could our action answer your extempore', and thereafter Posthaste's confidence in his ability to extemporize, and his pleasure in doing so, are kept constantly before us.

What form did this extemporizing take? Partly, no doubt, it was extempore rhyming and ballading on given themes; but was it also something like the improvisation of the *Commedia dell'Arte*, which Mundy had seen in Italy and perhaps also in France? If it was the latter kind of improvization, did Mundy organize his own company as *Histriomastix* seems to suggest? From all that we know of him, that seems more probable than that he should have been organized by others. If Mundy acted extempore with others, whatever their organization, it seems highly likely that he would have supplied some of the scenarios required, if not most of them. Mundy's production of scenarios may, therefore, have begun as early as 1581 or very soon afterwards. During the 1580's and 1590's he may have plotted a large number of plays, for a variety of companies. I think we may safely assume that a goodly proportion of any scenarios Mundy drew up before 1600 would have been on historical and patriotic subjects. In this way his influence on the development of the history play in the 1580's may have been considerable. Combined with the example and influence of his own historical plays, it may have been greater than that of any other single dramatist, though of course Mundy could not have been the only purveyor of scenarios; Greene and Nashe seem to have been others.[9]

Over the years, no doubt, companies that bought such scenarios would rework the superstructures built on them, pruning or expanding the action, and varying the dialogue, either themselves as best they could, or with the help of professional writers. But in spite of such re-working of details, the basic outline of plot and action—the original scenario—might well remain unaffected and substantially unchanged. This one would expect to have been particularly true of those plays which from the first were most successful for, unless the theatrical profession was then very different from what it is now, nothing is safer from revision, nothing is more un-changeable, than a stock success. How many plays by Shakespeare (and by other dramatists) are reinterpretations of old scenarios, too tried and too successful to be discarded or even departed from to any extent? How far were the new versions shaped and determined in advance by the success of the old scenario? How much does *The Merchant of Venice* owe to '*The Jew* shown at the Bull', or *Hamlet* to the 'ur-Hamlet'? How many of Shakespeare's 'source-plays' themselves are revisions of such scenarios? I often wonder whether certain of the so-called 'abridged texts' of early Elizabethan plays are not in fact versions of scenarios supplied originally by Mundy, Greene or some other dramatist, expanded and patched by a succession of actors and writers for the companies that owned and performed them. I find it much easier to explain in this way the state of the text of, for example, *The Famous Victories of Henry V*, than to accept theories of memorial reconstruction, imperfect reporting, and so forth.

Is it possible then that the basic plot and pattern, and general outlook, of Shakespeare's *King John* were dictated to him by the great success of *The Troublesome Reign*, and that behind the latter was an even earlier version, or versions, of the same scenario? Was there a similar history for Shakespeare's *Taming of the Shrew* and the anonymous *A Shrew*; and behind *King Lear* and *The Chronicle History of Leir*? Were Shakespeare's *Henry IV* and *Henry V* and their source-play *The Famous Victories*, partly conditioned by an 'ur-Henry'? Would that explain familiar references to 'Hotspur' and 'Owen Glendower' in *John a Kent* in 1589, or earlier?[10] These, of course, are only a few of the questions that might be raised. If there is anything in these specula-tions, their implications for students of the development of Elizabethan drama, and of Shake-speare's plays in particular, are far-reaching, perhaps disturbing. So I hasten back to the firmer ground of *Sir Thomas More*, Mundy's next surviving play.

There can be no doubt whatever, it seems to me, that the original draft of *Sir Thomas More* was conceived, as well as written, wholly by Anthony Mundy. This is not a mere impression. However, to set out the supporting evidence would require far more space than is available now, so I must, for the moment, present the conclusion alone.[11] But although I am convinced that Mundy was the author of *Sir Thomas More* in its original version, I am not at all sure that any-thing useful can be said about Shakespeare's connexion with its revision, because I do not see how we can hope to establish, on the existing evidence, that the famous three pages of Addition II are in Shakespeare's handwriting. Sir E. M. Thompson's arguments seem to me, at their very best, to prove only that the writer of the authenticated Shakespeare signatures *might* also have written the three pages in Hand D in *Sir Thomas More*. This is very far indeed from proving that he did. Some of Thompson's evidence is inconclusive—for example, he is wrong in sup-posing the famous 'spurred a' to be peculiar to these documents. Several different examples of it occur in various State Papers of the 1580's and 1590's; Thompson's arguments, moreover, are often literary and imaginative rather than palaeographical, and consequently anything but conclusive. This is particularly true of his attempt to fix the date of Mundy's writing in *Sir Thomas More* on what he calls palaeographical evidence, but what is in fact guesswork about Mundy based on the account current in literary histories. Thompson's conclusion that Mundy wrote *Sir Thomas More* about 1592 or 1593 may be correct, but it is not supported by anything that deserves to be called scholarly argument rather than wishful thinking. Thus the firmer ground to which we seemed to be moving when we turned to *Sir Thomas More* proves rather to be a quicksand, possibly a mirage, for students of Shakespeare's connexion with that play.

It is more profitable to consider what Shakespeare might have learnt either from *Sir Thomas More* or from similar history plays that Mundy doubtless wrote earlier and about the same date. *Sir Thomas More* is not a play about 'Evil May-day', as some discussions of it might suggest, but a portrayal of the career and personality of its protagonist. It is a study in character, comparing the behaviour of differing or opposing characters in the same situations, in the course of attempting a rounded presentation of an historical figure who was also a great man. In this it is unusually successful and convincing, for we feel Mundy's More to be not only an entirely credible human being but also a truly great man. Of course Mundy's success is due partly to the use he makes of Hall's *Chronicle* and Roper's *Life of More*, as Shakespeare later was helped by use of Holinshed and Plutarch. But it is important to note that Mundy's achievement in *Sir Thomas More* necessitated some at least of the same kind of insight and the same skill in handling source-material as we admire in Shakespeare. Moreover, if 1593 is near the correct date for *More*, Mundy can hardly have learnt any of this from Shakespeare, though the latter may have found useful lessons in method in Mundy's *More*. He may have learnt other lessons there also. Knowing what we do about Mundy's theologico-political standpoint we are compelled to admire his tolerant and broad-minded appreciation of More. Magnanimity of this order is not what we are taught to expect from an Elizabethan protestant, much less from a formerly active and convinced anti-Catholic agent; if it was as rare in the 1590's as our histories suggest, it may have had no little influence on Shakespeare's reading, and rendering, of history.

NOTES

1. A lecture delivered to the International Shakespeare Conference at Stratford-upon-Avon, 2 September 1959.

2. See 'Mundy's Birthdate', *Notes and Queries*, N.S. III (1956), 2–3; the arguments there advanced have now been confirmed by Mark Eccles in 'Anthony Munday' in *The English Renaissance Drama*, ed. J. W. Bennet and others (1959), and by Leslie Hotson in *Notes and Queries*, N.S. VI (1959), 2–4.

3. The evidence is conveniently reprinted in Celeste Turner's *Anthony Mundy* (Berkeley, 1928), pp. 58–9.

4. In dedicating his *Watchword* to Queen Elizabeth Mundy described himself as 'her Maiesties most humble Subiect and Seruant'; the book must have been sent to press in October 1584.

5. I have found no record of a payment to Mundy as Messenger earlier than one in the Chamber Accounts for the year ending 29 September 1586; the precise date of payment is not given (P.R.O., E. 351/542/membr. 83, dorse).

6. Cf. *Shakespeare Survey*, 8 (1955), 100.

7. The author of *Histriomastix* (Act II), and Ben Jonson in *The Case is Altered* (I, i).

8. See 'Stenography and Bad Quartos', in *Times Literary Supplement* (13 May 1960), p. 305, for other evidence that *plot* in Elizabethan English may sometimes mean 'scenario'.

9. In *Have With You to Saffron Walden* (1596) Nashe indignantly rejects the charge of having imitated Greene, 'he subscribing to me in anything but plotting Plays, wherein he was his crafts master' (McKerrow's *Nashe*, III, 131).

10. For 'Hotspur' see *John a Kent* (Malone Society Reprint), line 301; for 'Owen Glendower' see line 895.

11. The evidence will be detailed in a study of the *Sir Thomas More* problem which I hope to publish shortly.

MARLOWE AS PROVOCATIVE AGENT IN SHAKESPEARE'S EARLY PLAYS

BY

NICHOLAS BROOKE

There are a number of eruptions in Shakespeare's work of passages which are unmistakably Marlovian in tone and attitude, to a degree which would almost justify a disintegrator in identifying them as Marlowe's work. That can, of course, be said of Shakespeare's relations with other contemporaries, for he was always a magpie; but what makes Marlowe's influence quite a different matter from anyone else's is that he alone was a poetic dramatist of genius. That the laments over the 'dead' Juliet might have been a different thing without Kyd, only suggests that they might have been a better thing; but that Morocco's speeches in *The Merchant of Venice* would have been different without *Tamburlaine* leads forward into the evident development of Othello's distinctive utterance from Morocco's: and that is a line which can hardly be over-valued. It suggests a deliberate closeness to Marlowe's very distinctive manner which must involve an attitude to his equally distinctive moral values, except for the most vulgarly eclectic of imitators; and Shakespeare was not that kind of magpie. The significance of such passages is my principal concern in this essay.

They form, of course, only a loosely distinguishable group among the various familiar kinds of Marlovian influence. At one extreme, there are precise verbal echoes which are often without particular significance; such things as

> Peace!—how the moon sleeps with Endymion
>
> *(Merchant of Venice*, v, i, 109)[1]

whose evident derivation from Marlowe's Ovid (I, xiii, 43) only suggests to me how much more acceptable this side of *The Merchant* would be if Shakespeare had carried over Marlowe's irony with his imagery.[2] There is not much more to be said about the well-known tributes in *As You Like It*,[3] which in any case do not refer to Marlowe's dramatic poetry; Pistol's parody of Tamburlaine does that (*2 Henry IV*, II, iv, 176–8), but only in a very conventional form. Far more considerable is the derivation of Shylock from Barabas, or of Richard of Gloucester from Marlowe's Machiavels. To this I shall return; but for the largest case of all, the relation of *Edward II* to Shakespeare's Histories, I assume general acceptance of A. P. Rossiter's judgement[4] that Marlowe learnt from *Henry VI*, and Shakespeare reclaimed the debt in *Richard II*.

At the other end of the scale, it is universally acknowledged that the effect of Marlowe's verse is pervasive in Shakespeare's early work. Such general influence is not, of course, all of one kind: as F. P. Wilson has emphasized,[5] there is considerable variety in Marlowe's writing, and passages influenced by *Tamburlaine*, or *The Jew of Malta*, or *Dr Faustus* will not all be just the same thing. In any case, this pervasive influence is apt to prove elusive; but it can merge into the more direct imitation which I want to examine, and it is more often felt in some plays than in others. Such is the case with *2 Henry VI*, and here, though it may well be true that the verse is affected by Shakespeare's awareness of Marlowe, it is almost curious that it is not more so. Suffolk, Margaret, and York all have Machiavel tendencies; they might all with perfect propriety talk like the Guise. But though from time to time they approach hyperboles of power, the Marlovian rhythm never fully takes charge: the nearest approach, I think, is York's

> Ring, bells, aloud; burn, bonfires, clear and bright,
> To entertain great England's lawful king.
> Ah! sancta majestas, who'd not buy thee dear?
> Let them obey that knows not how to rule;
> This hand was made to handle nought but gold.
>
> (*2 Henry VI*, v, i, 3–7)

Momentarily, York suggests the ruthless *virtù* of Marlowe's heroes: but Shakespeare allows it no development, and one is left feeling that if Marlowe has been glanced at, he has been almost deliberately avoided (perhaps in favour of the stress on 'lawful'). And this kind of influence and avoidance remains the general fact in *3 Henry VI* and in *Richard III*.[6]

It is a very different thing when in *Titus Andronicus*, after a first act which (though its ill-repute seems to me exaggerated) certainly does not derive its imperial tone from Marlowe, we come on Aaron's soliloquy preluding Act II:

> Now climbeth Tamora Olympus' top,
> Safe out of fortune's shot, and sits aloft,
> Secure of thunder's crack or lightning flash,
> Advanc'd above pale envy's threat'ning reach...   (ll. 1–4)
> Then, Aaron, arm thy heart, and fit thy thoughts,
> To mount aloft with thy imperial mistress,
> And mount her pitch whom thou in triumph long
> Hast prisoner held, fett'red in amorous chains,
> And faster bound to Aaron's charming eyes
> Than is Prometheus tied to Caucasus.
> Away with slavish weeds and servile thoughts!
> I will be bright, and shine in pearl and gold.   (ll. 12–19)

It seems to me impossible to hear this, and not think of Marlowe.[7] Overall there is a sustained rhythmic splendour moving from hyperbole to hyperbole; but the relationship is patent also in every significant detail. Tamora's achievement of the imperial crown is not to Aaron (as it is to her) simply a useful means to private satisfactions of revenge and lust: for him, it places her like Tamburlaine beyond the limitations not only of human law, but of Nature's or Fortune's control as well. Aaron, in fact, values empery in terms of the human apotheosis, in the fullest contrast to the implied normality of 'slavish weeds and servile thoughts' (that Aaron is in fact a slave modifies, but does not alter, this general sense); and the richness of the speech depends always on the association of this concept of power with the wealth of pearl and gold[8] as well as on the insistent sensuality. It is an important point that when Aaron comes to mention a specific object for the exercise of power, although it is no less than the ruin of emperor and empire, it is clearly indicated as a falling-off from the full scope of his sensual triumph:

> To wait, said I? to wanton with this queen,
> This goddess, this Semiramis, this nymph,
> This siren, that will charm Rome's Saturnine,
> And see his shipwrack and his commonweal's.　　　　　(ll. 21–4)

The progression that leads through 'queen', 'goddess' to 'Semiramis' is really a regression: aurally she is splendid, but in mythological fact she is not a goddess, and so we move downwards through nymph and siren, to the cheaper sense of siren which is Tamora's power to lead Saturnine by the nose—a thought far removed from the delighted vision of wantoning with a goddess.

The point does not need labouring further: Aaron not only borrows Marlowe's utterance, he expresses through it a summary of the distinctive attitudes which gave that utterance its greatness in *Tamburlaine* and *Dr Faustus*. It is something that York's speech in *Henry VI* only faintly suggested: Aaron has it in full; but with one significant omission. He has no chance of grasping, here or anywhere else, the intellectual aspirations of Faustus, which Tamburlaine had (however strangely) anticipated, and to which the Guise has still some pretensions (e.g. in his dealings with Ramus). Barabas, whom Aaron is later to echo, has less inclination towards learning, but even he has a kind of intellectual pride which Aaron does not share (e.g. *Jew of Malta*, I, ii, 219–24). The very unlikelihood of Tamburlaine's philosophical reflexions on Nature is a clear indication of a kind of respectability in the hero; I do not mean of course an unconditional endorsement, for there is scarcely a criticism of the Tamburlaine figure which does not find strong utterance in Marlowe's later plays, to say nothing of Part II of *Tamburlaine* itself. But nobody I think doubts that such criticism in Marlowe's work goes with a fundamental sympathy. This is by no means so with Shakespeare: the element of 'respectability' is entirely absent from this speech of Aaron's, though imaginative potency is very much present.

Aaron's case differs somewhat even from Barabas'; they are alike in perfect malignancy later, but there is about Aaron initially none of the ambiguity we may feel in the Jew: he is, as Barabas is not, absolutely evil. The decisiveness of this judgement goes with the simple orthodoxy of Shakespeare's morality in all his early plays, and is quite alien to Marlowe. Shakespeare is committed to a total rejection of this imaginative force whose identity he establishes not only by a Marlovian figure, but by a fully Marlovian utterance. What is remarkable is that the moral rejection accompanies an imaginative recognition so strong as to generate a fully original creation, of words and character, in Marlowe's mode. If this is to be called pastiche, it must be with the recognition that it is re-creation with original force.

This is important, because it is directly from this vitality that Aaron develops into a force capable of disturbing the orthodox order of the play. *Titus* comprehends a multiplicity of tragic themes as deliberately involved as the variety of comic concerns in *The Comedy of Errors*. But the main pattern is developed from Ovid's *Metamorphoses*: Titus is translated from the noble hero of the opening to the sub-human revenger of the end; and the pivot of this change is his eruption into appalling laughter in III, i, 264. Aaron is the principal agent behind this metamorphosis, and he anticipates that laugh in generating a sense of horrid farce in his mockery of the Andronici in III, i. Subsequently he is made to emerge, contrapuntally to Titus' decline, revealing his vitality as a profoundly human instinct in defence of his black baby, for whose life he sacrifices with superb contempt first the midwife ("Wheak, wheak!" So cries a pig prepared to the spit'—IV, ii, 147–8), and finally himself. But this extraordinary vitality, however 'healthy', does not make Aaron 'good': his final gesture is still of contempt, based on his full imitation of Barabas' catalogue of evil (v, i, 125–44; *Jew of Malta*, II, iii, 175–201). Both speeches are fantasies of evil; but there is some difference of context between them. The Jew is partly 'making this up' for Ithamore's benefit; whereas it is Aaron's final self-identifying gesture. Consequently, Aaron can be finally condemned and committed to emblematic punishment without the latent equivocation which seems to attend the restoration of order in *The Jew* (which will be felt, I think, even if it is inadequately pointed in the text).[9]

The conclusion which this inspection of Aaron's place in *Titus* suggests is of a deliberate inclusion of the Marlovian figure in the tragic complex. His presence does much to distort the simple orthodoxy which I have claimed as characteristic: to that Shakespeare finally returns, from that indeed we have never supposed he would depart. But on the way he has indicated not only the utter degradation of his 'hero', but also what one might call the elevation of his major villain; a villain who takes on much of the character of one kind of tragic hero himself. The final orthodoxy is achieved only through a recognition that there is no necessary correlation between human vitality and the moral order, for Aaron is not even given the kind of psychological background with which Richard III accounts for his moral condition. And if it is acknowledged that elsewhere the verse of *Titus* rarely if ever suggests Marlowe in any significant way, then it seems to follow that the Marlovian utterance is here introduced as explicitly identified with the Marlovian ethos.

There is no other instance of such full-scale deployment of this kind of imitation; but hints of it in varying degrees occur in a number of very different plays and situations, at least as far as *Julius Caesar*. The closest parallel is obviously with the figure of Richard of Gloucester, developed consistently through *3 Henry VI* and *Richard III*. The ghostly Margaret places him in *Richard III* by an echo of Barabas which is obviously not mere coincidence:

> O Buckingham! take heed of yonder dog:
> Look, when he fawns, he bites.
>
> (I, iii, 289–90; *Jew of Malta*, II, iii, 20–1)

Marlowe's villain is still a felt presence behind Shakespeare's, and such a general relationship has always been recognized. But the Marlovian presence is, in fact, some way behind in *Richard III*: by then, Shakespeare has developed for Richard his own distinctive utterance, which is never precisely Marlovian, and it is notable that Richard's ambition for the crown includes no speculation at all on the possibility of rising above the common limitations of humanity. He is committed, more completely even than Aaron, to moral condemnation. What he has, Aaron-like in his Marlovian origins, is the vitality to dominate the play, and to give its orthodoxy a kind of excitement which Richmond alone would never provide. But Richard's vitality is always fully within the compass of his perversion, which Aaron's is not; Richard can, by his force, do something to distort the obvious values of the play, but he never sets a healthy human instinct at odds with the moral scheme.

In other words, in *Richard III* we have something derived from Marlowe, but entirely new-created to Shakespeare's own purpose in a very different context. There is not the implication I found in Aaron of deliberately involving the Marlovian experience as one among other dominant themes, and so there is no pastiche of Marlowe's verse to carry that sense. What is interesting is that when Richard was first brought forward in *3 Henry VI*, there was a much wider Marlovian absorption implied:

> And, father, do but think
> How sweet a thing it is to wear a crown,
> Within whose circuit is Elysium,
> And all that poets feign of bliss and joy. (I, ii, 28–31)

The reference to 'poets' is deliberately generalized, but there can be no doubt that the one most immediately in mind is Marlowe, and not *The Jew of Malta* here, but specifically *Tamburlaine* (I, II, vii, 12–29). This expresses the attitude which I find markedly absent from *Richard III*; but even here, were it not for the explicitness of the reference, one would hardly recognize the *tone* as decisively Marlowe: the idea is echoed, but not (or not convincingly) the utterance which gives it value. And indeed, even the idea itself fairly quickly disappears. It seems still to characterize Richard's reported battle-cries in I, iv, 16–17:

> 'A crown, or else a glorious tomb!
> A sceptre, or an earthly sepulchre!'

and leaves some mark on the first of Richard's major soliloquies:

> I'll make my heaven to dream upon the crown;
> And, whiles I live, to account this world but hell,
> Until my mis-shap'd trunk that bears this head
> Be round impaled with a glorious crown. (III, ii, 168–71)

But the stress is already more on the 'mis-shap'd trunk' than on the *glory* of the crown, and the rest of the speech turns more conclusively towards the utterance that characterizes Richard later. Marlowe is still very much present in:

> I can add colours to the chameleon,
> Change shapes with Proteus for advantages,
> And set the murd'rous Machiavel to school.
> Can I do this, and cannot get a crown?
> Tut! were it further off, I'll pluck it down. (ll. 191–5)

But here the crown itself has come within the orbit of Richard's contempt; *Tamburlaine* has disappeared in a selective absorption from *The Jew*. It seems unlikely, then, that Shakespeare in *3 Henry VI* ever contemplated a re-creation of Marlowe as deliberate as in *Titus*; and certainly, in the event, what does start as a general Marlovian ethos, narrows and transposes into a distinctive creation that still owes much to Marlowe, but much also to a particular purpose radically unlike Marlowe, the final identification of the Machiavel with an orthodox conception of evil. And in this process he withdraws not only the positive humanity of Aaron,[10] but also the Tamburlainish positiveness with which Richard had begun. The Marlovian figure subserves a purpose in the moral-historical pattern, and his most potentially disturbing aspects are not allowed to develop. For this reason, and because Marlowe's strongest verse is *not* imitated here, it would clearly be wrong to take the treatment of Richard as a direct comment on the Marlovian figure; the relationship is rather one of utility than the critical exploration which I think is involved in Aaron.

A distinctive critical attitude does, however, seem to be implied in the Marlovian utterances of Bolingbroke and Mowbray in the first scene of *Richard II*. Most commentary has been concentrated here on supposed anticipations of Richard's personal weakness, of which there does not seem to me to be any clear indication. I take

> We were not born to sue, but to command   (l. 196)

to have a rhythm natural to authority, and to comment with final force on the peculiar utterance of the dissentients. This question is too large for discussion here:[11] I make the point only to focus attention on that utterance, for more than once it suggests Marlowe to significant effect. Bolingbroke's initial insults are sufficiently rhetorical, but Mowbray's reply develops a rhythmic momentum that carries it far beyond reasonable bounds:

> I do defy him, and I spit at him,
> Call him a slanderous coward, and a villain,
> Which to maintain I would allow him odds,
> And meet him were I tied to run afoot
> Even to the frozen ridges of the Alps.   (ll. 60–4)

The point is not only that the alpine hyperbole is in Marlowe's rhythm, but that it makes of Mowbray's retaliation a gesture of personal supremacy in terms of heroic force and endurance. And Bolingbroke succeeds in out-daring the gesture:

> Which blood, like sacrificing Abel's, cries
> Even from the tongueless caverns of the earth
> To me for justice and rough chastisement.   (ll. 104–6)

The blood image, and Abel's murder, are recurrent themes in the play owing nothing important to Marlowe; but it is on the Marlovian tone in which Bolingbroke has delivered them that Richard, very pertinently, comments:

> How high a pitch his resolution soars!   (l. 109)

The justice or otherwise of their complaints becomes unimportant compared with the mode in which they utter them: soaring resolution is not a question of justice, but of the glorification of individual man. They express an attitude in direct conflict with the concept of ordered society, let alone sacred kingship, which the play is going to develop. The Marlovian ethos is invoked in Marlovian verse, but not in such a way as to disturb us: for the rhetoric is so decisively placed as blood-ruled ('wrath-kindled gentlemen') that it is felt almost as parody (not comic of course) rather than echo. The possibility of presenting insubordinate Lords in this way may well derive from the handling of Mortimer: but the difference is very large, for with Mortimer, though he is condemned, there is no question of parody; and Bolingbroke, on the other hand, is not subsequently identified with the attitude he here expresses. The play would be very different if he saw the earthly crown directly as a sweet fruition. The critical attitude engendered to Marlovian rhetoric has much more to do with the play's themes than it has with the development of the 'characters' of its main protagonists; and so this tone is disposed of here, and never revived.

General recollection of Marlowe is, I noted earlier, persistent in the play's debt to *Edward II*. Shakespeare reorganizes his borrowings into a pageant of Order: Marlowe may not have studied the Great Chain of Being, but Shakespeare certainly had. Such a change amounts to a radical criticism of the Marlovian ethos; but it seems to me that the Marlowe thus 'put in his place' re-emerges as a disturbing agent in at least one specific context, where there is perhaps less show of deliberation than in the play's opening scene. In the de-coronation scene (IV, i), Richard notoriously sustains the image of himself as Christ which Carlisle had initiated; but the self-complacence is countered by three somewhat elusive reminiscences of *Dr Faustus* within a space of twenty-five lines:

> O that I were a mockery king of snow,
> Standing before the sun of Bolingbroke,
> To melt myself away in water-drops!
>
> (IV, i, 260–2; *Dr Faustus*, V, ii, 183–4)

> Fiend, thou torments me ere I come to hell.   (l. 270)

> Was this face the face
> That every day under his household roof
> Did keep ten thousand men? Was this the face
> That like the sun did make beholders wink?
>
> (ll. 281–4; *Dr Faustus*, V, i, 98 ff.)

Ure[12] is mildly sceptical of this last, because the ten thousand men derive from Holinshed: but it seems to me beyond doubt that the rhythmic numerals have coalesced with the apostrophe to Helen in Shakespeare's verse. The cumulative significance of these three reminiscences is striking: the Richard who identifies himself with Christ, identifies himself also with the damned Faustus; or rather, like Faustus in his last speech, his reflexions oscillate between the visions of Heaven and Hell, and the shadow of Helen stresses the sensuality in Richard's narcissism. Richard has proved Tamburlaine's last warning to his son:

> The nature of thy chariot will not bear
> A guide of baser temper than myself   (2 *Tamburlaine*, V, iii, 242–3)

which has for context the Phaeton image (ll. 231 and 244) and the subject kings as jades to be bridled (ll. 203 and 238), which are presumably echoed in

> Down, down I come, like glist'ring Phaeton,
> Wanting the manage of unruly jades.   (*Richard II*, III, iii, 178–9)

When Richard sees his ultimate failure as damnable to himself as well as to those who supplant him, the possibility is envisaged, however obscurely, that his elevation was no more divine than Faustus'.

The distinction felt in *Richard II* between Shakespearian and Marlovian attitudes to State and Individual reaches much further than is obvious in general comparison with *Edward II*: *Tamburlaine* and *Faustus* are also remembered, and the awareness of Marlowe's power, which Shakespeare can criticize and parody in I, i, is not after all so easily disposed of: it re-emerges as a disturbing challenge.

Critical parody of a less important kind may be felt occasionally in the Bastard's speeches in *King John*: he deflates (at least in Acts I and II) rhetoric of any kind by setting it against his own distinctive 'plain speech', but it is again almost surprising how seldom there is any hint of Marlowe. One may suspect it in II, i when the elaborate formalities of Hubert (or 'first citizen') are taken off in terms more obviously Marlowe-like than what they parody:

> Here's a large mouth indeed,
> That spits forth death and mountains, rocks and seas,
> Talks as familiarly of roaring lions
> As maids of thirteen do of puppy-dogs! (ll. 457–60)

But the parody is of verbal hyperbole in general, and when the speech indicates this as out-of-date—

> Zounds! I was never so bethump'd with words
> Since I first call'd my brother's father dad (ll. 466–7)

—one is more likely to think of *The Troublesome Raigne* (if that is an earlier play) than of Marlowe. At any rate, this is purely linguistic parody, no question of Marlowe's *values* arises; so that it is not much more consequential than Pistol's pampered jades. Nor is there any repetition elsewhere in *Henry IV* of the significant references in *Richard II*. Glendower's eloquence (*1 Henry IV*, III, i) rolls shepherds and magicians together, and is open to Hotspur's laughter; but it does not suggest Marlowe. We get a little closer in *2 Henry IV*, IV, i, 113–29, when young Mowbray, explicitly recalling his father's part in *Richard II*, gives an account of the rebellion in glowing romantic rhetoric which is coldly set down by Westmoreland's

> You speak, Lord Mowbray, now you know not what. (l. 130)

But though the dismissal of rhetoric and attitude does reflect the scene in *Richard II*, the specific attitude and utterance here suggests Hotspur and even Hal more readily than Marlowe. Shakespeare has developed, as in *King John* and later in *Julius Caesar*, a process of invoking the literary criticalness of his audience to expose attitudes in the kinds of utterance that identify them. This technique itself may derive from the initial experiments in placing Marlowe by imitation and parody.

The only remaining play showing considerable imitation that I know of[13] is *The Merchant of Venice*; and as with *Richard II* this is no doubt affected by the general reminiscence of a specific play, this time *The Jew of Malta*, carrying with it other aspects of Marlowe's work. The language of Shylock, and the use made of him to criticize the hypocrisy of a Christian society, come from

The Jew; but Morocco and Arragon belong more widely, I believe, with Marlowe's heroic figures. The richness of Morocco's first speech:

> Bring me the fairest creature northward born,
> Where Phoebus' fire scarce thaws the icicles,
> And let us make incision for your love,
> To prove whose blood is reddest, his or mine. (ii, i, 4–7)

leads through

>   by this scimitar
> That slew the Sophy, and a Persian prince
> That won three fields of Sultan Solyman,
> I would o'erstare the sternest eyes that look. (ll. 24–7)

to self-identification with Hercules (ll. 32–8). The figure thus briefly re-created has no doubt reference to other Eastern heroes derived from Tamburlaine, but the quality of it is Tamburlaine's alone; and this is the more apparent when in ii, vii Morocco develops a lyrical address to Portia:

> The Hyrcanian deserts, and the vasty wilds
> Of wide Arabia are as throughfares now
> For princes to come view fair Portia. (ll. 41–3)

The last line is adapted like a refrain in l. 47, and so suggests Tamburlaine's lyrical 'To entertain divine Zenocrate' (*2 Tamburlaine*, ii, iv, 15 ff.). Morocco, in short, derives his nature and his utterance from Tamburlaine; whereas Arragon's

> I will not choose what many men desire,
> Because I will not jump with common spirits,
> And rank me with the barbarous multitudes. (ii, ix, 31–3)

is even more distinctively descended from the Guise's

> What glory is there in a common good,
> That hangs for every peasant to achieve? (*Massacre at Paris*, ii, 40–1)

These two figures, then, the heroes of scenes which are nowadays amongst the most glossily tedious of all Shakespeare's, derive their surprising poetic quality from deliberate invocation of Marlowe. They had, in the 1590's, far more force than now, since they presented the two basic hero-types, carefully distinguished but still associated in the common origin of their utterance; between their gold and silver lies the difference between the splendour of the Middle Eastern Alcides and the less glorious Western Machiavel.

The choice makes a judgement much too easily, for all its suggestion of a divine providence behind what they, like Mortimer, call 'Fortune'. The critical sense of their utterance, where we are made aware of a force and quality as well as of hollow arrogance, is more adequate; but still too easy against the recollection of Marlowe's plays that is invited. But perhaps in a comedy this is full enough development. In *Julius Caesar* that technique receives fuller, and more complex, development. It is in the case of Caesar himself that Marlovian rhetoric plays a significant part, used to discriminate between the valid greatness assumed to be his, and the vulgar egotism superficially indistinguishable from it. Reliance on Marlowe is by no means extensive, nor is it a matter of close imitation; but when Caesar says (II, ii, 71):

> The cause is in my will: I will not come,

we may recognize the attitude; and we feel it more strongly in the prelude to the murder, as Caesar's rhetoric gathers momentum (and hyperboles) against the appeals to mercy for Metellus:

> Know, Caesar doth not wrong, nor without cause
> Will he be satisfied. (III, i, 47–8)

This is not the nonsense Ben Jonson made of it in *Timber* ('Caesar did never wrong, but with just cause'),[14] but in *tone* the difference is not great; and that tone develops into the epic simile of the constancy of the North Star with its climax:

> Yet in the number I do know but one
> That unassailable holds on his rank,
> Unshak'd of motion; and that I am he. (ll. 68–70)

One further challenge, and the substitution of rhetoric for authority becomes complete:

> *Cin.* O Caesar—
> *Caes.* Hence! Wilt thou lift up Olympus? (l. 74)

He has arrived at a final self-identification with the Tamburlaine-type, in a single characteristic hyperbole; it is the pitch to which his resolution has been soaring, and its achievement is both the signal for, and the justification of, the murder.

The tragic irony of the play is most strongly felt when (in IV, iii) Brutus is moved to a similar rhetorical progression, quarrelling with Cassius, but revealing all too plainly the tones of jealous pride:

> Must I observe you? Must I stand and crouch
> Under your testy humour? (ll. 45–6)

The final climax is indicated by recollection of Caesar's words:

> A flatterer's would not, though they do appear
> As huge as high Olympus. (ll. 90–1)

I would not claim that the suggestion of Marlowe is anything like so full as in the earlier instances; but still here the climax of the exposure does remind us strongly, and significantly, of a differently valued self-assertion. The placing of Caesar's crazy ambition in the ascent of a Marlovian rhetorical mountain, startlingly echoed in Brutus' wrath-kindled speech later, is only one (and that the crudest) of the ways in which this play, more elaborately than others, doth make critics of us all. Again and again, we judge by quality of utterance the values represented by Cassius, Brutus, Antony and the other noble Romans. Brutus' speech to the crowd is rhetoric, but significantly restrained by prose; Antony pulls out every stop: the result is poetry of a high order, rhetoric of the most offensive kind (not Marlowe's, of course). The whole play, it seems to me, depends on discriminations of this kind, often subtler. The process I have been isolating as deliberate pastiche of Marlowe merges into this larger use of opposing kinds of utterance enforcing critical judgements on what they represent. It is not mere parody of mannerisms, but the evaluation of attitudes by reflexion on the utterances that represent them.

In *Julius Caesar* whatever is reminiscent of Marlowe is directly condemned; but it has still the power to disturb. That seems to me the significance of nearly all the passages I have quoted. The ethos that Marlowe created in *Tamburlaine* he himself submitted to increasingly acute criticism. The early Shakespearian ethos is of a radically different kind. The pattern of ordained degree so fully adumbrated by *Richard III* is manifestly in danger of complacent simplification. Against that tendency, the periodic eruptions of Marlowe stand as a vital force, disturbing always in their implications. This is true even of Richard himself, more so of Aaron; it is still true in *Richard II*, and though Morocco and Arragon do not much disturb *The Merchant*, Shylock does. Marlowe seems to have been for Shakespeare not only a great poet, as his tributes imply, but the inescapable imaginative creator of something initially alien which he could only assimilate with difficulty, through a process of imitative re-creation merging into critical parody. By *Julius Caesar* that element is at a minimum, and thereafter the process of assimilation is complete; reference to order is never again a matter of simple confidence, never asserted without a great reckoning with a complex of disturbing recognitions. But, however much they may owe indirectly to Marlowe, Shakespeare's later plays never (as far as I know) show any direct dependence. The provocative agent has taken his seat in the Establishment.

NOTES

1. For Shakespeare, line references are to the Oxford edition, quotations from the New Arden editions where available; for Marlowe from the Methuen series, except for *Dr Faustus* where I have used the 'conjectural reconstruction' by W. W. Greg (Oxford, 1950).

2. See also *3 Henry VI*, II, v, 114–15; *Jew of Malta*, III, ii, 11; and *Hamlet*, III, i, 79–80; *Edward II*, v, vi, 65–6.

3. III, iii, 7–17 and III, v, 81–2. *Merry Wives*, III, i, 17 ff. may be counted another kind of tribute.

4. See the Introduction to *Woodstock* (1946).

5. *Marlowe and the Early Shakespeare* (Oxford, 1953), p. 30.

6. Bakeless summarizes opinions on *Richard III* in *The Tragical History of Christopher Marlowe* (Cambridge, Mass., 1942), II, 245–8. His discussion of *3 Henry VI* depends on the now very dubious assumption that *The True Tragedie* was its source.

7. The only suggested specific echo is of Peele, in ll. 16–17; but the tone and quality are not Peele's.

8. See especially ll. 5–8.

9. See F. P. Wilson, *op. cit.* p. 68.

10. I do not mean that *Titus* is necessarily earlier than *Richard III*: the chronology of these early plays is so uncertain that I have avoided any decisive notion of sequence. Difference of purpose will explain different degrees of imitation, whichever was the earlier.

11. I am supported by Peter Ure in his introduction to his New Arden edition of the play (1955).

12. Commenting on the lines in his edition.

13. H. R. Walley argues that the first half of *Romeo and Juliet* differs largely from Brooke's poem because of Marlowe's *Hero and Leander*; no doubt there is a connexion, but a very remote one. A possible echo of *Edward II* ('Gallop apace', etc.) is insignificant. See 'Shakespeare's Debt to Marlowe in *Romeo and Juliet*', *Philological Quarterly*, XXI (1942), 257–67.

14. *Ben Jonson*, ed. Herford and Simpson (Oxford, 1947), VIII, 584; ll. 664–5.

THE TRAGEDY OF REVENGE IN SHAKESPEARE AND WEBSTER[1]

BY

HAROLD JENKINS

Some comparison between Shakespeare and Webster as writers of tragedy is made possible by their having both written tragedies based upon a type which was very popular in their day. It is true that a dramatic critic in the *Observer* has recently issued the warning that 'it is altogether too late for anyone to treat *Hamlet* simply as a revenge play'. Yet the meaning *Hamlet* has for us is inseparable from that traditional plot which gives it its unity of structure. It is with some observations about the structure of *Hamlet* that I begin.

The typical revenge plot, in its barest essentials, is one in which a crime is committed, usually a murder, and vengeance is wrought upon the perpetrator of the deed. The dramatic action therefore centres upon the opposition between the avenger and the murderer, the hero and the villain. In the old Danish story of *Hamlet*, as we know it from Saxo Grammaticus and as it was retold by Belleforest in Shakespeare's lifetime, a king was murdered by his brother, and the avenging of such a crime, notwithstanding all that may have been said by some Elizabethan preachers and some modern scholars,[2] is regarded by the story as a natural duty devolving upon the murdered man's son. To provide a cover for his designs of vengeance the Prince in the story pretends to be mad, and to get behind his guard of madness his uncle has recourse to various plots. First there is the woman who is employed to try to get his secret from him; next there is the King's counsellor who hides in the Queen's chamber; and finally there are the King's two ministers who escort Hamlet to England to be killed. It is obvious that we have here already adumbrated the roles of Ophelia, Polonius, and Rosencrantz and Guildenstern, and these all originate in that move and counter-move between the hero and the villain which gives the action of Shakespeare's play its excitement and its form. These essentials of Shakespeare's plot must have been already present in some sort in the old lost drama of *Hamlet* upon which we suppose Shakespeare to have based his own. It is probable that the lost drama also had, though the original story did not, the acting of a play at court. In Shakespeare at any rate a play-within-the-play is used to prove the murderer's guilt. But it simultaneously discloses to the murderer that his guilt is known. So that the thing which confirms the hero in his purpose of revenge also confirms the villain in his suspicion of the hero and brings the conflict between them thrillingly to a head. And this thing which brings the conflict to a head is, more precisely, the re-enacting of the murder itself. This crime, of which we learn in that tremendous narrative of the Ghost which makes the climax of the exposition, takes place once more, or rather twice, in the very central scene of the play. Nothing could be clearer than that it is around this crime and its avenging that Shakespeare's dramatic art has organized his play.

It is a frequent principle of Shakespeare's dramatic organization that the main action of the drama is interwoven with others which repeat or contrast with it. In *Hamlet* the killing of the

45

counsellor who hides behind the arras provides occasion for a second revenge action. And in this secondary plot of course Hamlet, who in the main plot is called to avenge his father, becomes the murderer and the object of revenge by the murdered man's son. Through the interweaving of these two revenge situations the play moves to its catastrophe with the hero in an ambivalent role, killed as the victim of Laertes' revenge at the moment when he achieves his own.

There is yet a third revenger in *Hamlet*. When we see Fortinbras at the head of his army, it is true that his campaign has nothing to do with avenging his father. Yet when we first heard of him in the opening scene, it was as a youth whose father had been killed, and killed moreover by Hamlet's father. It is clear enough in what character Fortinbras as well as Laertes first took root in the dramatist's mind. Shakespeare's imagination, stimulated by what is essential in Hamlet's situation, the need to avenge his father, creates these other situations to be related to it. This is apparent from the design of the exposition. The big court scene (I, ii) which gives us our first sight of the villain and the hero shows the hostility already lurking between them. But the tension between these two should not so wholly absorb us as to obscure the significant conjunction of the three young men with whom King Claudius deals in turn: first Fortinbras, next Laertes, and then Hamlet, in ascending order of importance. Criticism has usually remarked that the business of Fortinbras and Laertes here, by holding us in suspense, heightens the effect of the King's first words to Hamlet.[3] But is it not as important to observe how the three revengers are from the beginning juxtaposed? Fortinbras and Laertes are here made to lead up to Hamlet because their situations are designed to reflect his. No doubt three young men avenging dead fathers would have been too much; and when in the next court scene (II, ii) we hear that Fortinbras's rebellion is over, it is clear that the idea of using him as a revenger has been relinquished. In the early stages of a play Shakespeare is often prolific in seeds for future action not all of which can subsequently be let grow.

By contrast the role of Laertes blossoms. He was first drawn to our attention when the King addressed him by name four times in nine lines. And though this may, as the critics tell us, show the King's graciousness towards him,[4] its more important dramatic effect is the obvious one: it impresses him indelibly on our minds. And before he is allowed to disappear from Denmark we see him again with Ophelia and Polonius. The purpose of this scene (I, iii), it may be said, is to introduce the love-plot. But if this had been its only purpose, Ophelia's conversation with Polonius might have been sufficient. The scene also shows Laertes as a brother and a son. He requests and twice receives his father's blessing. And the father's advice to his son, though often regarded as a set-piece of dubious relevance, is not too long for its function of showing father and son in their natural relation with one another. In a play which turns upon sons avenging fathers, this will be of some importance. There is presently another little scene (II, i), in which Polonius sends a messenger to inquire out his son's doings. And this, too, prepares for later events. It shows Polonius with that propensity for spying which will bring him to his death; and it sustains our interest in the absent son who will presently return to avenge him.

When he does return, he is all the situation calls for, the revenger of a simple standard type. Irrupting into the palace with a mob at his heels, he threatens the King in fury: 'I'll be revenged most throughly for my father.' When he learns that the slayer is at hand he at once cries,

> Let him come.
> It warms the very sickness in my heart,
> That I shall live and tell him to his teeth,
> Thus diest thou.

(Though our texts follow the Second Quarto and the Folio in reading 'Thus diddest thou', I have not the slightest doubt that 'Thus diest thou' is what Shakespeare actually wrote.)[5] These instinctive reactions of Laertes show what Hamlet's reactions might have been if his native 'resolution' had not been 'sicklied o'er' with thought. When Laertes proclaims, 'Both the worlds I give to negligence, Let come what comes', we remember Hamlet pausing to consider what might come 'when we have shuffled off this mortal coil'. We have seen Hamlet's will confounded by 'the dread of something after death', but Laertes can say, 'I dare damnation'. The behaviour of Laertes exhibits to a superlative degree what the code of revenge demands, and it throws all Hamlet's doubts and hesitations into high relief.

So also does the behaviour of Fortinbras when at this stage in the play he likewise re-emerges in its pattern. For although Fortinbras has not grown into a revenger, his role has not been discarded, only changed. With Laertes sufficiently sustaining the role of the second revenger Fortinbras has become available for a contrast with the hero on a very much broader front. Still the leader of an army, we may note, he scorns death and danger not in pursuit of revenge but 'even for an eggshell', while Hamlet, with his so much more urgent cause, 'a father killed, a mother stained', lets all sleep. Hamlet's reflexions upon Fortinbras echo of course his earlier soliloquy on the Player, who had worked himself into a passion over the imaginary woes of Hecuba, a mere 'fiction', while Hamlet, with his so much greater 'cue for passion', could 'say nothing'. The very difference between the Player and Fortinbras, the one an actor reciting a speech and the other a prince leading an army, only serves to emphasize the one thing that they have in common and in which they are unlike the hero of the play. They give themselves wholeheartedly to their vocation and Hamlet neglects his. The comparisons between them and him, though Waldock argued otherwise,[6] are therefore organic to the play. They help to give to Hamlet's revenge a representative character as a great duty in which a man is inactive. Indeed the duty of revenge is not simply the fact which holds the plot together; from the character it assumes in the imagination the profoundest meanings of the play arise.

Hamlet's duty is set from the first in the widest possible context. It has its sanction from the tie which binds the son to the father in the workings of the natural law. Enjoined on the hero by the dread voice that comes from beyond the grave, it acquires also the mysterious compulsion of the eternal world. And it is a duty to which all the good in Hamlet's nature, whatever his misgivings and frustrations later, instinctively responds:

> Haste me to know't, that I, with wings as swift
> As meditation or the thoughts of love,
> May sweep to my revenge.

Even before the murder is disclosed Hamlet's 'prophetic soul' has already discerned his uncle as the destroyer and his foe. In his first soliloquy he has seen his father and his uncle as Hyperion and the satyr. And if we perceive the significance of this, we shall not argue for five pages, as Wilson Knight does, that Claudius is 'a good and gentle king', who happens to have committed a murder but is not really a criminal type at all.[7] A satyr is of course a creature half-man half-beast, while Hyperion is the god of the sun in human form. The figures of Hamlet's father and uncle bring into dramatic opposition the opposite elements in man's dual nature, the god and the beast, and the play becomes receptive at every point to ideas concerning good and evil, which struggle together in human life. It is the crime of Gertrude that having been united with the god, she has replaced him with the beast. And in so doing, she has become no better than a beast herself: 'A beast that wants discourse of reason Would have mourned longer'. One aspect of the evil in human nature, as the play presents it to us, is, then, the suspension of the 'discourse of reason' when man surrenders to the gross animal instincts within him which his reason should control. This bestiality further appears in the 'swinish' reputation—it is Hamlet's word—of a court whose drunken revel disturbs the solemn night even as we wait for the Ghost to appear. The Ghost denounces Claudius not only as a murderer but as 'that incestuous, that adulterate beast' who 'won to his shameful lust' the 'seeming-virtuous Queen', making of 'the royal bed of Denmark' 'a couch for luxury and damned incest'. Later, in the Queen's chamber, when Hamlet reveals 'the inmost part' of her, he shows her how Hell mutinies in a matron's bones when 'reason panders will'. This we may see as the condition of Denmark which makes it a 'prison' to Hamlet, as he tells Rosencrantz and Guildenstern it is. What is in prison is that quality of man which Hamlet praises, also to Rosencrantz and Guildenstern, in a eulogy which begins 'How noble in reason' and ends 'How like a god'. Again, when Hamlet reflects upon Fortinbras, it is to contrast 'divine ambition' with a state of being in which the 'godlike reason' is allowed to 'fust' in man 'unused', and he becomes 'a beast, no more'. What 'is rotten in the state of Denmark', we may say, is that Hyperion is slain and the satyr rules. If Hamlet's task is in one aspect to kill his father's murderer, in another it is to rid the world of the satyr and restore it to Hyperion. Is it any wonder that he finds the task beyond him?

The reason why the task must be beyond him may also be suggested by the situation of the play. When Hamlet tersely states the plain fact of his mother's incest, 'You are . . . your husband's brother's wife', he adds, 'And (would it were not so) you are my mother'. The outrage that he feels at her beastliness is more even than the revulsion that he feels at the violation of a natural law. It comes from the knowledge that she who has thus shown it in her to unite herself with the beast is the woman who, by giving him life, has given him her nature. Without wishing to press into symbolism every detail of the play, we may note that he stays in the prison of Denmark in obedience to her. 'I shall in all my best obey you, madam.' His obedience to her springs from that same law of nature as requires him to avenge his father. The evil he is called to cleanse from the world is in himself. As he tells Ophelia, 'virtue cannot so inoculate our old stock but we shall relish of it'. Hamlet's awareness of this taint in him is what poisons his love for Ophelia. His early gifts to her were accompanied by 'holy vows of heaven', but when she reminds him of his love for her, he can only retort, 'Why, wouldst thou be a breeder of sinners?' It is to avoid this fate that she must get her 'to a nunnery'. His own thoughts have turned to suicide as the only escape from the defilement of living and he is given to reflexions on the mysterious destiny of man, a being stirred by the loftiest aspirations but infected by life's evil.

It is Hamlet's destiny, then, to share the guilt that he is called upon to extirpate, and this is what makes appropriate his dual role of avenger and the object of revenge. As the enemy of Claudius he is the upholder of good; but *vis-à-vis* Laertes he is himself the evil-doer.[8] Yet though he fights Laertes at Ophelia's grave, this is because he has loved her. And before the final fencing-match he makes Laertes that curious apology in which he says that the injury he has done Laertes was done by him in madness and not by his true self. And since, as he explains, 'his madness is poor Hamlet's enemy', it follows that Hamlet and Laertes are of the same 'faction' and not really one another's enemies at all. For this quibble Hamlet has been much blamed, by Dr Johnson[9] and others, but if it outrages your sense of propriety and seems a clumsy device on Shakespeare's part, that makes it the more important to understand why the device was necessary. For there are sometimes occasions, and I take it this is one of them, when the demands of characterization have to submit to the action's overruling design. While their antithetical revenges seem to force Hamlet and Laertes on to opposite sides, in a more fundamental way they are not to be seen as opponents. On the contrary, Hamlet says, 'By the image of my cause I see The portraiture of his'. The duty of the son to avenge the father is the same in either case, and the thing that puts Hamlet and Laertes at enmity in a deeper sense unites them. Even the contrast between them in the way they conduct their revenge must finally give way to our sense of their common cause. So Hamlet sees that he has hurt his 'brother' and it is a 'brother's wager' that they play. And although they kill one another, they die forgiving one another. Instead of telling him in his teeth, 'Thus diest thou', Laertes says to the dying Hamlet, 'Mine and my father's death come not upon thee, Nor thine on me', to which Hamlet replies, 'Heaven make thee free of it'. Though Laertes makes the thrust which kills the hero, he puts the final blame elsewhere: 'The King, the King's to blame.' For the King there is no forgiveness any more than there was any repentance. What he was at the beginning he is when Hamlet at length kills him, 'Thou incestuous, murderous, damned Dane'. Hamlet, reconciled to Laertes and to his own fate, with all his questionings at length stilled in his submission to the 'divinity that shapes our ends', has come to accept the inevitable condition of human life in which evil has a part along with good. But evil is still recognized for what it is, and with evil itself there can be no reconciliation.

The importance of a literary archetype comes from what the imagination discovers in it. We may readily agree that *Hamlet* is something more than a revenge play. Yet it is through the archetypal revenge plot that Shakespeare reveals to us that larger pattern, whose outline—with some inevitable simplification but I hope not too much distortion—I have endeavoured briefly to trace, a pattern concerning the good and evil which coexist in human life. What the revenge plot suggests to Webster is something very different. His two important tragedies make use of the revenge plot, but in using it Webster reverses its emphasis in a way that may only have been possible to one who came late in the history of the revenge tradition. His protagonists, Vittoria Corombona and the Duchess of Malfi, do not pursue revenge; they suffer it. Shakespeare's secondary action has now become the main one. This is the originality of Webster; but this shift in the centre of dramatic interest involves him in certain difficulties. For those who suffer revenge and who are now to engage our sympathy must still commit the deed for which revenge is to be exacted. The dramatist's dilemma is particularly manifest in *The White Devil*. The puzzling nature of this play appears in the widely diverse critical comments it has received, and I speak of it with much diffidence.

It is significant that Webster begins farther from the archetype. In place of the primitive story of a blood revenge, his plots are taken from recent Italian history. They have nothing to do with sons avenging fathers, and the revenge lacks that sanction of righteousness that in Shakespeare's more orthodox situation was fundamental. The precise source of *The White Devil* is unknown, even after the skilful analysis by Gunnar Boklund[10] of the numerous existing versions of Vittoria's story. But the events of her life were familiar, and even without an identifiable source the contemporary accounts enable us to see broadly what attracted Webster to the story and what innovations he made in giving it dramatic shape. In none of these accounts do Francisco and Lodovico begin revenge against Vittoria until after Brachiano's death, but Webster's dramatic instinct makes them the killers of Brachiano also, and moreover advances them into prominence at the beginning of the play. When an early scene (II, i) shows Brachiano denounced by Francisco even before his wife is done away with, the destined revenger and his victim are already thrown into opposition; and it is Lodovico, the deathsman of Vittoria, who begins the play as well as ends it. We are not kept waiting for a dying confession to tell us of his forty murders; in the very opening dialogue we learn that he has 'acted certain murders here in Rome, Bloody and full of horror'. And to the tale of his crimes Webster adds a comparison of him to a 'meteor' and a legend that he was 'begotten in an earthquake'. Of the menace of this sinister figure we can have no doubt, and it is of Brachiano and Vittoria that he says, 'I'll make Italian cut-works in their guts If ever I return'.

The play, then, rests its structure on the clear-cut opposition of revengers and their victims. And in elaborating its details Webster is guided by the example of preceding revenge plays. Vittoria's brother Flamineo, the murderer of her husband, is built up into a full-scale Machiavellian villain. Isabella dies through kissing a poisoned picture; when her brother is planning to revenge her, her ghost opportunely appears; there is even a mad mother bewailing a dead son after the model of *The Spanish Tragedy*, though partly in the language of Ophelia. One cannot but notice here, though, that the corpse the mad mother bewails is not one for which revenge is taken. And this is but one indication that Webster's elaborations, unlike Shakespeare's in *Hamlet*, do not spring out of the central situation. They are imported from the stage tradition. This tradition is admittedly helpful in creating the world of violence and evil in which Vittoria and Brachiano move; yet in this world of many crimes the particular murders for which Vittoria and Brachiano are to suffer receive a diminished emphasis.

This is one of the paradoxes of the play. The murders of Vittoria's husband and Brachiano's wife are carried out with fiendish ingenuity and with full theatrical spectacle; and as in *Hamlet* they are given in dumb-show. But whereas in *Hamlet* the dumb-show and the play which follows it bring into the conflict between murderer and revenger a double reflexion of the crime we already know to be its cause, the dumb-shows in *The White Devil* are much less organic. Webster supplies, so to speak, in a sort of dramatic shorthand what Shakespeare writes out in full and in the centre. The murders in *The White Devil* we see *only* in reflexion, and they make on their watching perpetrator no such emotional impact as the image of the crime in *Hamlet* makes upon both villain and hero. While the murder in *Hamlet* is brought closer to us, the murders in *The White Devil* are set farther off. There is, moreover, some confusion about what is being avenged. For Camillo's murder Vittoria is apprehended, but though the play, through the neat invention of her dream, has stressed her culpability in advance, the murder is never brought home to her and she is sentenced as a whore. The murder of Isabella is not even discovered till after Vittoria has been sentenced, when the play is already half over. Yet it is *this* murder which at length gives the revengers their chance to set to work. Francisco is Isabella's brother, and Lodovico, when he has once cast his shadow across the play, is subsequently linked with her by a series of little afterthoughts. He is in her train when she is murdered and we are afterwards told he loved her. If this seems a trifle perfunctory, it may serve to show once more the art of that early scene in *Hamlet* between Laertes and his father. Webster does not construct like Shakespeare, and though this need not mean that he constructs less well, I confess to thinking that he does, since I have failed to discover in his apparent inconsequentialities the design that others may see in them. It is as though his sources, with the murder of Camillo as well as Isabella, and the revenge tradition, with its ghosts and poisonings and mad scenes, have supplied him with too much material, which his imagination cannot effectively control. And one reason why it cannot, I think, is that Webster is using the idiom of the revenge play when his imagination is really engaged by something else.

The direction in which his imagination is drawn is already clearly suggested by that dynamic opening which flings Lodovico on to the stage. This man of dreadful menace hurls his threat at Vittoria and Brachiano before *their* crimes take place. Though he is a revenger, he is an unholy one. We cannot suppose that in a play which begins like this revenge will have anything to do with even a wild justice. Francisco, with his sister's ghost, is a more orthodox revenger; but he recruits his assistants from the Cardinal's book of 'notorious offenders', 'agents for any villainy', and when he gloats over revenge achieved he says, 'Tush for justice'. The revengers share guilt with their victims. So it is not merely that Webster has changed the dramatic emphasis by centring his interest in the sufferers of the revenge; he has broken from that type of revenge situation in which Shakespeare could find imaged a contest between good and evil.

Vittoria and Brachiano suffer for their evil; but what drives them into evil is what drives them into love. They live superb in the vitality of their passion. This is their greatness, but it is also their fate. Is it not this which engages Webster's imagination—the progress of passionate life through its fulfilment to its inevitable destruction? In this imaginative rhythm the particular crimes, even those upon which the plot appears to turn, can become almost incidental. What may be as important to notice, though this too the plot structure does not emphasize, is that it is in the celebrations of his marriage that Brachiano receives his agonizing and terrible death. And his ghost bears like an emblem a pot of lily flowers which are rooted in a skull.

It is with the shadow of Lodovico already cast upon him that Brachiano first enters, saying 'Quite lost, Flamineo'. As he and Vittoria come together in delight, there is still the suggestion of their helplessness. Even Vittoria's dream which inspires the murders, since we must surely take it as a dream and not as a fabrication on her part, is something that arises in the mind unsought. Their guilt is born in their enchantment to begin their course towards ruin. The full complexity of this situation is suggested in that scene (I, ii) where Brachiano woos in talk of jewels, while Flamineo supplies accompaniment in gross jests of copulation and Vittoria's mother arises from the background with her curse. None of these things can we forget as we follow Vittoria, still splendid, to her trial, her imprisonment, and her death, till we behold her on the brink of eternity 'like to a ship in a dark storm' driven she knows not whither.

What the play expresses, then, most powerfully, through these central figures, is the doom that hangs upon their lives. In focusing upon the sufferers of the revenge, Webster has enlisted for them our pity and our admiration. But as they are still the perpetrators of crime, we still see

Claudius and Gertrude in them. And although Webster has not based his plot upon the opposition of good and evil, he has not been able to free himself entirely from the predilections of such a design. On the contrary, as the opposition between good and evil disappears from the central conflict between murderers and revengers, we find him introducing it elsewhere. That this is done designedly is evident because it is done through episodes which are not offered by the original story. When Webster amalgamated in Flamineo the brother who murdered Vittoria's husband and the brother who died with her, he removed the need for any second brother at all. Yet he still retained Marcello as a good brother to set against the bad. As Flamineo is in the service of the wrongdoer, so is Marcello in the service of the revenger. He attacks Flamineo for his villainy and Flamineo kills him for his pains. Similarly, Brachiano's son is given a boyish virtue to contrast with his sinful father; he mourns his mother's death; he bids Flamineo be penitent; and when at the end he inherits, we see him dispensing justice. But this antithesis of good and evil which Webster has woven into his play, at any rate as I see it, does not complement, it rather criss-crosses that other pattern in which Vittoria and Brachiano appear as the hapless, if splendid, creatures of their human destiny. Some confusion, I think, is evident in the ambivalence with which all the chief characters are presented. The ambivalence of *The White Devil* is quite different from that of *Hamlet*. For when Hamlet appears both as revenger and as object of revenge, he has a dual role and a dual situation; and Vittoria has only a single ambiguous one. It was Lamb who spoke of Vittoria's 'innocence-resembling boldness' at her trial, and though the play never conceals that she is guilty, she is allowed to behave as if she were not. At the beginning of this famous scene she ridicules the prosecuting lawyer for his 'hard and undigestible words' in a passage that one might compare with Hamlet's mockery of Osric just before the fencing-match. But Osric is the villain's messenger and can be the object of our ridicule without upsetting the moral balance of the play. When the Cardinal accuses Vittoria, she wrests the initiative from him, and one of the ambassadors—significantly the English one—remarks that 'the Cardinal's too bitter'. All this has the effect of swinging us to her side, and when she is finally sentenced as a whore, her superb disdain of the judgement has the air of a moral triumph. It is very different from Gertrude's collapse when she is taxed with *her* sins. Earlier Vittoria's paramour has suffered the Cardinal's rebuke, in words that may remind us of the Ghost's about Claudius, for giving himself to a 'lascivious' and 'insatiate bed'; but he daunts his accusers with the authority of his bearing and all Webster's wit in retort. When Claudius sees his crime enacted, he is put into confusion, but Brachiano is never more majestic than when he leaves the trial—and his cloak—in scorn behind him. He retains his majesty even in terror of death—'On pain of death, let no man name death to me: It is a word infinitely terrible'—whereas Claudius' death is wholly ignominious. Yet Brachiano is taunted and reviled as he goes into perpetual damnation. Vittoria recognizes the scene as 'hell', and at her own death she says, 'My greatest sin lay in my blood. Now my blood pays for it'. When her persecutors have disregarded justice and she is being driven she knows not whither, she sees perhaps too clearly that this is retribution. *The White Devil* does not, I suggest, like *Hamlet*, combine two patterns; it remains uncertain what its pattern is to be.

But perhaps we may say that in writing *The White Devil* Webster had discovered the pattern that his imagination sought. And that he could extricate it from the tangle is revealed in the play which followed. Though I say this with some trepidation, this seems to me a more homogeneous play and I may speak of it more briefly. I do not want to join in the critical game of contesting which of the two is the greater, but I have little doubt that *The Duchess of Malfi* is what it is because *The White Devil* had preceded it and Webster was artist enough to learn from his own mistakes. The similarity in the plots and character-groupings of the two plays is obvious. Again we have the central figure of a woman who, through taking a lover, arouses the enmity of a powerful Duke and Cardinal, who wreak their vengeance through a tool-villain. But, with the source no doubt assisting, the plot stands out more clearly. Webster resists, at any rate till the last act, his fatal tendency to complication. There is now no ghost, no mad wailing mother, no good brother to be killed by a bad. The overlapping roles of Lodovico and Flamineo are skilfully amalgamated in the single person of Bosola. And if there is introduced the not very satisfactory subplot of Julia and the Cardinal, at least this contributes to the Cardinal's villainy and provides a vicious woman to contrast with the virtuous Duchess. The effect of all this is to make the opposition between the good and evil characters complete, so that it reinforces instead of confusing the opposition between those who revenge and those who suffer revenge. But as compared with *Hamlet*, good and evil have of course changed sides. The direction of our sympathy to those who suffer is now taken to its logical conclusion by making the revengers evil and the sufferers innocent. *The Duchess of Malfi* becomes that unique thing, a revenge play without a crime. The Duchess has, of course, to commit the deed which provokes revenge; but the deed is no longer a murder, it is unexpectedly a marriage—or perhaps not so unexpectedly if we remember the linking of Brachiano's marriage and death.

It is true that the Duchess was a widow and that she marries beneath her; and much critical ink has been spent on citations from Elizabethan literature to show that on both these counts her marriage could be regarded as a transgression against right social and moral conduct.[11] To this I can only answer that it is not so presented in the play. The play knows all the conventional objections, but it goes out of its way to deny them their validity. Indeed it is here that it makes its most significant deviation from its source. The story as told by Painter in *The Palace of Pleasure* repeatedly speaks of the Duchess's 'wanton flesh', 'her libidinous appetite', her 'shameless lusts, for which she did the penance that her folly deserved'. But Webster, contradicting this, makes his Duchess a being of

> so divine a continence
> As cuts off all lascivious and vain hope.
> Her days are practised in such noble virtue
> That sure her nights, nay, more, her very sleeps,
> Are more in Heaven than other ladies' shrifts.

This is one of the most eloquent passages in Webster, and its function in the exposition of the play I should have thought unmistakable. It establishes the Duchess's perfection. And the 'divine continence' and nights in Heaven establish it especially in her sexual nature. Here, where a tragic flaw is sometimes seen, Webster has insisted on the opposite. It is true that the speaker is Antonio, the man she is to marry, but to find irony in this would be to go against the spirit of the play. Antonio himself is praised for his nobility, and his perception of the Duchess's character is a sign of it; and it makes him her fitting partner. When she herself puts the conventional objection, 'He was basely descended', Bosola retorts that she should examine not men's pedigrees but their virtues; and his reaction to her marriage is one of stupefaction at such extraordinary goodness as prefers a man for his mere worth. This marriage for which the Duchess suffers is not merely innocent; it is the very flower of her resplendent virtue. Her tragedy is that of a noble woman, eager for love and life, but doomed by the very fact of the life which glows within her to a lingering suffering which brings her 'by degrees to mortification'.

The Duchess of Malfi, like The White Devil, introduces us in its opening to the baleful figure who is to shadow the heroine's life and finally destroy her. Bosola is in Painter's story only the slayer of Antonio at the end; but the dramatist advances him, like Lodovico, to the beginning. From Lodovico no doubt he derives his aura of murder, but his relation to the principals in the action is much more carefully given. Receiving gold from Ferdinand, he says 'Whose throat must I cut?' and is planted in the Duchess's household. The character of his employers is also fully impressed on us. A fertile imagery of toads and spiders and so on suggests their living corruption as they set themselves against their radiant sister's marriage. Again, as in The White Devil, the shadow is cast before the deed is committed; so that it comes as no surprise when the very marriage-proposal is made in the image of a will and testament and the consummation of the Duchess's love is a 'dangerous venture' into the 'wilderness'. With Bosola lurking beside her, her marriage has its fruition, the reports of which drive Ferdinand into tempests of promised destruction. He never visits her without talk of poniards, bullets, or fire. The dead man's hand, the feigned corpses of her husband and children, which make their macabre sensation in the theatre, are only the climax of these portents. The whole play moves like a ritual, fore-ordained, controlled by what it symbolizes. The antics of the madmen which prelude the Duchess's death have recently been connected, in a most illuminating article by Miss Inga-Stina Ekeblad,[12] with the tradition of the antimasque and more especially with the charivari, the grotesque discordant music which serenades an incongruous marriage. What is incongruous about the marriage of the Duchess of Malfi will appear not when it is judged by the conventions of society but when it is seen against the law of life. In the charivari of the madmen we hear voices from another world which ridicule those hopes for happiness of life which the marriage has shown. And in the last act the dying, as they look back upon life, reveal through a variety of metaphor a significant unanimity. Ferdinand, sunk into an animal in the horrors of remorse, accounts 'this world but a dog-kennel'; Antonio, the loving husband now destroyed, asks, 'Pleasure of life, what is't? only the good hours Of an ague'; Bosola, the tomb-maker, speaks from the mist,

In what a shadow or deep pit of darkness
Doth womanish and fearful mankind live.

And finally they are all united in oblivion. Cariola, whom the Duchess once called superstitious, gives assurance of reunion with loved ones in another world, but the Duchess's voice when it echoes from the ruins denies this.

The fundamental contest in Webster's tragedies, though the revenge plot may disguise this, is not one between good and evil, but one between life and death. And since this is one in which the grave must have the victory, the action of The Duchess of Malfi shows not movement and counter-movement but an uninterrupted progression. Webster's interest in life's victims was shown in the new turn he gave to the traditional revenge plot; but it was only when he completely reversed this plot that he clearly discovered, or at least expressed, what I take to be his tragic vision. What moves me in Webster is the tragedy of the passionate human creature which reaches out towards life but advances slowly to decay until its radiance is shrouded in extinction. His is, I think, a smaller and less harmonious vision than Shakespeare's if only because it sees more of death than of life. It stresses suffering, but not reconciliation nor forgiveness.

NOTES

1. A lecture delivered to the International Shakespeare Conference at Stratford-upon-Avon, 2 September 1959.

2. See L. B. Campbell, 'Theories of Revenge in Renaissance England', *Modern Philology*, XXVIII (1931), 281 ff.; F. T. Bowers, *Elizabethan Revenge Tragedy* (1940), pp. 12–14, 93–4, and *passim*.

3. e.g. Dover Wilson, *What Happens in Hamlet* (Cambridge, 1935), p. 31; Granville-Barker, *Prefaces to Shakespeare* (1937), III, 39.

4. As above.

5. See 'Two Readings in *Hamlet*', *Modern Language Review*, LIV (1959), 393–5.

6. A. J. A. Waldock, *Hamlet: a Study in Critical Method* (1931), pp. 85–6, 91–5.

7. *The Wheel of Fire* (1930), pp. 36–41. This remarkable passage remains substantially unaltered in the later editions. Instead of the 'genuine penitence' which Wilson Knight discovers, Claudius' attempt to pray shows, in his own words, a 'bosom black as death' which 'cannot repent'.

8. In stressing this aspect of the relationship between Hamlet and Laertes, I do not wish to suggest that there are not others, nor that Laertes has not himself a dual role. If he is the secondary revenger, he is of course also the tool-villain in the main revenge plot. But our impression of Claudius and Laertes as partners in treachery should not obscure the distinction between them which the end of the play makes.

9. *The Plays of William Shakespeare*, ed. Johnson (1765), VIII, 303: 'I wish Hamlet had made some other defence; it is unsuitable to the character of a good or a brave man, to shelter himself in falsehood.'

10. *The Sources of the White Devil* (Uppsala, 1957).

11. See especially M. C. Bradbrook, *Themes and Conventions of Elizabethan Tragedy* (1935), pp. 198 ff.; C. Leech, *John Webster* (1951), pp. 69 ff. and 'An Addendum on Webster's Duchess', *Philological Quarterly*, XXXVII (1958), 253–6. The contrary view is put by F. W. Wadsworth, 'Webster's *Duchess of Malfi* in the Light of Some Contemporary Ideas on Marriage and Remarriage', *Philological Quarterly*, XXXV (1956), 394 ff.

12. 'The "Impure Art" of John Webster', *Review of English Studies*, IX (1958), 253 ff.

THE SIMPLICITY OF THOMAS HEYWOOD

BY

MICHEL GRIVELET

The time is past when it was possible to maintain, with Hazlitt, that 'Heywood's plots have little of artifice or regularity of design to recommend them'. The complaint, it is true, could still be heard not so long ago: even in *A Woman Killed with Kindness*, it was said, 'the subplot continually interferes with and interrupts the important main action' and the author 'might better have employed the "two hours traffic" of his stage in filling out the story of the Frankfords'.[1] But the use of double plots is a thing we have learnt to know among other conventions of Elizabethan art. No one today, it may be assumed, would miss their significance.

In Heywood's case in particular, as Miss Townsend has shown,[2] it is clear that they meet artistic requirements. The story of the Mountfords, in his best-known play, is hardly less important than that of the Frankfords: main plot and subplot are bound together by common themes into a complex whole which must be considered in its entirety if the play's dramatic purpose is to be grasped at all. To those who have studied it in this new light, *A Woman Killed with Kindness* has yielded evidence of its thoughtful intricacy of structure and given scope for renewed interpretation.[3]

However, this technique of the dramatist has not always been vindicated in such a way as to do much for his reputation. Miss Townsend, for her part, is mainly concerned with the 'artistry' of his double plots, and only incidentally with their dramatic meaning. Of the seven plays which she considers, three only, in her estimate, can be regarded as combining two plots 'which complement each other, or which taken together, illustrate some central theme'. A second class comprises two other plays 'whose plots are related by a cause-and-effect relationship'. The remaining two—that is, *The Captives* and *The English Traveller*—are works 'in which there seems to be no thematic or causal relationship between the two plots'. Thus, in the majority of cases, there would be only the most outward connexion, or even no connexion at all, no relationship of any significance between the two stories which the author puts together.

Now, if this is true, there is little cause to praise Heywood's powers as a play-maker. Some cleverness, perhaps, may be detected in his way of handling supposedly unrelated plots. He is shown indeed, by Miss Townsend, to practise 'the psychological art of arousing just the proper amount of interest', for 'too much interest in the action about to be dropped must generate in his audience impatience with that about to be taken up; too little, meant a lack of suspense and a reluctance to return to the first action when the second had been carried, in its turn, to the breaking-off point'. But what, one may wonder, is the point of such 'art'? Can there be anything more idle than to combine stories whose combination, however skilful, makes no sense?

It is hardly surprising, then, that criticism of Heywood should remain mostly condescending. Even the renewal of interest in *A Woman Killed with Kindness*—the one play to be repeatedly singled out for serious study—scarcely works to his advantage. It would rather seem to encourage the view that so exceptional a work owes even more to chance than to the conscious

56

endeavours of its author. *A Woman Killed with Kindness*, we have been recently told, 'is a very remarkable work, just great enough to give us a glimpse of reaches of thought and feeling which remained, alas, inaccessible to its honest maker'.[4] This is not markedly different from traditional praise given to Heywood for a few pathetic scenes, in terms which recall Lamb's commendation of the 'prose Shakespeare', and from related denunciations of his 'peculiar oafish simplicity' which is said to account for pages of 'utter drivel' in practically every one of his plays.[5]

But it remains to be seen whether this simplicity—Shakespearian or oafish—is really Heywood's. One cannot help feeling that this belief owes much to the persistent habit of considering his double plots merely as clumsy, padded-out single plots. It will not seem superfluous, therefore, to insist that none of these plays is gratuitously double, none without a dramatic meaning that can be expressed only through the interplay of contrasted stories.

The English Traveller will serve to prove this better perhaps than any other of these dramas. For though it was originally 'reserved' by the author himself among the many productions in which he claimed to have had 'either an entire hand, or at the least a maine finger', no one, it seems, has ever cared to seek the import of both plots jointly considered. And Miss Townsend, who finds no thematic or causal connexion in the play, adds the further remark that it is the only one 'which fails in the opening act to provide a natural transition from one action to the other, to make it appear, at the beginning, that the second action is in some sense an outgrowth of the first'. No dramatic piece of Heywood would be actually more disjointed, if it were not for the texture of ideas which holds its parts together.

This is not to say, of course, that uncommon mental powers should now be claimed for the author. The investigation may as well lead to a clearer view of the bias and limitations of his talent. But just as the true greatness of Shakespeare is never more striking than when he is seen as one of the Elizabethans, so modern misunderstanding need not be regarded as a certain proof of Heywood's incompetence.

What relation there may be between the two plots of *The English Traveller* does not, it must be admitted, appear at first sight—especially if the play be taken, as it usually is, for a mere re-handling of the basic situation in *A Woman Killed with Kindness*, a kind of remake of the former success. The injured husband, this time, is not the real husband but, after the solemn exchange of 'verba de futuro' between Mrs Wincott and Young Geraldine, the would-be husband of the erring wife. Geraldine, like Frankford, is betrayed by his friend; he discovers the guilty pair in similar circumstances and his forbearance also leads to the wife's repentance and death.

If this is the main argument, can the Plautine subplot have any bearing upon it? Closely imitated from *Mostellaria*, it shows what a good time Young Lionel has at home while his father risks his life at sea to increase his wealth. Yet the prodigal will be spared the unpleasant consequences of Old Lionel's sudden return, thanks to the stratagems of the wily servant Reignald. Like Tranio in Plautus' comedy, Reignald persuades the old man that the house, where the son is hiding with his mistress and merry companions, is haunted by the ghost of a murdered man. He even succeeds in having the father pay the debts of the son under the false pretence that the money borrowed from a usurer has been used to buy a new house. Undeceived at last, Old Lionel will forgive the repentant prodigal and the treacherous, if resourceful, servant. Between this farcical second plot and the serious, elegiac, main action, the discrepancy seems absolute.

The title of the play, however, gives a first hint of what they have in common. Young Geraldine's travels to Rome and Jerusalem, though copiously discussed in the opening scene, might seem of little relevance to a domestic story of betrayed friendship and adultery. But they are, in fact, no fortuitous incident. It is while the English traveller was away on his Grand Tour that the girl whom—from their childhood almost—he had regarded as his future wife, became Mrs Wincott:

> In those times,
> Of all the Treasures of my Hopes and Love,
> You were th'Exchequer, they were Stor'd in you;
> And had not my unfortunate Travell crost them,
> They had bin heere reserved still.

Much in the same way, it is during a second absence of his friend, 'abroad At London, or else where', that Dalavill, who has treacherously contrived everything, seduces Mrs Wincott. And when Young Geraldine discovers that he has been duped by the 'viperous brood of Friend and Mistress', he exclaims:

> You have made mee
> To hate my very Countrey...
> ...First I'le leave this House
> And then my Fathers, Next I'le take my leave,
> Both of this Clime and Nation, Travell till
> Age snow upon this Head.

Fate, and something too perhaps in his character, an impulse to fly, to go away, have sealed his sad destiny. Travelling, more exactly unfortunate travelling, is inseparable from Geraldine's story.

Our attention is thus directed by the title to something in the main plot which is not the mere repetition of Frankford's drama. Neither is this title unadapted to the subplot. Old Lionel too is an English traveller whose absence, as he himself remarks, 'hath begot some sport' for others, while resulting in no small loss for himself. But the Plautine fable rather emphasizes the luck and good sense of such as stay in the house, like Young Lionel, to enjoy themselves with a sweet mistress. To them, the house proves first a palace of pleasure, and then a sanctuary in which they manage to weather the storm raised up by the father's sudden return.

How closely the lot of a young man can be associated with a house, his nature and fate identified with it, is stated at length in Plautus' comedy by Philolacles whose long soliloquy Heywood has skilfully adapted and put in the mouth of Young Lionel, in the first act of his own play:

> To what may young men best compare themselves?
> Better to what, then to a house new built?
> The Fabricke strong, the Chambers well contriv'd.

Then comes 'that lasie Tenant, Love' who brings the house to ruin, submits it 'to every storme and Winters blast'. Moral symbols are not lacking either in Plautus or Heywood. The haunted house, out of bounds for the father, figures the son inhabited by the wild passions that keep out all filial feelings. And the newly bought house, though a mere fiction and stratagem, somehow heralds the recovery by the father of what he lawfully possesses. In other words, it announces he return of the prodigal, for now that he has sown a few wild oats he is willing to renounce he blandishments of riotous love and to be his own father's again. Indeed, the house idea is as essential to Young Lionel as its counterpart, the travel idea, is to Young Geraldine. And both plots, through similitude and contrast, fall within the same perspective.

But the pattern of symmetries thus revealed between the two plots is more intricate than a first glance can discover and a much closer investigation would be needed to trace it out. The author has left a clue to the less obvious design of his work in the names of the characters. Somewhat cryptic, they are certainly intended as pointers to a deeper, hidden meaning of the play, for it should be noted that here Heywood owes everything to himself. The only name he retains from Plautus is that of the very minor character of Scapha, the bawd, whose part, though not entirely negligible, is merely episodic. As for the main plot, its prose version in *Gunaikeion* gives no proper names. The wife is 'a beautiful and well-bred young gentlewoman' married to an 'elderly gentleman' and the English traveller is 'the son of a neighbour who had travelled far and wide' and who had a 'best friend'. Even if, as is probable, the plot is not derived from this narrative and the real source to be sought elsewhere, this source is unlikely to have had such quaint names as those we find in the play.

Of those, there is one at least whose artificiality is conspicuous. To her seducer, who has just said: 'See, I am Dalavill', the repentant Mrs Wincott replies:

> Th'art then a Devill, that presents before mee
> My horrid sins.

Dalavill is all devil. In a manner scarcely less ostensible, Geraldine is an angel. At the same crucial moment, Mrs Wincott says of him:

> ...hee like a good Angel sent from Heaven
> Besought me of repentance.

It is indeed Geraldine's violent outburst, after much forbearance, that has brought about Mrs Wincott's conversion:

> Die, and die soone, acquit me of my Oath,
> But prethee die repentant; Farewell ever,
> 'Tis, thou, and onely thou hast Banisht mee,
> Both from my Friends and Countrey.

So that the exact anagram of Geraldine's name fits his dramatic function very well: he is a 'dire Angel'.

Dire, because Geraldine's resentful love, together with a strangely tender, other-worldly, concern for her salvation, prompt him to utter the cruel words which will kill the false beloved. But dire also, if angel—and here the celestial epithet is clearly not without irony—because Geraldine has his own large share of responsibility in Mrs Wincott's undoing. It is hardly loyal of him to say: 'thou, and onely thou hast Banisht mee', since his first 'unfortunate travel' was none of the young woman's devising. Now, it is precisely while and because Geraldine was away that she got married to Old Wincott, whose very name suggests the wintry season, the wintry house, where her youth soon found itself imprisoned in the unequal match of Januar and May. As the Clown puts it to Geraldine in the first scene:

Small doings at home, sir, in regard that the age of my Master corresponds not with the youth of my Mistris, and you know cold January and lusty May seldome meet in conjunction.

Essentially one who travels and, in the end, a 'messenger', an 'Angel sent from Heaven' Geraldine is also, and is first in point of time, one who fails to be where and when he is wanted who fails to be human. This, of course, is Dalavill's opportunity, Dalavill who 'beares away the substance' while Geraldine 'doate(s) upon the shadow', Dalavill who is the traveller's best friend and, we may say, his *alter ego*. There can be no clearer condemnation of a love that misguidedly ignores the claims of human nature, body and soul, that aims at a pseudo-Platonic sublimity and, while pretending to be ideal, falls only too readily under the subjection of the flesh. One is reminded of Montaigne:

Ils veulent se mettre hors d'eulx, et eschapper à l'homme; c'est folie; au lieu de se transformer en anges, ils se transforment en bestes.[6]

From the very first scene, in which Geraldine and Dalavill carry on a seemingly pointless conversation about the former's visits to Rome and Jerusalem, both friends—and the whole play—are placed under the dramatic sign of travel. There is already about Geraldine, associated as he is with the holy cities, a suggestion of the divine, an angel-like quality which Dalavill is lacking, he who has stayed at home to read in books of what Geraldine has seen. And when Dalavill says: 'I have the Theoricke, But you the Practicke', one cannot help taking this as an ironical anticipation of Bess' words to Geraldine:

> You beare the name of Land-lord, but another
> Injoyes the rent; You doate upon the shadow.

There is, however, another reversal at the end. In spite of appearances, Dalavill also is a traveller. After Mrs Wincott's repentance and death, the Clown reports that he has fled on horseback 'as if hee were to ride a Race for a Wager'. 'All our ill lucks goe with him, farewell hee', comments Wincott; and Young Geraldine echoes:

> It calles me from all Travell, and from henceforth
> With my Countrey I am Friends.

The (evil) spirit of travel has gone with Dalavill, and Geraldine is a traveller no longer. But the full meaning of his metamorphosis can only be understood through the experience which the subplot provides in the happy lot of that lucky home-bird, Young Lionel—the prodigal who never left his father's house. Young Geraldine is now what Young Lionel never ceased to be. He has become human.

Such a view of the hero may seem hard to reconcile with the often repeated opinion which makes him 'one of the truest gentlemen of Elizabethan comedy'.[7] But this is precisely where one should remember that the play is a dual play and that it cannot be rightly interpreted if this duality is left out of count. For the irony provided by the main plot at the expense of Geraldine's character is strongly supported by the subplot.

Apart from Scapha, the bawd, and Blanda, the prodigal's mistress, the dramatis personae in the story borrowed from Plautus have apparently quite innocent English names. Why Latin Tranio has become English Reignald may seem of no consequence, until one realizes that Reignald is the almost exact anagram of Geraldine. There is little doubt that Heywood wants us to look for some symmetry between the two characters. It is not therefore with Young Lionel only, nor chiefly with him perhaps, that Young Geraldine must be compared. Much rather, Young Lionel, securely enjoying his fair mistress under his father's roof, resembles Dalavill, the happy lover of Mrs Wincott, in Wincott's house. And just as Reignald, by sheer astuteness and renewed stratagems, manages to prevent the old man from interfering, so Dalavill takes advantage of Geraldine's ill-judged reserve and gullibility to dupe him as well as Old Wincott. Dalavill and Geraldine on the one hand, Lionel and Reignald on the other, are associates. But while Reignald, a mere servant, is devoted to his young master and, being partly responsible for his disorders, resolves to stand by him to the very end—

> Ile stand it at all dangers; And to recompense
> The many wrongs unto the young man done—

Dalavill, on the contrary, repays Geraldine's friendship with ingratitude. Though very different and even opposed, Geraldine and Reignald play similar roles. And, to be sure, there is a way in which the gentleman's innocence does not compare favourably with the servant's cunning. Little harm is done to his masters, young and old, by the wily unscrupulous knave, whereas the ambiguous virtue of the English traveller proves deadly to the woman he loves.

The names of the characters are only a means, of course—one which, one imagines, would call for more visual devices in the staging—of directing our attention to the pattern of symmetries between the two plots. They help to define the play more clearly as a kind of image reflected in a mirror, and illumined in its turn by this very reflexion. But it is in this subtle reverberation of light between the two pictures that the essence and unity of the action chiefly reside. Within each plot, the travel idea and the house idea are contrasted. And, from plot to plot, the contrasts are in their turn contrasted. Themes and images reappearing here and there, from time to time, in different circumstances, weave an intricate web of mental reference between the two parts of the dramatic composition.

Heywood has been at pains to give scope to this interplay of contrasted ideas, as is clearly seen in the only major addition he has made to his Plautine subplot: the burlesque episode of the shipwreck on land, borrowed from Athenaeus and later imitated by Cowley in his *Naufragium Joculare*. The purpose of this adjunct is not merely to increase the boisterousness of an already rowdy story. Besides, whether it really belongs to one plot more than to the other is not so easy to decide. It belongs to the subplot in so far as it is Young Lionel and his associates who, after copious eating and drinking, 'out of [their] giddy wildnesse' conceive

> The Roome wherein they quafft, to be a Pinnace,
> Mooving and Floating; and the confused Noise,
> To be the murmuring Windes, Gusts, Marriners;
> That their unstedfast Footing, did proceed
> From rocking of the Vessell.

But the ridiculous incident is narrated in Act II, scene 1, within the frame of the main plot, by Young Geraldine, just before his interview with Mrs Wincott and the exchange of their vows. It is only after this—apparently—quiet, serenely happy scene that we return to Lionel and his merry companions whom we find 'as newly wak'd from sleepe' and commenting on the 'stormy night' they have had, still under the delusion that they have actually weathered a storm, when suddenly they learn that a worse tempest threatens, for Old Lionel is 'landed and at hand'.

Thus, the episode provides the first material link between the two plots which have been kept entirely separate throughout Act I. They are now for the first time united, not of course for the mere reason that the proximity of the Wincott and Lionel houses has enabled Young Geraldine to be informed of the shipwreck on land, but because his narrative, placed as it is, reveals something of the inward coherence of the two stories. Not the least irony of it, indeed, is that it should be told by Young Geraldine.

There is a first paradox in the idea that a house may prove as unsafe as a 'Pinnace' on a 'Turbulent Sea'. But the storm, which is no other than that of the prodigal's riotous life, was not unexpected. Young Lionel, in his soliloquy, had warned us that the 'house new built', when the 'lasie Tenant, Love, steps in', is bound to be shaken by 'every storme and Winters blast'. Young Geraldine, however, who, rather reluctantly and in derision, tells the story as a mere 'Jeast, that askes a smoother Tongue', is obviously unaware of the moral symbol that Young Lionel would be prepared to see in it. Still farther from him is the idea that he, the English traveller, might do well to learn the lesson for himself. Yet he is also, in his way, a house new built. The insistence with which Old Wincott presses him to stay comes from that paternal feeling which, according to the subplot, urges parents to 'build' their sons. 'Wee are', Young Lionel says,

> those houses made,
> Our Parents raise these Structures, the foundation
> Laid in our Infancy; and as we grow
> In yeeres, they strive to build us by degrees.

Old Wincott, who is childless, envies Geraldine's father and strives more or less, in fact, to rob him of his heir. 'I would have you', he says to the young man,

> Thinke this your home, free as your Fathers house,
> And to command it, as the Master on't.

The old man, obviously, has a large share of responsibility in the drama, for the dangerous situation from which so much unhappiness will result for everyone is largely due to his own possessiveness.

These baser motives are glanced at, somewhat cryptically as usual, in the first lines of Act III. The Wincotts are expressing their thanks to Old Geraldine for having 'lent' them his son. 'By trusting him to me', says Wincott,

> of whom your selfe
> May have both use and pleasure, y'are as kind
> As money'd men, that might make benefit
> Of what they are possest, yet to their friends
> In need, will lend it gratis;

his wife adding that they are 'indebted more than they can pay'. This kind of talk goes on for some time, until Dalavill remarks:

> What strange felicitie these Rich men take,
> To talke of borrowing, lending, and of use;
> The usurers language right.

Its implications are disclosed further with the 'Usuring-Rascall' episode in the subplot, which follows close upon this section of the main plot. Old Geraldine is a kind of usurer who wants his money back, and gets it, for Dalavill has lost no time to play on his half-conscious feeling of resentment at seeing his son stay 'so seldom' with him, and the English traveller is immediately ordered 'to forbeare the house' of Old Wincott. And just as Old Lionel pays heavily for a house that cannot be his, Old Wincott, though now deprived of the son he regarded as his own, is about to suffer great wrongs.

No less indeed than Young Lionel, Young Geraldine is dramatically represented by a fair house which the covetousness of others as well as the storms of his own passions threaten with ruin. Or better, perhaps, if we keep in mind how essential to his character is the travel idea, it should be said of him, in his father's words:

> You are growne perfect man, and now you float
> Like to a well built Vessell; 'Tweene two Currents,
> Vertue and Vice; Take this you steere to harbour,
> Take that, to eminent shipwracke.

What irony, then, in his amused and disdainful account of the shipwreck suffered on land by Young Lionel and his crew! And, placed as it is between this narrative and the re-emergence in the subplot of the storm-theme, how precarious the peaceful, the loving interview between him and Mrs Wincott, how ill-advised and doomed beforehand the passionate exchange of their mutual promise, their vows of future marriage!

Enough has been said perhaps to show that, whatever the discrepancies, the utter heterogeneity even of the two plots, on the level of outward happenings, there runs throughout *The English Traveller* a strong unifying current of dramatic interest. Once our attention has been drawn to the deeper moral argument inherent in both of them, we have no real sense of a break and change in the trend of our thoughts when we leave one series of events for the other. The effect is not merely one of balance and variety, it is also cumulative: what strength and tension has been gathered on one side is soon brought to bear upon the other. And though there are two different stories, it can hardly be said that there is more than one action.

The way Thomas Heywood has of building his drama on recurring themes and images is, of course, nothing exceptional. There is not one perhaps among his contemporaries that does not use this kind of language. And how effective it can be, how rich in sense and suggestion, has been more than once demonstrated in the case of Shakespeare. But whereas in Shakespeare the continuity of imaginative thought is embedded and as it were concealed in a coherent, if complex, fable, with Heywood it is made to bridge the gap between two otherwise unrelated examples of human conduct. And though the human interest centres upon the main story—the subplot, which always winds up in the fourth act, being clearly subordinate—though it is for Geraldine and scarcely for Lionel that we are concerned, the unity of the play really lies in the mental interference between the two developing situations.

This is why dialogue in Heywood sounds so often unconvincing and even idle enough some-times to be mistaken for 'utter drivel', when it is actually very far from such dramatic pointless-ness. Time and again—when, for instance, the Wincotts and Geraldines tediously indulge in 'the usurers language'—we feel that what the characters say scarcely proceeds from themselves. Their talk, instead of flowing naturally from within, seems, so to speak, put on from without. It is, in fact, largely dictated by the exigencies of plot. It does not mean so much what it says as what it stands for in the complex scheme of the double plot. One might almost think of it as a kind of algebra, or dramatic shorthand. It is not surprising that it should often seem flat and uninspired, lacking the ease and freedom, the deeper poetry of spontaneous emotion. With Shakespeare, on the contrary—and here we have a measure of his greatness—no discrepancy appears between immediacy of feeling and deliberateness of structure.

Heywood leans heavily on the side of abstract speculation. He relies too much on careful devising and mere ingenuity in the building of his plays. As the author of *The Great Assises Holden in Parnassus* already observed in 1645, he expects elaborate structure to do duty for poetry itself:

> Shakespear's a Mimicke, Massinger a Sot,
> Heywood for Aganippe takes a plot.

But surely, if there is a fault he should not be charged with, it is thoughtlessness. Deliberation can least of all be dispensed with where the dramatic action cannot possibly be left to the natural unfolding of a single human story. The very selection of the elements which are to go into the complex whole requires an awareness of the hidden possibilities of each plot, a vision of the way in which they must be shown to correspond, of the interplay of ideas which will have to develop between them. No one could be farther from the truth of the matter than Hazlitt when he says of Heywood that 'He writes on carelessly, as it happens, and trusts to Nature and a certain tranquillity of spirit for gaining the favour of the audience'.

It is true that, in some cases, little rehandling will be found necessary to bring two stories significantly together into one play, if they have been selected with thoughtful care. In *The English Traveller*, as Allan H. Gilbert notes, 'the plot taken from Plautus is little modified by its combination with the other story'.[8] Indeed, Heywood merely includes Plautus' first act in his own first act, Plautus' second act in his own second. Rearrangement occurs only after Act III, scene i of the Latin comedy, and it consists mainly in the compression of the rest of it into the fourth Act of the modern play. The Plautine material has been adapted to the purpose of the English dramatist with only the slightest manipulation, or in his own phrase, the few rapid touches of 'a maine finger'.

But Heywood's method does not exclude the 'entire hand', the more thorough process of original creation. The prose version of Geraldine's story, though told in *Gunaikeion* (pp. 193–6) as 'a modern history, lately happening, and in [the author's] own knowledge', is much more likely to derive from the play than the reverse, just as the story of Lady d'Averne in *The Captives*, which is known to have been borrowed from a novella by Masuccio di Salerno, must have anticipated rather than followed the narrative presented in *Gunaikeion* (pp. 253 f.) as the 'true history' of a Lady in Norwich.[9] And Heywood may well have given as much care to the elaboration of Geraldine's drama as the study of the sources of *A Woman Killed with Kindness* shows him to have done in the case of the Frankfords.

The debate which is still going on about the various possible origins of this story[10] bears not only upon the genesis of the play but also upon its intentions. There are those who insist on its homiletic descent and the lesson of patience and forgiveness it is meant to give, while others, who derive the plot from Italian novelle, point to the revengefulness and insidious cruelty it implies. *A Woman Killed with Kindness* has even been recently interpreted as a 'dark', pessimistic play in which, with the exception perhaps of the servant Nicholas, no one is blameless, every character acting on mistaken or base motives.[11] And, as we have just seen, the view which the author takes of human nature in *The English Traveller* does not appear to be unreservedly encouraging.

The truth is that the response called for by such works is bound to be ambiguous. Made of symmetries and contrasts, patterned in many perplexing ways, they baffle the reader's judgement, they body forth the elusiveness, the endless ironies of life. A student of Heywood should always take care not to read his own simplicity into the complex plays of the dramatist.

NOTES

1. H. H. Adams, *English Domestic, or Homiletic Tragedy, 1575–1642* (New York, 1943).
2. 'The Artistry of Heywood's Double Plots', *Philological Quarterly*, xxv (April 1946), 97–119.
3. See, for instance: Peter Ure, 'Marriage and the Domestic Drama in Heywood and Ford', *English Studies*, xxxII (October 1951), 200–16.
4. Peter Ure, in *Études Anglaises*, xII (January 1959), 66–7.
5. F. L. Lucas, *The Complete Works of John Webster* (1927), III, 136.
6. *Essais*, III, xiii.
7. A. W. Ward, *A History of English Literature* (1899), p. 565 n.
8. 'Thomas Heywood's Debt to Plautus', *JEGP*, xII (1913), 593–611.
9. See M. Grivelet, *Thomas Heywood et le Drame Domestique Elizabéthain* (Paris, 1957), pp. 83–4.
10. See Waldo F. McNeir, 'Heywood's Sources for the Main Plot of *A Woman Killed with Kindness*' in *The English Renaissance Drama* (1959).
11. Patricia Meyer Spacks, 'Honor and Perception in *A Woman Killed with Kindness*', *Modern Language Quarterly*, xx (December 1959), 321–32.

THE TRAGIC VISION OF FULKE GREVILLE

BY

IVOR MORRIS

The outstanding feature of Fulke Greville's writings—apart from their complexity—is the witness they bear to the sustained intensity of their author's 'cosmic vision'.[1] In his ranging spirit of metaphysical inquiry and reference, Greville is the most Elizabethan of all the Elizabethans. That he was the worst dramatist of them all needs no urging. His poetic idiom is baffling. The speculative bent of his intellect swamped what dramatic instinct he may have had. And perhaps a characteristic dislike for what he termed 'horrible periods of exorbitant passions'[2] had already precluded success in this field—though his Hala, Rossa, Alaham and Soliman are hardly to be described as passionless. Nevertheless, though his dramas are unactable, there is no denying their imaginative integrity, and their latent power.

In one important respect, *Alaham* and *Mustapha* are deserving of attention. The function of drama, with Greville, is to make apparent and explicit the forces that are operating in man and society, not to create the living characters and situations from which, among other Elizabethan authors, those forces are to be inferred. He was a playwright with the instinct of an essayist, concerned with the contemplation of human life rather than its portrayal, to 'trace out the high waies of ambitious Governours'[3] rather than to enact 'the despair, or confusion of mortality'[4] in the high-wrought passions of the contemporary tragedy. Thus he cannot write a play without making clear its significance in the light of his own opinions: and tragedy and tragic vision receive simultaneous dramatic expression, the latter principally in the Choruses, which are unique in the objectivity and completeness of the view of man's situation that they put forward. We therefore have in these two plays an unparalleled statement of that innermost understanding of life whence a tragedy derives its being.

Some critics, confronted with what purports to be a 'tragic vision', are of a mind to declare, with Macbeth, that

> There's no such thing:
> It is the bloody business which informs
> Thus to mine eyes,

and speak of tragedians as literary craftsmen and dramatic illusionists. But the vision is not so easily dispersed. Not only must a dramatist frame actions and sentiments that are meaningful in terms of his audience's concepts, but what he writes must necessarily be at one with the range of possibilities that he sees himself. For effective dramatic creation he is limited to the scope of his own outlook, and must at all times be submitting the symbols of life he is dealing with to personal standards of appropriateness and significance. In this process the tragic vision must consist; but the writer of tragedy is concerned with the outcome of the process, and is hardly in a position, even if he consciously wished to do more, to give other than marginal and fleeting expression to his intimate convictions.

That is the substance of what Bradley says in approaching the subject of a tragic order implicit in Shakespearian tragedy: Shakespeare's concern is with the concrete world, with life as it is experienced and reacted to. Though his works contain numerous supernatural and religious notions, 'these ideas do not materially influence his representation of life, nor are they used to throw light on its tragedy'.[5] Bradley was of course handicapped by the belief that the Elizabethan drama was almost entirely secular; we are more accustomed, by the present time, to the Elizabethan habit of cosmic reference. Yet Bradley's instincts were more powerful than these convictions, and few can have been unimpressed by his puzzled disquisition on the order that must lie behind the world of the tragedies. The tragic fact is piteous, fearful, mysterious: yet the tragedies do not leave us crushed or rebellious. The tragic order therefore is not a moral order; yet it cannot be indifferent to human happiness. 'Such views contradict one another', declares Bradley, 'and no third view can unite them.' We get the impression that the heroes are helpless and doomed, but also that they are free agents, albeit in a deceptive world. The fearsome, disproportionate, and often unmerited suffering that tragedy brings in its train bears no relation to justice. It is true that the tragedy always springs from some evil, that the order seems to react against a fault in the hero, and that evil itself always is revealed as negative; but it cannot, therefore, be held that the order must in some way be akin to good. For evil is part of the system, as are the heroes with their glories and failings; the system is the beginning and the end of the tragedies it produces. If it demands perfection from human beings, it is tyrannous and remorseless in an impossible demand; and, for whatever purpose it operates, it wastes and destroys its own being in the process.[6] Thus Bradley declares in the same breath his apprehension of a tragic order in Shakespeare and his utter failure to understand it.

The primary purpose of this article is to put forth clearly and briefly the substance of the thought contained in the Choruses of Greville's plays. Since the object is to arrive at the view of things that existed simultaneously with the creation of tragedy, reference is made to other of Greville's writings only where it is necessary to clarify statements in the Choruses or to bring out an implied meaning. It is also proposed to consider a possible basis for postulating a tragic vision in Shakespeare not essentially different from the vision that now emerges—to consider, in fact, if there might be a 'third view' that can reconcile conflicting reactions to the tragic fact.

For Greville, the most significant fact about human existence is that it is momentary: time is meaningless to him, and the revolution of centuries but the 'New-borne childe of Planets motion', a progression of futility, a laughable monster with its tail held firmly in its own mouth. Yet so narrow is the range of human understanding, so prone are men to allow their minds to be dazzled by what their eyes look upon, that they conceive time, the things of time and the little lives of men to be the 'measure of *Felicitie*'; and they make the course of fleeting days and years their standard of permanence. That which seems to be most real to earthlings, and the goals to which they bend their labours as they pay their breath to time and mortal custom, are in fact products of a false vision. Worldly knowledge is a delusion, and men's laws, their arts, their sects, their mitres and their monuments are based upon pale probabilities, which could not keep their reputation in their eyes were it not for the revolutions of time producing novelty, and daubing the beggarly approximations of human wit —'Those mortal forms, moulded of humane error'—with the gaudy colours that 'Natures erring *Alchymie*' can distil. It is man's time-serving accommodations that lead him to think he is ague-proof.

Despite chance and change and imperfection, therefore, men cling to the values they have chosen for themselves and struggle for the glittering prizes that the world apparently offers them. The affairs of men and nations are governed by time's dictates; unworldly joys lose their appeal, and those who try to apply other standards to the game of human existence meet with Fortune's frown, and are despised. Those who are in the world, and of the world, have to adopt the garb, the manners and the coin of the world; but, intent as they are on acts that have no relish of salvation in them, it is not theirs to count upon success and prosperity. All too often they are struck down by misfortune, but there is none to whom they can complain: time and the things of time are worthless to man, whether he gains them or loses them. The infelicities that they bring in their train are a just reward for him who has sought them, for they make his error manifest to him—and is it for mortal man to ask more? The world's imperfections merely demonstrate to those who would jump the life to come that its claims have no validity and signify nothing: that mankind, vainly building

Vpon the mouing Base of selfe-conceipt,

has lived and is living in error. If only humanity could understand thus far, they would not make it their master.[7]

Man's understanding is marred, however, by the operation upon him of dark forces that are the agents of evil, waiting upon human thought. These agencies are urged on by a restless desire to spoil Creation and reduce mankind to their own wretchedness—to abuse and damn them, in fact. They have nothing to offer man, for they can do nothing except deprive him of the good that is his birthright and his true happiness: evil is nothing but the privation of good.[8] Yet it is by calling upon him to be fully himself and attain his true good—to be the same in his own act and valour as he is in desire—that these powers entice him to destruction. What kind of world would it be, these evil powers propose to the successors of Adam, where men fall through pride of courage and rise through meek obedience; where greatness is glorified littleness, and the reward for virtue is to have a cheek for wrong? That is what men must expect if they choose to be 'good'; but is this mediocrity worthy of human greatness and merit? Weaklings alone can desire the safety of such a '*lasy calme*'. But the rarer spirits among mankind, who wish to realize their natures to the full in a span of triumphant assertion, must boldly enter into evil, make it their element and enact deeds of dreadful note; for

The glory of the skilfull shines, where men may go amisse.[9]

Thus men are deafened with the storming shout that prosperity on earth is the only creed worthy of their natures. Were they calmly to consider what these dark powers propose, they would realize that the triumphs of evil dissolve even as they are attained: that the course of wickedness is in the end no more than a progress from ill to ill, and that the successful wrongdoer soon discovers that to be thus is nothing. Whatever is obtained through evil is ever dearly bought, since the disorder through which it is gained destroys the value it had when it was first desired, and all is spent in gaining what is naught to have. Whether evil succeeds or fails in its immediate aims, therefore, all its efforts serve only to waste its energies and disclose its essential ugliness. But despite the manifest emptiness of all its works, the clamours of iniquity still seize hold of mankind. For it is not truth that man desires, but the doctrines that fit the bent of his earthy nature.[10]

The fault cannot lie elsewhere but in man. For since all experience shows that reality lies with good, and that evil is negation and unreality, we are driven to one vital question:

> The obiect then it is, from whence this oddes doth grow,
> By which the ill o'reweighs the good in euerything below.
> And what is that but Man? A crazed soule, vnfix'd;
> Made good, yet fall'n, not to extremes, but to a meane betwixt.[11]

The evil agencies that mar man's estate, though part of an order as inscrutable as it is dark, nevertheless draw part of their being from human nature. And so they must remain as long as man's primary error—his 'forming his God out of his owne powers'—is perpetuated, for his misplaced desire for greatness will lead him to forsake his conscience and do evil, and his corrupt reason will recommend to him as just, actions which violate duty and honour. He will be beset with numberless furies of his own creating:

> A feare in *Great* men still, to lose their might;
> And in the meane, *ambition* infinite;
> *Truth*, in the witty held but as a notion,
> *Honour*, the Old mans God; the Youths promotion.

(How much of Shakespearian tragedy, one might wonder, lives in these lines?) Despite all the forces of evil, however, humankind cannot become utterly corrupt; for the greater part of them are sustained by a mysterious force that prevents them from merging with the darkness they choose for themselves[12] (whose operation might even be apparent to a Shakespeare as a daily beauty in their lives). But it does not keep them from straying from goodness, and so they doom themselves to labour   with shaddowed light of imbecillitie,
> To raise more towers of Babel vp, aboue the Truth to be.

They try to regulate their error, and frame laws in an attempt to strengthen the sagging structure of their society; but it is in vain. Their laws are propounded out of their own faults—they are 'but corrupt reason'[13]—and arouse new lawlessness in the process of putting down the old.[14]

The governments of mankind—'those theaters of clay'[15]—are monuments to men's depravity, founded upon vice, and more unstable than the creature they rule. So imperfect is men's fallen condition that authority can hardly be instituted until it has 'So aboue Nature rais'd the Lawes of Might' as to make possible all manner of crime and error. Once it is established, its subjects ascribe greater glory to their ruler than to their Creator. They fashion God in their crazed imaginations 'as if from Powers Throne he took his being', and, blind to its iniquities, they offer up their freedom at the feet of their pompous idol,[16] awed by the kingliness of every inch of it.

Some among mankind bear the privilege of nobility; but their positions of authority in the state are not signs of health. The nobility aspire toward the honours that are granted from the throne rather than to the gifts of the heavenly kingdom. Their seeking to rise to greatness is the beginning of their downfall, for in their impressed servility they become the tools of tyrants. Inferior princes and magistrates abandon their reason in their rush for the dignities of office, and all too rarely do they perceive that the robes in which they strut majestically with their peers are in fact the livery of servitude. They

> live like clouds in middle regions blown
> Which rise and fall to make their mover known,[17]

and ebb and flow with the moon.

Yet thrones themselves, which have the power to crush or corrupt all beneath them into compliance, are in their very nature unstable: the more tyrannously they show their strength, the more they contribute to their own overthrow. Their power is founded upon the people's submission; but it does not follow that the greater obedience of their subjects is a guarantee of their permanence. A nation will submit to a king's authority so long as it respects him, but its implicit obedience can tempt him to acts of vice or despotism that destroy the popular awe and arouse contempt:

> So when *Excesse* (*the maladie of Might*)
> Hath (*Dropsy-like*) drown'd all the stiles of right,
> Then doth *Obedience* (else the *food of Power*)
> Helpe on that dropsie Canker to deuoure.[18]

Obedience, that was the food of monarchy, becomes its poison; and when it adopts tyranny in order to magnify itself, it puts itself in the hands of its people. Usually, however, the latter do not stir when they are provoked, either through a mistaken sense of duty or natural servility, so that rulers continue in their abominations and people in their misery.[19] Nevertheless, the secret of successful government lies in the people, and no monarch who does not hear their cries can be safe, no matter how exalted or clever he may be.

> Yet if Kings be the *head*, we be the *heart*;
> And know *we loue no soule, that doth not loue vs*.[20]

If man were not in the first place oppressed by his fallible nature, says Greville, he would not allow kings to oppress him further.[21] But kingdoms perpetuate the human error on which they are founded, and deny the laws of God, and of human kindness; and the doctrines of the Church, teaching obedience to anointed rulers and patience under misfortune, encourage evil rulers in their tyrannies. It is hard for the virtuous man, stung into anger and despair by the cries of the suffering, not to denounce the Church for its shortcomings—to contrast the 'painted heavens' which it preaches to the multitude with the torments which true believers are suffering under its very eyes, and which it is helpless to prevent. How can that doctrine be true that urges men to go meekly to their deaths at the hands of evildoers? Every heart testifies that this is an unnatural proceeding: the laws of nature, that speak to men through their consciences, must surely be a better guide to right action than the compromised principles of mundane religion,[22] which must ever, in this world, be 'mixt of base things and sublime'.[23]

But, although the wicked doings of their fellows may lead men to denounce the Church for its doctrines of patient resignation, and incite them to fight against what they know to be evil in the world, they cannot conquer evil by themselves, for it is part of their natural condition; and virtue cannot so inoculate our old stock but we shall relish of it. Every man, it is true, is wedded to spiritual truths and laws; but at the same time he is subject to the faulty laws of mankind, and to the dictates of a nature fundamentally imperfect. Passion and reason are locked in combat within his breast, and more often than not it is too much for him, being passion's slave, even to distinguish the virtuous impulse from the corrupt, let alone to carry it out when it is known. Man, though spiritually obligated, is bound no less rigidly to the laws of the flesh, and, though perhaps indifferent honest, he lives in a state of error and evil,[24] crawling between heaven and earth. Only those

> Who living in the world, yet of it are not[25]

can meet the challenge of human existence. But natural man, at war with himself, finds that there are no easy ways to good, and that his best efforts are unavailing;[26] and despairingly he asks

> Why God commanded more than man could do,
> Being all things that He will, and Wisedom too.[27]

For this man the time is out of joint; and he will continue to ask this question so long as he remains a worldling. So long as he remains one, he will not find an answer. But those who are not worldlings—

> Those Angell-soules in flesh imprisoned,
> Like strangers liuing in Mortalitie—[28]

do not ask that question, because they do not have to. They have come to rely upon a will mightier than their own, and a reason above their own (which will perhaps bring them to see Providence in the fall of a sparrow). When they have come to that stage, then although they will still be in the world, they will not be of it. Greville does not say that flights of angels will sing them to their rest; but if he means what he writes, a conclusion of this sort can scarcely be in question.

How such people come to see thus far, and find themselves living apart in a corrupt world like the spies of God, is a great mystery. It must, however, come about first of all through 'a light, a gift, a grace inspir'd' that is 'not of us, a spirit not of earth'.[29] Certainly their worldly reasonings must die before their faith can live: '*For God comes not till man be ouerthrowne; Peace is the seed of grace, in dead flesh sowne*'.[30] and the sowing cannot take place, presumably, until a man is as filled with 'contempt for his own subtle brain and once devious ways'[31] as the Providence-proclaiming Hamlet. And until that moment, a man must remain unspiritual. His stature may be God-like in terms of worldly powers,

> Yet without God, a slave of slaves is he;
> To others, wonder; to himself, a rod.[32]

Thus it follows that the path to spiritual insight cannot be by way of worldly success or attributes, but their opposite. Those who are ready for the journey would seemingly term what they meet on the way adversity or affliction, 'man's true glass'[33] for Greville and all the Elizabethans. But to those who are unprepared for spiritual adventure, affliction must bear the brows of tragedy. In the scope of Greville's tragic vision, misfortune can open eyes blinded by habit to the true nature of worldly existence and can direct the mind toward spiritual endeavours. The uses of adversity are traditionally sweet for the writers of the age:

> *Afflictions* water cooles the heate of *sinne*,
> And brings soule-health.[34]

To attempt to ascribe to their origin the ideas contained in the foregoing account would be a large undertaking. What is relevant to the present purpose is that we have here an outlook essentially Christian and basically world-forsaking. At the risk of some inexactness, Shakespearian phraseology has been occasionally resorted to in the account in order to suggest that this philosophy is one which Shakespeare could to some extent have shared. But to say that Shakespeare echoed some of these ideas is not to say that they are in his personal creed; you cannot prove what Shakespeare believed from what he says. We have hints, of course, in 'this nether world' that Lady Macduff sees before her assassination, where values are hideously topsy-turvy, or in Lear's preternatural characterization of the world as a great stage of fools, or in Hamlet's unweeded garden inhabited by things rank and gross in nature. But, Shakespeare being what he is, it would be truer to say that it is the impressions of Lady Macduff, Lear and Hamlet, and not of Shakespeare, that are here in question.

Again, particular studies of the imagery can unquestionably show whither Shakespeare's thoughts are tending; but imagery is far too much part of a play's texture, and therefore far too diffuse and inexplicit in its operation, to provide sufficient objectivity for a study of the writer's personal convictions. An investigation of the imagery, further, can hardly re-create the full imaginative impact of a play—can hardly assess the interplay and force of character, for instance, or of dramatic sequence. Certain features of a play may be more eloquent than others, but it is in its entirety that a play truly speaks. If there is one thing we can be sure of, it is that the whole of a play directs the poet's pen. What we must seek is the cumulative yet hidden eloquence and appeal that springs from what a play is in itself. And that is obtainable only by reflexion from the understanding of the reader or beholder.

Some minds have been able to react totally and uninhibitedly to the impressions of Shakespearian tragedy, and have combined the gifts of analysis and imagination—the disintegrating and the plastic powers—to a significant degree. The best of them was Bradley's; and it is here suggested that the reaction of such an intellect to the multifarious impressions of Shakespearian tragedy offers the most direct means of gaining an idea of its tragic vision. It is also suggested that the idea thus gained bears some resemblance to the tragic vision of Fulke Greville.

The order behind the tragedies—the custodian of Fate—is distinguished for Bradley, as we have seen, through its creating evil though being averse to it, cherishing good without being akin to it, and implanting in all its achievements the seeds of its own ruin. Of this order, he further declares, the characters represented form but a feeble part; for apart from being so vast and complex as hardly to be understood or controlled, and so definite that one change produces inexorable consequences, it also determines the dispositions, circumstances and actions of men. These, as Bradley sees them, are the characteristics of what is for Shakespeare the ultimate power in the tragic world.[35]

Beyond this point Bradley's approach must be subjective; but the picture already begins to resemble Greville's murky arena.

It is through what he calls 'impressions beyond the tragic', present at the end of *King Lear* but present also at the close of other tragedies, that Bradley approaches closest to the tragic vision. One is that the heroic being, though outwardly a failure, is yet in another sense superior to the world in which he appears, strangely untouched by the doom that overtakes him, and 'rather set free from life than deprived of it'. This feeling implies the existence of an idea which, if taken in isolation, would transform the tragic view of things.

It implies that the tragic world, if taken as it is presented, with all its error, guilt, failure, woe and waste, is no final reality, but only a part of reality taken for the whole, and, when so taken, illusive; and that if we could see the whole, and the tragic facts in their true place in it, we should find them, not abolished, of course, but so transmuted that they had ceased to be strictly tragic,—find, perhaps, the suffering and death counting for little or nothing, the greatness of soul for much or all.

A second impression concerns the world which greatness of soul overcomes in its ascent. The gods of that place do not interfere in its workings. They do not show their approval of their own by defending them

from adversity or death, or by giving them power and prosperity. These, on the contrary, are worthless, or worse; it is not on them, but on the renunciation of them that the gods throw incense. They breed lust, pride, hardness of heart, the insolence of office, cruelty, scorn, hypocrisy, contention, war, murder, self-destruction. The whole story beats this indictment of prosperity into the brain.

Lear's great speeches in his madness proclaim this indictment. But in this play, as in *Timon*, we see that

the poor and humble are, almost without exception, sound and sweet at heart, faithful and pitiful. And here adversity, to the blessed in spirit, is blessed. It wins fragrance from the crushed flower. It melts in aged hearts sympathies which prosperity had frozen. It purges the soul's sight by blinding that of the eyes. Throughout that stupendous Third Act the good are seen growing better through suffering, and the bad worse through success. The warm castle is a room in hell, the storm-swept heath a sanctuary. The judgement of this world is a lie; its goods, which we covet, corrupt us; its ills, which break our bodies, set our souls free;

> Our means secure us, and our mere defects
> Prove our commodities.

Let us renounce the world, hate it, and lose it gladly. The only real thing is the soul, with its courage, patience, devotion. And nothing outward can touch it.

These impressions, declares Bradley, are not the whole spirit of the tragedy.

But still this strain of thought, to which the world appears as the kingdom of evil and therefore worthless, is in the tragedy, and may well be the record of many hours of exasperated feeling and troubled brooding.

The strain of thought is one which, if it were allowed to dominate, would destroy the tragedy by depriving it of the presuppositions concerning the reality and worthwhileness of human life on which they are based. But,

Pursued further again, it leads to the idea that this world, in that obvious appearance of it which tragedy cannot dissolve without dissolving itself, is illusive.[36]

In his claiming it to be 'in the tragedy' that the external world out of which tragedy arises is wrapped in illusion and unreality, and that reality inheres in the soul and not the suffering, Bradley, it is here believed, is on the way to his 'third view'. His failure to perceive this, or pursue the matter, is due partly to the limited expression it finds in Shakespeare, partly to its intangibility and the perilous degree of subjectivity needed for its apprehension, and mainly to the realization that these thoughts are utterly opposed to the tragic mood, and are tending outside the province of the play. His fears are eminently justifiable; and yet in a sense he is too scrupulous on the latter point. For whatever our beliefs or faith, we are but men, and in our purgatorial state of devout worldliness must be grieved when we are shown the waste of good and the suffering of the innocent. However far Bradley had pursued his inquiry, he could not have loosened tragedy's hold upon the action. But in the process he might certainly have had to admit new possibilities concerning the function of tragedy, or concerning matters transcendent.

If the above conclusions are correct, our approach to Shakespearian tragedy cannot be unaffected. A new appreciation of the sphere of human activity must imply a reappraisal of the attributes, concepts and deeds of men. If, for example, the entirety of worldly existence is flawed, are we realistic in looking for tragic flaws of character? If from the pathetic briefness and error of our lives—'What are mens lives', asks Greville, 'but labyrinths of error, Shops of Deceit, and Seas of misery?'[37]—it is evident that we are such things as dreams are made on, dare we idolize the tragic heroes, and make them standards of greatness? (Is it not man's characteristic sin and failing, according to Greville, to form a God out of his own powers?) What should our opinion be? Should we say, 'How beauteous mankind is!' and invite Prospero's possible rebuke of *naïveté*, or should we declare, 'Man delights not me' as we note the tragic span of this quintessence of dust?

These questions apply only if what is put forward in this article can ever be more than a suggestion. But one thing is beyond all doubt. Before we can be sure that we understand Elizabethan tragedy, we must be sure we have the means of taking into account lines as characteristic of Elizabethan thinking as the following:

> Thus though *Affliction* be no welcome *Ghest*
> Vnto the *world* (that loves nought but her *weale*)
> Of me, therefore she shalbe loved best,
> Because to me she doth the *World* reveale,
> Which *worldly welfare* would from me conceale:
> It is a gainefull *skill* the *World* to know,
> As they can tel that with the *World* doe deale,
> It cost them *much* ere *proofe* the same doth show,
> Which knowledge fro *Afflictiō* streight doth flow.
>
> *Affliction*, Ladie of the happy life,
> (And Queene of mine, though my life happlesse be)
> Give my Soule endlesse *peace*, in endlesse *strife*,
> For thou hast powre to give them both to me,
> Because they both haue residence in thee.[38]

NOTES

1. See G. Bullough, *Poems and Dramas of Fulke Greville*, Introd. vol. 2.

2. *Life* of Sir Philip Sidney, ed. N. C. Smith (1907), p. 151.

3. *Ibid.* p. 221.

4. *Ibid.*

5. A. C. Bradley, *Shakespearean Tragedy* (1937), p. 25.

6. *Ibid.* pp. 25 ff.

7. *Mustapha*, Third Chorus.

8. *Ibid.* Fourth Chorus, ll. 11–16.

9. *Alaham*, Third Chorus, ll. 19–40; and First Chorus, ll. 35–40.

10. *Ibid.* First Chorus, ll. 71–4, 86, 91–2.

11. *Ibid.* ll. 19–22.

12. *Ibid.* Second Chorus, ll. 12, 135–8, 87–94.

13. *A Treatise of Monarchy*, st. 242.

14. *Mustapha*, Fourth Chorus, ll. 15–16, 62.

15. *A Treatise of Religion*, st. 66.

16. *Mustapha*, Second Chorus, ll. 47, 98.

17. *A Treatise of Monarchy*, st. 340.

18. *Mustapha*, First Chorus.

19. *Ibid.* Second Chorus, ll. 201, 192–8.

20. *Alaham*, Fourth Chorus, ll. 15–16.

21. *Mustapha*, Second Chorus, ll. 209–10.

22. *Ibid.* Fifth Chorus (Chorus Tartorum).

23. *A Treatise of Religion*, st. 51.

24. *Mustapha*, Final Chorus (Chorus Sacerdotum).

25. *Treatise of Religion*, st. 111.

26. *Mustapha*, Final Chorus (Chorus Sacerdotum).

27. *Treatise of Religion*, st. 76.

28. *Alaham*, Prologue, ll. 66–7.

29. *Treatise of Religion*, st. 3.

30. *Ibid.* st. 75, and *Caelica*, XCVI.

31. Harley Granville-Barker, *Prefaces to Shakespeare*, Third Series (1937), p. 172.

32. *A Treatise of Religion*, st. 6.

33. *Ibid.* st. 103.

34. John Davies of Hereford, *Microcosmos* (Oxford, 1603), p. 79.

35. *Op. cit.* p. 30.

36. *Ibid.* pp. 323 ff.

37. *An Inquisition Upon Fame and Honour*, st. 1.

38. John Davies of Hereford, *op. cit.* pp. 82, 80.

SHAKESPEARE *v.* THE REST: THE OLD CONTROVERSY[1]

BY

T. J. B. SPENCER

Shakespeare's own attitude to his professional rivals was one of astonishing modesty, if we may take seriously his despondent description of himself as

> Desiring this man's art and that man's scope.

By the time he had written this, however, in his early thirties, when Francis Meres published his *Palladis Tamia*, Shakespeare is already firmly among his contemporaries:

These are our best for Tragedie, the Lorde *Buckhurst*, Doctor *Leg* of Cambridge, Doctor *Edes* of Oxforde, Maister *Edward Ferris*, the Authour of the *Mirrour for Magistrates*, *Marlow, Peele, Watson, Kid, Shakespeare, Drayton, Chapman, Decker*, and *Beniamin Iohnson*.

And on the next page we read:

The best for Comedy amongst us bee, *Edward* Earle of Oxforde, Doctor *Gager* of Oxforde, Maister *Rowley* once a rare Scholler of learned Pembrooke Hall in Cambridge, Maister *Edwardes* one of her Maiesties Chappell, eloquent and wittie *Iohn Lilly, Lodge, Gascoyne, Greene, Shakespeare, Thomas Nash, Thomas Heywood, Anthony Mundye* our best plotter, *Chapman, Porter, Wilson, Hathway*, and *Henry Chettle*.[2]

Such was the race-card towards the end of the sixteenth century, and it is by no means clear who are the favourites—though the increasing publication of Shakespeare's writings during the next few years shows where the reading-public was beginning to put its money. And by the time that *The Return from Parnassus* is written (in which Shakespeare's name appears among half a score of candidates for fame) it is possible to express stronger opinions. There, Kemp and Burbage are talking and give their point of view:

Why heres our fellow *Shakespeare* puts them all downe I and *Ben Ionson* too.[3]

Shakespeare succeeded in making a strong impression among his contemporaries. It was one of distinctness and individuality—Ben Jonson, in his lines prefixed to the Folio, gave his strikingly expressed testimony that Shakespeare's personality was to be felt in his writings:

> Looke how the fathers face
> Lives in his issue, even so, the race
> Of *Shakespeare's* minde, and manners brightly shines
> In his well torned, and true filed lines.

The praise bestowed upon him in his monument in Stratford Church is outside time. It asserts that Shakespeare was in worldly wisdom a Nestor, in natural genius a Socrates, in literary art a Virgil:

> Judicio Pylium, genio Socratem, arte Maronem.

The words are powerful. But in fact he had not been regarded as unique. Those who had praised him had naturally judged him in relation to other writers of his time, and therefore some of the praise (for instance, that of Webster in his preface to *The White Devil*) may sound rather condescending. But in the seventeenth century, until Dryden, they were not able to decide and define exactly what the impression was. Shakespeare was a lively and fluent writer; of great fancy and versatility; also, diligent. But the careful collections that have been made of references to Shakespeare in the seventeenth century show how many writers paid little or no attention to him. G. E. Bentley has made it clear, in his valuable study of the reputations of Ben Jonson and Shakespeare, that Jonson, if we are to judge from the printed testimony, was the more popular during two-thirds of the seventeenth century.[4] It was only after that that Shakespeare drew level and triumphantly outstripped him. There were good reasons for this. Ben Jonson was manifestly a 'writer'. He produced 'literature'. He published his *Works*. He was a man of intellectual authority, a scholar and a philosopher, with qualities making him seem important and appealing to the young and pretentious. Jonson was, moreover, the most vocal literary critic of the early seventeenth century, and found Shakespeare a convenient contrast to himself, for the purposes of that rough-and-ready miscellany of Renaissance literary theorizing which Jonson compiled or conveyed. He gave Shakespeare a kind of typological significance: the naturally gifted writer, who fails to discipline himself. Jonson, in spite of all his splendid praise of Shakespeare, turned him into a kind of sparring partner, whom he could use in order to justify his own rather laborious critical position.

Of course, in contrasting himself with Shakespeare, Jonson saw something that was really there. But from Jonson derived the facile commonplace about Nature and Art, which for long proved to be a pertinacious and unproductive theme of Shakespeare criticism. It was picked up by Milton in his thoughtless youth, when he complimented Shakespeare:

> to th' shame of slow-endeavouring art,
> Thy easie numbers flow.

The plausible commonplace about nature and art impeded even the more intelligent critics, and went rolling down the years, reaching, perhaps, critical rock-bottom when Burns, in a misguided moment of national zeal, announced to an Edinburgh audience:

> Here *Douglas* forms wild Shakespeare into plan.[5]

In the age of Dryden and of Rymer, the comparison between Shakespeare and his contemporary dramatists was a matter of balanced critical activity. Dryden himself, looking back upon 'the last age', made several efforts to differentiate 'the Giant Race, before the Flood'; to allot merits of different kinds among them. The lesser candidates for fame have now dropped out. Of the score or so of starters, only three are now running, Shakespeare being definitely the pacemaker. In his *Essay of Dramatick Poesy* Dryden gave his well-known 'characters' of Shakespeare, Beaumont and Fletcher, and Ben Jonson. These became classics of their kind; that is to say, they became (like most of Dryden's critical aperçus) deteriorating clichés of literary criticism for the next hundred years. In comparison with Shakespeare, Beaumont and Fletcher 'understood and imitated the conversation of gentlemen much better; whose wild debaucheries, and quickness of wit in repartees, no poet before them could paint as they have done'. Or, in his lines to Congreve:

> In easie Dialogue is *Fletcher*'s Praise:
> He mov'd the Mind, but had no Pow'r to raise.
> Great *Johnson* did by strength of Judgement please:
> Yet doubling *Fletcher*'s Force, he wants his Ease.

When Dr Johnson called Dryden 'the Father of English Criticism', he meant more than a vague panegyric—something more precise than is commonly supposed. Dryden was the stallion that begat most of the hobby-horses and mares' nests of criticism in England in the eighteenth century; and his statements (or guesses or ventures) became normal doctrine, repeated by all the Dick Minims of the time. Pope mocked at these worn-down counters of criticism:

> In all debates where Criticks bear a part,
> Not one but nods, and talks of Johnson's Art,
> Of Shakespear's Nature, and of Cowley's Wit;
> How Beaumont's Judgment check'd what Fletcher writ.[6]

Among the more curious and curiously persisting of Dryden's differentiations between Shakespeare and his contemporaries was his comment that the 'excellency' of Shakespeare was 'in the more manly passions; *Fletcher*'s in the softer: *Shakespeare* writ better betwixt man and man; Fletcher, betwixt man and woman: consequently, the one describ'd friendship better; the other love'.[7] Shakespeare's supposed deficiency in female characterization (and the greater success of Fletcher in this) became a traditional comparison. It was, surely, contrary to theatrical experience. For, in fact, the female characters in Shakespeare's plays had, ever since a woman appeared as Desdemona with Killigrew's company in 1660, provided scope for subtle and admired theatrical interpretation—although the parts were often fattened in the acting versions of the plays. It was well known, of course, in the eighteenth century that on Shakespeare's stage the women's parts were taken by boys. This fact was sometimes brought forward to account for the comparative inferiority, as it was supposed, of Shakespeare's women-characters. 'What Grace, or Master-strokes of Action' (asked Colley Cibber in 1740) 'can we conceive such ungainly Hoydens to have been capable of? This Defect was so well considered by *Shakespeare*, that in few of his Plays, he has any greater Dependance upon the Ladies, than in the Innocence and Simplicity of a *Desdemona*, an *Ophelia*, or in the short Specimen of a fond and virtuous *Portia*.'[8] According to later taste (especially the taste of the nineteenth century) Dr Johnson was astonishingly imperceptive on the subject of Shakespeare's women. This was not personal insensitivity, for the opinion was shared by the men of sensibility of the time. William Collins, in his verse *Epistle Addrest to Sir Thomas Hanmer on his Edition of Shakespear's Works* in 1743, picked up Dryden's equable comparison between Shakespeare and Fletcher and converted it into biased praise of Shakespeare—he awards the palm to the gentle Fletcher for his powers of expressing

> Each glowing Thought, that warms the Female Mind;
> Each melting Sigh, and ev'ry tender Tear,
> The Lover's Wishes, and the Virgin's Fear.
> His ev'ry strain the *Smiles* and *Graces* own;
> But stronger *Shakespear* felt for *Man* alone.

The opinion of Shakespeare's inferiority to Beaumont and Fletcher in drawing female characters was still being repeated and excused by Sir Walter Scott in the early nineteenth century.[9]

Much of Coleridge's Shakespeare criticism was spoken in a tone of exasperation. His rejection of *this* long-persisting critical delusion determines the mood of his more enthusiastic expressions of admiration for Shakespeare's women. It was, in fact, Coleridge's great discovery, which was exploited throughout the nineteenth century, that Shakespeare's women characters were remarkable in that you felt like marrying them. Moreover, when you come to think of it, there were very few women of whom a vivid, rounded portrayal was given—not only in Elizabethan drama, but anywhere in the world's literature (at that date)—that you *did* feel like marrying. A few moments' consideration revealed the surprising fact that even in Greek literature there was hardly anyone sufficiently attractive to be desired as a partner for life. What could Homer offer? Helen? Certainly not—even though Mr Gladstone, who displayed a lifelong kindness towards erring women, thought she was 'a production never surpassed by the mind or hand of man', and was so bold as to say on several occasions that in her 'Paganism comes nearest to the penetential tone and profound self-abasement that belong to Christianity'.[10] Penelope was all very well in her way, but a little more warm-heartedness was needed. Nausicaa, though charming, and Andromache, though tender, were too slightly sketched for you to feel sure. There was not much to be said for any of the women in Greek drama. The only really admirable ladies in the extant thirty-three plays were two: Antigone and Alcestis. But their positions were very peculiar, and their characters, if brought to the test of normality, were somewhat ambiguous, so that a genuine admiration for their merits hardly went so far as a desire to marry either of them. And if Greek literature failed us, where were we to look? Not among the shadowy Petrarchan or pastoral or Amazonian heroines of romance. And not anywhere in Elizabethan drama outside Shakespeare. Coleridge vigorously condemns the old notion that Fletcher felt for women and Shakespeare alone for men. Indeed, in the plays of Beaumont and Fletcher (he tells us) the female characters, with very few exceptions, 'are, when of the light kind, not decent; when heroic, complete viragos'.[11] Of all writers for the Elizabethan stage, Coleridge affirms, Shakespeare alone 'has drawn the female character with that mixture of the real and of the ideal which belongs to it.... There is no one female personage in the plays of all his contemporaries of whom a man, seriously examining his heart and his good sense, can say "Let that woman be my companion through life: let her be the object of my suit, and the reward of my success".'[12] Of Shakespeare's ladies you could say that.

Coleridge's opinions about Shakespeare's females have been visited with a good deal of ridicule in modern times. But this ignores the fact that his method of expressing himself on this subject was deliberately combative. The record is mostly from reports of his conversation or of his lectures; if our post-prandial conversational sallies and lecture-room vagaries were to be chronicled, as Coleridge's have been, who shall escape the scourge of folly?

This, at least, was the end of one of the critical notions—the superiority of Fletcher to Shakespeare in the presentation of love and of the female heart—which Dryden had ill-advisedly put into circulation. Unfortunately the most brilliant part of Dryden's work failed to establish a tradition: the criticism of particular plays, as unified works of art, was slow off the mark. His analysis of *The Silent Woman* in *An Essay of Dramatick Poesy* seems to have had no successors. There was no comparable analysis of a single Elizabethan play until the mid-eighteenth century; and then for a long time it was only Shakespeare who was accorded that distinction.

The disappearance of the Elizabethan, Jacobean, and Caroline playwrights, apart from a few plays of Ben Jonson and a few of Beaumont and Fletcher, from the normal reading of educated people from Dryden's time onwards was justified by critical opinion. A typically enlightened view of the cultural defects of Shakespeare's contemporaries was to be found in Hume's *History* (from 1754 onwards), a work which was constantly reprinted and soon translated into other European languages. After his account of the reign of King James I, Hume discusses the state of culture in England at that time, including literature; and so he comes to Shakespeare and the drama. Ben Jonson, he tells us,

possessed all the learning wanting to Shakespeare, and wanted all the genius of which the other was possessed. Both of them were equally deficient in taste and elegance, in harmony and correctness. A servile copyist of the ancients, Jonson translated into bad English the beautiful passages of the Greek and Roman authors, without accommodating them to the manners of his age and country. His merit has been totally eclipsed by that of Shakespeare, whose rude genius prevailed over the rude art of his cotemporary.[13]

In 1736 Joseph Spence, then Professor of Poetry at Oxford, published an edition of *Gorboduc*, which he dedicated to the Earl of Middlesex (a descendant of Sackville); and he was able to quote the testimony of the most distinguished living English poet to the merits of the play. Spence tells us that Pope approved of *Gorboduc*, commending its regularity, and lamenting that Sackville's contemporaries did not follow in the same track:

that the Writers of the succeeding Age might have improv'd themselves by copying from this Tragedy a Propriety in the Sentiments, an unaffected Perspicuity of Stile, and an easy Flow in the Numbers; In a Word, that Chastity, Correctness, and Gravity of Stile, which are so essential to Tragedy; and which all the Tragic Poets who follow'd, not excepting Shakespeare himself, either little understood, or perpetually neglected.[14]

Spence was also impressed by the position held by Thomas Sackville at the Queen's Court, and observed his resulting superiority to Shakespeare:

'tis no wonder, if the language of kings and statesmen should be less happily imitated by a poet than by a privy councillor.

—an insinuation which has a premonitory ring of Baconianism about it.

Even the scholarly men of letters of the eighteenth century had little regard for Shakespeare's contemporaries in the drama. Dr Johnson gave more quotations from Shakespeare than from any other writer in his *Dictionary*, as an authority for the usage of words. In fact, about fifteen per cent of the quotations are (it is said) from Shakespeare, and they come from all the plays, though not, apparently, from the *Sonnets*. And Johnson read and used the works of other interesting Elizabethan authors: Sidney's *Arcadia*, Chapman's *Homer*, Spenser's prose, Puttenham, Drayton, Daniel, Donne, Raleigh's *History*, and so on. But in the *Dictionary* hardly anything is to be found from the dramatists outside Shakespeare, except a little Ben Jonson. In the early years of the century there had been a booksellers' edition of Ben Jonson and of Beaumont and Fletcher. Theobald planned critical editions of these authors as a natural development of his work on Shakespeare; but he died before he had got very far. In the 1750's there was a slight revival of activity. There appeared a scandalously garbled edition of Beaumont and Fletcher, which was reprinted in 1778; in 1756 a booksellers' *Ben Jonson*; and in 1759 (more remarkable) a *Massinger*, which was reprinted twenty years later. As regards the works of Shakespeare's playwright contemporaries, that was about all.

There was, however, another category of things, which were not 'works', not literature, not poetry, and rarely even drama. There were certain things called 'Old Plays'. Being badly printed, flimsy, ill-stitched and rarely bound, they ran many perils; their survival value was slight. They soon lost their blank leaves, and if they lost their title-pages, they became mere waste paper. (The demand for waste paper, for a variety of domestic and other uses, has, until comparatively recent times, been heavy and continuous and urgent and far in excess of the supply. The consequences for English literature have been serious.) Old playbooks came to be collected by people interested in the theatre, or by bibliophils as ephemeral curiosities. It was one of these ample collections of old playbooks that came into the possession of Garrick, was augmented by him, and eventually came to the British Museum. In 1744 Robert Dodsley, the enterprising publisher and bookseller, felt that there was sufficient public curiosity for him to venture to open a subscription-list for the publication of a selection of them. He obtained five hundred subscribers, including Mr Pope and Mr Garrick; and he modestly submitted his pioneer work to the public:

My first End was to snatch some of the best Pieces of our old Dramatic Writers from total Neglect and Oblivion. . . . Several of these being not unworthy the present, nor indeed any Stage.[15]

He proposed to print fifty plays; but he was encouraged by the response of his subscribers to add a further two volumes and bring the number up to sixty plays. The twelve volumes served a need for a long time. It was probably the most important single step towards a just understanding of Shakespeare; the clarification of the admiration of Shakespeare was to come from the growth of an interest in the dramatists who were his contemporaries.

Dodsley, and his successors in the publication of old plays, provided the material for the destruction of one of the critical commonplaces misbegotten by Dryden, who had said that Shakespeare 'found not, but created first the stage'.[16] Even if we ignore the hack compilations of theatre-gossip of Downes, Curll, and Chetwood, essentially this opinion was reinforced by the pioneer accounts of dramatic history. Dodsley himself, writing in 1744 his modest essay on the early history of the English stage, does not combat the prevailing opinion:

Now, as it were, all at once. . . the true Drama received Birth and Perfection from the creative Genius of *Shakespear, Fletcher* and *Johnson*.[17]

Much the same story was told by Bishop Percy in his essay 'On the Origin of the English Stage', which he published in his *Reliques of Ancient English Poetry* (1765); by Johnson in his *Shakespeare* (1765);[18] by Thomas Hawkins in the preface to his collection *The Origin of the English Drama* (1773); and even by Malone in his *Historical Account of the Rise and Progress of the English Stage and of the Economy and Usages of the Ancient Theatres in England*, which he published in 1790 and included subsequently in the Variorum editions of Shakespeare. Malone begins:

The drama before the time of Shakespeare was so little cultivated, or so ill-understood, that to many it may appear unnecessary to carry our theatrical researches higher than that period.

The titles of the plays before 1592, when Malone supposes Shakespeare commenced dramatic writer, 'are scarcely known, except to antiquaries; nor is there one of them that will bear a second perusal'. They are, he says, 'contemptible and few', and he enumerates thirty-eight (excluding the mysteries, moralities, interludes, and translations). His list of the 'contemptible and few' includes *The Spanish Tragedy*, and the plays of Lyly and Marlowe.

By the beginning of the nineteenth century, then, whom among Shakespeare's rival playwrights could the intelligent reader come to know without too much trouble?[19] The answer is: very few. In one of Charles Lamb's letters we have an interesting piece of evidence how difficult it was, at that time, to set about reading the older dramatists. In 1804 Wordsworth, for reasons of his own, wrote to Lamb in London saying that he wanted to get to know the early playwrights and asking him to try to obtain the books for him. And Lamb replied:

The books which you want, I calculate at about £8. Ben Jonson is a Guinea Book. Beaumont & Fletcher in folio, the right folio, not now to be met with; the octavos are about £3. As to any other dramatists, I do not know where to find them, except what are in Dodsley's Old Plays, which are about £3 also: Massinger I never saw but at one shop, but it is now gone, but one of the editions of Dodsley contains about a fourth (the best) of his plays.... Marlow's plays and poems are totally vanished; only one edition of Dodsley retains one, and the other two, of his plays: but John Ford is the man after Shakespeare. Let me know your will and pleasure soon: for I have observed, next to the pleasure of buying a bargain for one's self is the pleasure of persuading a friend to buy it. It tickles one with the image of an imprudency without the penalty usually annex'd.[20]

The new generation of men of letters were soon at work to remedy this situation. Gifford edited Massinger in 1805, and this may be regarded as the first of the nineteenth-century editions. But this was playing safe. And there is no doubt that (so far as publication was concerned) Lamb should be considered the pioneer as an admiring critic of the poetry of the old plays. His *Specimens of English Dramatic Poets, who lived about the Time of Shakespear: with Notes* appeared in 1808, and had been meditated for some time. Secondly, there was the powerful influence of the scholarly tastes of Sir Walter Scott. Scott published his *Ancient British Drama* in 1810, in three large volumes. By the title *Ancient British Drama* he meant those plays up to 1640 which had lost possession of the stage. He omitted Massinger and Ford—the one recently re-edited by Gifford and the other soon to be collected and published by Scott's friend, Weber. What Scott produced was a kind of popularization of Dodsley; more readable and less expensive; with good critical notes from his own pen—and Scott was one of the best critics of his generation. And he encouraged others; among them Henry Weber, a curious character. A German, born in Russia, he arrived in Scotland and was befriended by Scott, who set him on to various literary tasks. He brought out his *Ford* in 1811. It was the first 'collection' of the works of one of the old dramatists. Although it has defects, it is not nearly as bad as his censorious reviewers stated. Weber also re-edited Beaumont and Fletcher in 1812, and these were followed by Gifford's *Ben Jonson* (1816) and his *Ford* (an important advance upon Weber's) in 1827; and G. Robinson's *Marlowe* in 1826. The great editor, Alexander Dyce, appeared on the scene with his *Peele* (1828), *Webster* (1830), *Greene* (1831), *Shirley* (1833), which was completing the work begun by Gifford, and *Middleton* (1840). Collier edited Thomas Heywood for the Shakespeare Society in 1842; Halliwell-Phillipps' *Marston* appeared in 1856 and F. W. Fairholt's *Lyly* in 1858. Chapman and Dekker, however, had to await R. H. Shepherd in 1873 for adequate reprints of their plays. Many of these editions were laborious pioneer achievements, comparable to the achievements of the eighteenth-century editors of Shakespeare.

The early years of the nineteenth century were the age of personal enthusiasms for the dramatists, irradiated by a sense of discovery or rediscovery, which we can only envy. Francis Jeffrey, reviewing Weber's edition of Ford in the *Edinburgh Review* in 1811, said:

All true lovers of English poetry have been long in love with the dramatists of the time of Elizabeth and James; and must have been sensibly comforted by their late restoration to some degree of favour and notoriety.

Ford (says Jeffrey) belongs to 'a class of writers, whom we have long worshipped in secret with a sort of idolatrous veneration, and now find once more brought forward as candidates for public applause'.[21] Charles James Fox when a young man came across a copy of Massinger; 'he read it, and, for some time after, could talk of nothing but Massinger'.[22] Henry Mackenzie, the Man of Feeling himself, discovered Webster and wrote about him in eulogistic terms. Shelley was a great admirer of *The Duchess of Malfi* and thought the scene of the murder of the Duchess 'equal to anything in Shakespeare'.[23]

Gradually, indeed, other dramatists began to intrude their merits into the simple hierarchy that had been inherited from Dryden. Lamb believed that Ford was the man after Shakespeare. Leigh Hunt thought differently: 'I take Webster and Decker to have been the two greatest of the Shakspeare men, for unstudied genius, next after Beaumont and Fletcher; and in some respects they surpassed them.'[24] Marlowe (who had been thought frenzied by Lamb) begins to increase in reputation. The *Edinburgh Review* was telling its readers in 1823 that Marlowe 'was undoubtedly the greatest tragic writer that preceded Shakespeare'.[25] Indeed, Walter Scott was glancing at the fashionable reading at the time of his Waverley novels, when he prefixed to his chapters so many quotations from what he called 'Old Plays'. And the increasing esteem is clearly demonstrated by the change of titles for the collections. They were, indeed, formerly 'Old Plays'. They now became *The British Drama* or *English Dramatic Poetry*. Dodsley's *Old Plays* was reprinted with modifications in 1820 and the traditional title was naturally retained; and among bibliophils and antiquarians the phrase survived (as in the *Old English Plays* of Charles Wentworth Dilke, Keats' friend, a six-volume supplement to Dodsley in 1814–15, and in J. P. Collier's two separate collections of *Five Old Plays*). But as objects of criticism the whole body of writing had been elevated from the category of 'Old Plays' to 'the Ancient British Drama'.

The publication of readable editions of the dramatists now made possible the comparison of their merits with Shakespeare's—to judge him in his context among his fellow playwrights. The problem had been succinctly stated by Lamb in the preface to his *Specimens*: it was necessary to decide

how much of Shakespeare shines in the great men his contemporaries, and how far in his divine mind and manners he surpassed them and all mankind.

Or, to take Coleridge's formulation of the problem:

No one can understand Shakespeare's superiority fully, until he has ascertained, by comparison, all that which he possessed in common with several other great dramatists of his age, and has then calculated the surplus which is entirely Shakespeare's own.[26]

Gifford had already begun the comparison and provoked controversy in the preface to his edition of Massinger in 1805, affirming that Shakespeare's superiority to his contemporaries rested on his superior wit; and that in his other dramatic excellencies (sublimity, pathos, and so on) he was equalled by Ben Jonson, Beaumont and Fletcher, and Massinger. Beaumont was as sublime, and Fletcher as pathetic, as Shakespeare.[27] Henry Weber, in his introduction to his *Beaumont and Fletcher* in 1812, expressly stated that *Philaster* 'possesses excellencies little inferior to those of *Macbeth, Lear* and *Julius Caesar*'.[28] This sort of opinion was becoming fairly common. Miss Mitford scribbles to a correspondent in 1816:

Many of his [Shakespeare's] immediate successors approach him very nearly in tragic powers; Massinger equals him in declamation; Ford in sublimity; Fletcher in pathos; but no one comes near to him in wit.[29]

Lamb and Hazlitt, although not so extravagant as Gifford and Weber in their claims, were generally regarded as being responsible for the new literary elevation of the old dramatists. Hazlitt in his *Lectures chiefly on the Dramatic Literature of the Age of Elizabeth*, which he published in 1820, argued powerfully for the greatness of Shakespeare's contemporaries. He overlooks them, certainly; but he does so from the table-land of the age in which he lived. 'He towered above his fellows, "in shape and gesture proudly eminent"; but he was one of a race of giants, the tallest, the strongest, the most graceful, and beautiful of them; but it was a common and a noble brood.'[30] A few years later (1827) Lamb, when he was preparing his *Extracts from the Garrick Plays*, used rather similar language.

Why do we go on with ever-new editions of Ford, and Massinger, and the thrice-reprinted Selections of Dodsley? What we want is as many volumes more as these latter consist of, filled with plays...of which we know comparatively nothing. Not a third part of the treasures of old English dramatic literature has been exhausted. Are we afraid that the genius of Shakespeare would suffer in our estimate by the disclosure? He would indeed be somewhat lessened as a miracle and a prodigy. But he would lose no height by the confession. When a giant is shown to us, does it detract from the curiosity to be told that he has at home a gigantic brood of brethren, less only than himself?[31]

Thus does Dryden's metaphor of 'the Giant Race, before the Flood' begin to come back again into currency.

In short, some of the new admirers of the old dramatists began to express themselves, it was felt, without a sense of just proportion, and gave the impression that there were many dramatists of Shakespeare's time who were nearly as good as he was and occasionally his equal. Such opinions could not be received without dissent, and Coleridge, for one, vigorously protested. To correct perspective was one of Coleridge's important critical tasks, and it was in this spirit that he included in his prospectus for his lectures for the London Philosophical Society in 1811–12:

a critical *Comparison* of SHAKESPEAR, in respect of Diction, Imagery, management of the Passions, Judgment in the construction of his Dramas, in short, of all that belongs to him as a Poet, and as a dramatic Poet, with his contemporaries, or immediate successors, JONSON, BEAUMONT and FLETCHER, FORD, MASSINGER, &c. in the endeavour to determine what of SHAKESPEAR's Merits and Defects are common to him with other Writers of the same age, and what remains peculiar to his own Genius.[32]

Coleridge consistently resisted the elevation of Shakespeare's contemporaries to a plateau or mountain-range or race of giants with him. He claimed to have a full appreciation of the merits of those other dramatists; but Shakespeare's eminence was his own, and not that of his age; his style only superficially resembled that of the contemporary dramatists.[33] And Carlyle, with comparatively little knowledge of the subject, encouraged the same attitude to Shakespeare's singularity, in comparison with his fellow-dramatists, 'whose *Tamburlaines* and *Island Princesses*, themselves not destitute of merit, first show us clearly in what pure loftiness and loneliness the *Hamlets* and *Tempests* reign'.[34]

But the most respectable and consistent opposition came from one who was the most thorough student of the literature of Shakespeare's age; from Alexander Dyce, the admirable editor of many of the dramatists under discussion. The careful perusal, he tells us, of every existing drama of the reigns of Elizabeth and James only convinced him of

the immeasurable superiority of Shakespeare to all the playwrights of his time. I am not, I trust, insensible to the invention and power displayed by Fletcher, Jonson, Ford, Webster, Massinger, Dekker, Tourneur, Heywood, Chapman, Middleton, and the rest of that illustrious brotherhood; but I feel that over the worst of Shakespeare's dramas, his genius has diffused a peculiar charm, of which *their* best productions are entirely destitute; and to insinuate that any of his contemporaries ever produced a play worthy of being ranked with his happiest efforts,—with *Othello* for instance, *Macbeth*, *Lear*, or *Hamlet*,—seems to me an absurdity almost unpardonable in any critic.

And in reply to the remark that Shakespeare belonged to a race of giants, Dyce could only retort:

A falser remark, I conceive, has seldom been made by critic. Shakespeare is not only immeasureably superior to the dramatists of his time in creative power, in insight into the human heart, and in profound thought; but he is moreover utterly unlike them in almost every respect,—unlike them in his method of developing character, in his diction, in his versification.[35]

The same kind of discussion went on in Germany. Both Schlegel and Tieck contributed to it; and Goethe, following his theories that the great writer owes much to the spirit of the age in which he lives, declared that Shakespeare was like Mont Blanc: put that mountain in the middle of the plain of Luneberg Heath, and we should find no words to express our wonder at its magnitude. But seek it among its neighbours, the other great Swiss peaks; then Mont Blanc, while remaining a giant, will no longer produce such wonder in us. So was Shakespeare among his contemporaries. Besides, remarked Goethe to Eckermann,

let him who will not believe that much of Shakespeare's greatness appertains to his great vigorous time, only ask himself the question, whether a phenomenon so astounding would be possible in the present England of 1824, in these evil days of criticizing and hair-splitting journals.[36]

After visiting Goethe at Weimar in 1829, Crabb Robinson wrote in his diary: 'He was fully aware that Shakespeare did not stand alone.'[37]

There was, however, a grave objection to the full acceptance of the drama of Shakespeare's time as an adjunct to his works and as an estimable part of English poetry. The large scholarly editions of the dramatists were expensive and their circulation was comparatively restricted.

They were also unsuitable for that Victorian institution, family reading. The moral tone of the old drama was inevitably observed with some alarm, and occasionally with consternation.

Sir Walter Scott had shown a certain sensitivity to this censure when he published his *Ancient British Drama* in 1810, and he wrote in his introduction, rather defensively:

Coarse and indelicate passages may be found by those who love to glean for them; but the general tenour of our more ancient Plays is highly virtuous: nor had the Stage at any time, or in any country, so good a title to be considered as a school of morals, as in England, during the reigns of Elizabeth, James, and Charles the First.[38]

Scott set himself vigorously against the expurgation of the older literature. When he was editing Dryden in 1805, he wrote to a friend:

I will not castrate John Dryden. I would as soon castrate my own father, as I believe Jupiter did of yore. What would you say to any man who would castrate Shakespeare, or Massinger, or Beaumont & Fletcher?[39]

But in this respect Scott was writing against the spirit of the age. Dr Thomas Bowdler was about to appear upon the scene: first, in 1808 (a tentative castration), and more fully with the *Family Shakespeare* in 1818, producing one of the most widely read books of the century.

The plays of Shakespeare's contemporaries (far more than Shakespeare's) were a problem from this point of view. *The Literary Gazette* in 1830 explained the difficulty:

The works of our...elder dramatists are wholly and entirely unfit to be placed, as hitherto edited, in the hands of young persons, or of females of any age, or even to be thought of for a moment as furniture for the drawing-room table and the parlour-window, or to form the solace of a family-circle at the fireside.... What lady will ever confess that she has read and understood Massinger, or Ford, or even Beaumont and Fletcher? There is hardly a single piece in any of these authors which does not contain more abominable passages than the very worst of modern panders would ever dream of hazarding in print—and there are whole plays in Ford, and in Beaumont and Fletcher, the very essence and substance of which is, from beginning to end, one mass of pollution.[40]

It was to remedy this difficulty that John Murray began to publish a series of expurgated editions of the playwrights. In 1830 appeared: *The Plays of Philip Massinger, adapted for Family Reading, and the Use of Young Persons, by the omission of objectionable passages.* And a similar edition of Ford followed in 1831. The editor (who was William Harness, Byron's school-fellow and friend— a name still remembered in connexion with Shakespeare studies) in his preface explains his purpose: 'The Old English Dramatists, the friends and contemporaries of Shakespeare, have contributed one of the most valuable portions to the poetic literature of our country.' Why then are they 'unknown to the generality of readers, and are only found in the hands of an adventurous few...? The neglect of these authors, in an age so favourable to works of imagination as the present, can only be ascribed to that occasional coarseness of language which intermixes with and pollutes the beauty of their most exquisite scenes.' It is proposed, therefore, to publish editions of the plays 'omitting all such scenes and passages as are inconsistent with the delicacy and refinement of modern taste and manners'. These expurgated editions of Massinger and Ford seem to have filled a real need. They were promptly pirated in New York (as Harper's

Family Library), were later reprinted, and circulated widely; for they are still often to be found on library shelves.

It is not easy, nevertheless, to admire these expurgated editions. Nor can the modern reader feel much affection for the Victorian reprints outside the expensive library sets—for the double-columns of small print in the bulky volumes of Hartley Coleridge's *Massinger and Ford* and George Darley's *Beaumont & Fletcher*; or (even worse) Cunningham's reprints of Gifford's *Ben Jonson* and *Massinger*; or Shepherd's *Chapman*. What was needed to make the dramatists really popular reading were attractive cheap editions. It was that lively character Edward Vizitelly who provided them. Vizitelly was a journalist with a flair, and later a publisher with a sense of what the public wanted. In 1887, prompted by Havelock Ellis, he began one of his most success-ful ventures, publishing half-crown volumes of the old dramatists, with critical prefaces by lively and advanced young men; not unpleasantly decorated in a mature Victorian or Ninetyish style: the famous Mermaid series.

But poor Vizitelly had many difficulties with his Mermaids. In the early volumes he put the words 'Unexpurgated Edition' prominently on the title-pages. By January 1889 he was promising to remove this inscription—on the grounds that it was by now well known that the Mermaids gave the full text of the plays. The *Marlowe* in 1887, edited by Havelock Ellis, con-tained a complete reprint of Richard Baines' famous testimony against Marlowe ('concernynge his damnable opinions and judgement of Religion and scorne of God's worde'). This had been discovered long ago and printed by Joseph Ritson,[41] but only a much bowdlerized version had been given by Dyce and by Bullen.[42] Soon Vizitelly was apologizing for it on a slip inserted in later volumes in the series:

Objections having been made in various quarters to passages having reference to certain religious opinions attributed to Marlowe, contained in the Appendix to the above work, the Publishers beg to announce the issue of a new edition in which the passages excepted to have been suppressed. Book-sellers and others desirous of being furnished with cancel pages in lieu of pages 429, 430 and 431 of the first edition are requested to apply to the Publishers.

So your Mermaid *Marlowe* may contain either a complete or a bowdlerized version of Baines' testimony.

Meanwhile, Vizitelly was in prison, for publishing Zola. In October 1888 he was appre-hended for issuing a translation of *La Terre*, and during his trial he printed an entertaining pamphlet, *Extracts principally from English Classics, showing that the legal suppression of M. Zola's novels would logically involve the bowdlerising of the greatest Works in English Literature*. He was heavily fined; but he was unrepentant, and next year he began a reissue of Zola's works. In May 1889 he was sentenced to three months' imprisonment. He was by now 69.

Amid the misfortunes of Zola, the Mermaid dramatists were small beer. Vizitelly was driven out of business and the series passed to another publisher (Fisher Unwin), who sacked the general editor, Havelock Ellis,[43] and eventually to Ernest Benn.

It was in these unpromising circumstances that the Mermaids took root and flourished, sturdy creatures. They were widely read, and the old poetic drama rapidly became a pervasive influence in the new English poetry. Moreover, they are still being reprinted; what other Victorian cheap reprints have received such an astonishing honour? And university students still quote in their essays the blunders in those critical prefaces written by Vizitelly's advanced young men. There can, I suppose, be few of us who did not do a good deal of our early reading of the dramatists in that row of Mermaids which, affectionately worn, still adorn our shelves.

It was good fortune that the dramatists who were Shakespeare's contemporaries were launched on the twentieth century, for the general reading public, in this pleasant, rather daring form, free from pedantry and pretentiousness; not too firmly enshrined as classics of English literature.

NOTES

1. This article is based on a paper delivered to the International Shakespeare Conference in Stratford-upon-Avon, 4 September 1959.

2. *Francis Meres' Treatise 'Poetrie', A Critical Edition*, by D. C. Allen (Urbana, 1933), pp. 78–9.

3. Second Part, IV, iii.

4. *Shakespeare and Jonson. Their reputations in the seventeenth century compared* (2 vols. 1945).

5. *Prologue spoken by Mr Woods...1787*; *Poetry*, ed. Henley and Henderson, II, 145.

6. *Imitations of Horace*, The First Epistle of the Second Book, ll. 81–4.

7. Preface to *Troilus and Cressida* (1679).

8. *An Apology for the Life of Colley Cibber* (1740), chapter 4, pp. 76–7.

9. *Life of Dryden* (1808), chapter 1.

10. *Studies in Homer and the Homeric Age* (3 vols. 1858), II, 571, 580–1; *Homer* (1878), p. 133.

11. *Coleridge's Shakespearean Criticism*, ed. Raysor, I, 133.

12. II, 127–8.

13. *History of Great Britain* (1754).

14. Dodsley, *Old Plays* (1744), II, 2.

15. I, p. xxxv.

16. Prologue to *Troilus and Cressida*.

17. I, p. xxi.

18. *Johnson on Shakespeare*, ed. W. Raleigh, p. 40.

19. Robert D. Williams, 'Antiquarian Interest in Elizabethan Drama before Lamb', *P.M.L.A.* LIII (1938), 434–44, collects some information.

20. 13 October 1804; *Letters*, ed. E. V. Lucas (3 vols. 1935), I, 378.

21. August 1811, p. 275; reprinted in *Contributions to the Edinburgh Review* (1852).

22. *Recollections of the Table-Talk of Samuel Rogers* (1856), p. 90.

23. Thomas Medwin, *The Life of Percy Bysshe Shelley* (2 vols. 1847), II, 32–3; rev. H. B. Forman (1913), p. 256.

24. *Imagination and Fancy* (1844), p. 220.

25. February 1823, p. 187; an article on English Tragedy à propos of Knowles' *Virginius* and Beddoes' *The Bride's Tragedy*.

26. *Table-Talk*, 12 May 1830; Raysor, II, 353.

27. Introduction, p. li; 2nd ed. (1813), I, p. lxxix; cf. Coleridge, *Miscellaneous Criticism*, ed. Raysor, p. 41.

28. Introduction (vol. I), pp. xiv and lxxiii; cf. Coleridge, *op. cit.*

29. 20 October 1816; *The Letters of Mary Russell Mitford*, ed. R. Brimley Johnson (1925), p. 136.

30. Lecture I ('General view of the Subject'); *Works*, ed. Howe, VI, 180–1.

31. Note to *The Two Angry Women of Abingdon*; *Works*, ed. E. V. Lucas(1904), IV, 424.

32. Raysor, II, 26–7; a facsimile of the prospectus is given in *Shakespeare Quarterly*, IX, 1 (winter 1958), frontispiece.

33. *Miscellaneous Criticism*, p. 42.

34. *The Nibelungen Lied* (1831), in *Miscellanies*, III, 127.

35. *The Poems of Shakespeare* (Aldine ed. 1830), 1872 ed. p. lxiii; *The Works of Shakespeare* (1857), 1886 ed. 1, 149–50.

36. *Conversations with Eckermann* (2 January 1824).

37. Henry Crabb Robinson, *Diary, Reminiscences, and Correspondence*, ed. T. Sadler (3 vols. 1869), II, 434.

38. I, p. vi.

39. *The Letters of Sir Walter Scott, 1787–1807*, ed. H. J. C. Grierson (1932), p. 264 (to George Ellis).

40. *The Literary Gazette*, no. 686 (13 March 1830), p. 169.

41. *Observations on the three first volumes of the History of English Poetry* [by Thomas Warton] *in a familiar letter to the author* (1782), pp. 40–2.

42. And even by F. S. Boas in his edition of Kyd (1901), pp. cxiii–cxvi.

43. Havelock Ellis, *My Life* (1940), pp. 166–9; Arthur Calder-Marshall, *Havelock Ellis, A Biography* (1959), pp. 107–10.

SHAKESPEARE'S GENTLENESS

BY

HERBERT HOWARTH

There is only one adjective in Ben Jonson's lines to the Reader of the First Folio: 'gentle' in the phrase 'gentle Shakespeare', which has become a byword. What did he mean by that solitary and therefore telling, qualification? Possibly it was no more than a conventional expression of esteem. But the tribe of Ben liked obituaries in which a keyword characterized both the man and his style. When he himself was commemorated in the next decade, Falkland and Duppa called their volume *Jonsonus Virbius*. 'Virbius' is, to be sure, as unusual as 'gentle' is usual; but they were dealing with a learned poet, and had to find a correspondingly learned word; and they used it to imply at once his learning, his two-man-size physique, and his literary ideal of chastity (of which the address *To the Reader*, refusing all adjectives but one, is an example). I believe that in the same comprehensive manner Jonson intended 'gentle' to recall Shakespeare's struggle to establish his father's gentle rank; to endorse the grant of the patent by the College of Arms; to recall the civil demeanour with which he attempted to impress his gentility on his acquaintance; and to record how the gentle style had first distinguished his writing from his rivals', and had remained his most supple strength.

In the Shakespearian tradition, 'gentle' has been detached from the style and has come down to us only as a description of the man, forming that household image in which he appears wise and sympathetic. The purpose of these notes is, unavoidably, to resume some well-known details of biography, but more, to recover the history of an important Shakespearian style and to indicate its charm for an elite audience and its yet greater charm for the general audience. 'Gentle' is certainly associated with style in Jonson's more elaborate ode *To the Memory of my Beloved, the Author*; in the discovery of Shakespeare's 'brave notions, and gentle expressions'; and in the claim of Heminges and Condell that their dramatist 'as he was a happie imitator of Nature, was a most gentle expresser of it'.

Our dominant problems are those handed down by our fathers: their involuntary legacy of unfulfilled ambitions. Shakespeare's mother was a gentlewoman. His father had desired to be called a gentleman. He was one of those goodmen, so numerous according to the *Institucion of a Gentleman* of 1555, who were seeking the higher status. He negotiated for a gentleman's coat-of-arms, and as long as he was prosperous had hopes of a result; his 'credit' was a point in his favour—he would be able to sustain the rank if it were conceded. The mood in the Stratford home when Shakespeare could first understand his parents' talk was probably ebullient; he must have received the impression that the grant of the coat-of-arms was imminent and that it was merited. Instead there followed the depression of his father's fortunes, and he grew up in the lean years, with the natural consequences that he determined to be prosperous, never to have to bear domestic hardship again, and that he set a high valuation on the unachieved coat-of-arms and the status it represented. He wanted to secure the coat-of-arms for his father as a consolation in old age, and he wanted the title to reflect on himself and prove him 'William Shakespeare, gentleman'.

Prosperity was the first objective; and it had to be prosperity rather than mere sufficiency, for, as Hotson has remarked, securing a patent was an expensive affair. It is part of the paradox of the Shakespearian, and of the human, situation, that in order to become, what he was sure he deserved to be, Shakespeare the gentleman, he had also to become Shakespeare the business-man, and a part of him was so exhilarated by the management of money that he remained Shakespeare the (sometimes ungentle) business-man long after the pressure of necessity had relaxed. On his dramatic method the first effect of his problem was that he learned, with speed, to cultivate the box-office. He fed into his plays those pieces of deliberate showmanship which gratified and multiplied the crowds: pieces of pageantry and spectacle; quasi-legendary episodes of history; a masque; pieces of pathos, Blanche deciding between husband and family, Arthur pleading for his eyes. In fact the early plays are careless, or ignorant, of overall structure, and they go forward or turn course as Shakespeare sees opportunities for strokes that will please the crowd, whether or not scene be consistent with scene. Later he learned to integrate the wilfully popular scenes with the evolution of a play's question; part of his strength was to succeed in his errors, not to abandon them but to find purposes for them. And his common touch was as excellent as his gentleness. I am not for a moment decrying his capture of the public, nor the inventiveness, simplicity, and ultimately the proportion of the strokes of showmanship; his assault on the box-office was, in the strictest sense, *crafty*. But in the early days in the theatre he probably himself classified these clever passages as something apart from, even hostile to, the voice in him which was practising the language of a gentleman. Although the working-out of a problem always gives a poet pleasure, and to that extent he enjoyed their execution, he thought of them as an intermediate step to economic success, and of that as an intermediate step to social recognition.

A man seeking a favour in Elizabethan London, whose motions we can best understand if we think of it in terms of an oriental city, needed something else besides money: the support of friends. Shakespeare found himself requiring not merely the patron-in-general that every poet wanted, but a protector who could shorten his lobbying with the College of Arms. This is the situation that lies behind *Venus and Adonis*. Shakespeare looked round for a promising quarry, and found him in Southampton: young, attractive, and, best of all, close to the court favourite, Essex. But the interest of Southampton and his group could not, he fancied, be gained by box-office techniques. He must write a courtier's poem, a poem of dazzling elegance. Particularly, since he desired support in the application for the gentleman's crest, he must write a poem that manifested him a gentleman. *Venus and Adonis* is a deliberate first display of the gentle style.

If a test of beauty is 'fitness for purpose', *Venus* is a beautiful poem. To prove its writer the master-poet it demonstrates every weapon in the Renaissance poet's equipment. It offers to equal Ovid in English, by providing an English *Metamorphoses*, and does so with such triumph that the cry goes up 'The English Ovid!' It proves its writer a gentleman by the ease of its brilliance, the disinvolvement, the *sprezzatura*. Addressed to young men, it must be wanton; but addressed by a gentleman to noblemen, it must be free from crudity; and it is both, by dint of a technique of transposition, the attachment of the erotic words not to the protagonists but to the landscape, the undergrowth, the wild boar. It makes poetry of the gentleman's occupations: his hunting, horses, coursing, and discoursing. Above all, it exhibits the art of discourse. When young men like Valentine and Proteus and Southampton went to court, they expected to hear sweet discourse and to learn the skill of it. *Venus and Adonis* is a display of discourse to enchant the ear.

While Shakespeare was apparently interested only in the gentle side of his lineage, he owed a great deal to the combination in him of the gentle and the yeoman strains: owed his energy to it, and his success. He succeeded in most things that he attempted (except the handing-down of his name and the prized coat-of-arms through the male line; that was life's Greek revenge). Certainly he succeeded with *Venus and Adonis*. We know he obtained Southampton's attention, because the 'graver' *Lucrece* followed, according to promise. And is it not significant that the date of the first draft of the College of Arms award to John Shakespeare is 20 October 1596, when Essex' popularity was at its height after the fun at Cadiz? Shakespeare, the actor, knew the art of timing, and he pressed his noble friend to press *his* noble friend for a decisive word at the ideal moment.

Is there an equivalent to *Venus* in the theatre? I seem to see a sudden, plenitudinous exhibition of the gentle style in *A Midsummer Night's Dream*, and I suspect, while admitting the tangles of the dating problem, that in this comedy Shakespeare exhilaratedly converted the art of the Latin *Metamorphoses* and the English *Venus and Adonis* into theatrical terms. Requiring inventions as brilliant as those in *Venus*, but *dramatic* inventions, he concocts a plot and characters to allegorize the metamorphosis of English literature in his time. In his time and through him, and not least through this play that tells about it, the literature grown in the native sand during the middle ages wed the neo-classical literature which had lately immigrated from the warm south. We are told, in the voice of a wife's complaint of infidelity, that poetry has stolen away from fairyland to live the Theocritan idyll

> Playing on pipes of corn and versing love
> To amorous Phillida

and that had been the frequent truancy of Shakespeare's sixteenth-century predecessors, but now the very poetry that makes the complaint is both the poetry of the Italian flute and the poetry of medieval fairyland. We know Ovid's star is over the play from the name Titania, from the metamorphosis of Bottom, and from this major metamorphosis of our literature which the play dreams. The poetry, with a range of styles which the poet enjoys switching and commanding, is impeccably gentle in the courtier's sense when courtiers are the speakers, and gentle in the sense of easy and brilliant in the fairy scenes. In the class of brilliant fancy there is no poetry lovelier than the calendar of the freak seasons

> hoary-headed frosts
> Fall in the fresh lap of the crimson rose,
> And on old Hiems' thin and icy crown
> An odorous chaplet of sweet summer buds
> Is, as in mockery, set....

Look at that from one angle and it is Ovid in English; look at it from another, and it is no such thing but medieval personification; and in fact, as I have suggested, it is a marriage of the two. And the blent poetry has that easy and delighted carriage that was the signature of *Venus and Adonis*; it is only more delighted, more mobile and easy. The lines are warm—and even the frosts!—with the pleasure of the new adept in managing his art.

For all its success, there is a lamentable contradiction in the early gentle style: the style is *exhibited*; and it is not permissible for a gentleman to exhibit. The English image of the gentleman and his gentleness is closely related to the national practice of understatement (and to the morality, which perhaps grows out of it, of doing good by stealth). Though Shakespeare revelled in his first manner, he soon saw that it would not do. He dropped the ostentation and worked his way towards a deeper gentleness.

He found it in the plays of his 'early middle' period. Here he has passed from the brilliance of courtliness to the charity of courtesy. As occasion serves, he makes a character speak with modesty, good will, mercy, kindness, in words that could not be more telling yet could not be less ostentatious. Sometimes the gentleness lies precisely in that check on ostentation or power, that conscious moderation. Like the words, the music of the style betokens power controlled, though also sweetness of disposition. I will quote two instances from *The Merchant of Venice*. Bassanio, just now conqueror of Portia's hand and her estate, and therefore already entitled to welcome guests in her home, uses his title; but the moment he has spoken he detects in himself an unmannerly haste, and gently moderates his pretensions:

> Lorenzo and Salerio, welcome hither;
> If that the youth of my new interest here
> Have power to bid you welcome. By your leave,
> I bid my very friends and countrymen,
> Sweet Portia, welcome.

If ever we attempt this kind of modest self-correction in our private talk, we may have to do it by using the pattern Shakespeare has struck here: the recapitulation of our rash statement in qualified terms. A little later in the same scene Bassanio uses the same tone of modesty, and a similar structure of repetition and qualification, though this time his gentleness is that he is confessing faults while claiming an essential innocence at their heart. For love's sake, he says, he has concealed his debts:

> Gentle lady,
> When I did first impart my love to you,
> I freely told you, all the wealth I had
> Ran in my veins, I was a gentleman;
> And then I told you true; and yet, dear lady,
> Rating myself at nothing, you shall see
> How much I was a braggart....

With these gentle, chastened locutions, and the winsome compliments into which they often grow, Shakespeare captivated his audiences. The noblemen could, if vain, flatter themselves that they were faithfully reflected; if wise, appreciate a felicity beyond their own. And what about the general spectator? Castiglione had swept England just before Shakespeare was born, and for fifty years there was a national craving, permeating all classes but especially the less privileged, to speak with the grace of the courtier (whose style, thought Sidney, was the soundest style). Eager to educate himself in a pleasing diction, the general spectator was glad to take his lessons from the stage. Shakespeare's plays were the three-dimensional Courtesy-Books of Everyman.

Perhaps there was an additional reason for the popularity of this style. Perhaps the secret of the English attitude to art is a reverence for moral music; when the English hear morality and music in indissoluble fusion, they are struck to silence, overwhelmed. Of course they love the immoral and amoral too, but then they are conscious that they are adventuring, and part of their joy is the joy of the margin, the perilous brink. Shakespeare's gentleness of the deeper second variety is a moral music right at the centre of the English experience. He had come to it as the result of the refinement of the first literature of his social ambitions by his growing sensibility. Now, as he heard the audiences sigh with pleasure at it, he recognized, astonished perhaps by the revelation, that it was even more beneficial to the box-office than those pieces of showmanship with which he had first wooed the crowd.

Had Shakespeare been a complacent man, he might have continued to the end of his life writing gentle lines for the profit and the satisfaction of watching them score their effect on the audience. But he was an experimenter; and his world-picture was changing. A new intention can be traced in *Much Ado about Nothing*. He has designed the play in two parts: in the first Don Pedro is the pattern of gentleness; in the second, victimized by malpractice, he allows himself to swerve from it. He is gentleness pre-eminent when Beatrice cries heigh-ho for a husband. 'Lady Beatrice, I will get you one', he offers. And she, in her madcap pertness:

I would rather have one of your father's getting. Hath your grace ne'er a brother like you? Your father got excellent husbands, if a maid could come by them.

That is asking for a princely husband, and with another prince it might be asking for a royal rebuff. But Shakespeare's view is that royalty does not rebuff, and Don Pedro accepts the petition with the utmost charm: 'Will you have me, lady?' and Beatrice, who realizes that her wit went too far, comes back with the proper light-hearted refusal, followed by a modest apology, which the Don again turns with courtesy. But after the scene at the window the Don thinks his friend wronged and holds himself responsible, and gives himself to the atrociously ungentle plan to repudiate Hero at the altar. Hardin Craig has told us not to be offended, because Hero was, to all appearances, violating the sacrament of marriage by coming to it stained, and Shakespeare's audience would consider Claudio justified. I would crawl on my knees from Pennsylvania to Missouri to listen to Hardin Craig, but I think that here, as in his whole conception of representing Shakespeare as the vehicle of Renaissance norms, he eliminates half the drama. Shakespeare was not a conformist; he was an inquisitive man who, as Hardin Craig has elsewhere so well observed, likes to balance the pros and cons of a question. Hardin Craig justifies Claudio, but Beatrice does not:

What, bear her in hand until they come to take hands; and then, with public accusation, uncovered slander, unmitigated rancour,—O God, that I were a man! I would eat his heart in the market-place.

Of the operation in 'unmitigated rancour' of the Latin word for 'gentle' Shakespeare would be more aware than we can be. Gentleness has been worsted; and through Beatrice's anger—and she, though a madcap, is never guilty of wrong feeling—Shakespeare says that he does not like its defeat, does not like Claudio's conformist retaliation against Hero. Ah, what a hero *he* had been, if he had continued patient and the Don gentle. (But Shakespeare does not lay down a definite ruling. For an objective of his art by this time is to set his audience arguing the unresolved question: to have them carry the play with them to the tavern or to bed, not in print, of course, but in their warring souls and on their tongues. How good to have housewives and apprentices protracting the play in their memories as they debate who was right: Claudio or Beatrice?)

This brings us to the mature Shakespeare. What happens to gentleness in the tragedies? Where is it when Othello roars for the handkerchief which caused his pain, when Hamlet tears down the Humanist icon of angelic man, when Thersites satirizes war and lechery? The gentle style is present and active in the tragedies. There is no finer illustration of it in the repertoire than some of the exchanges between Hamlet and Horatio. It is present in the subdued proportion life actually allows, present in the fleeting time available for such a word. It is not asserted, nor does Shakespeare any longer invite admiration for it, though he may express love through it. He uses it as a good tool among a number of good ones he has mastered. An experimenter gives his special interest to new tools whose resources he has not yet fully explored. At the very period, 1594 to 1599, when he was most exploiting gentleness as his best stock-in-trade, he began to develop, as if by an inner protest, non-gentle energies. He remembered a very early, crude sketch of non-gentle energy, the Bastard, and built him into Hotspur. Hotspur is energy naked, energy that rejects the insulation of gentleness, energy that rejects gentle poetry and offers in contrast a poetry with the harsh metallic ring of real life. So strong was Shakespeare's intuition of an alternative to his current mask of gentleness, that it billowed out, in the same play, into Falstaff and his cronies. Shakespeare first drew them, as he thought, in dislike, weaving them coarsely from recollections of the anti-social impulses of his youth and observation of the contemporary footloose, factious younger sons whom Trevor-Roper has described in *The Gentry 1540–1640*. He created them in dislike, but that Anti-Man in his stomach still sympathized with them and insisted on a value, perhaps the power of the vulgar hold on life, in them. And he found that his audiences, regardless of their fashionable Courtiering, detected his unconscious sympathy and shared it and responded to it and loved what he had devised in contempt.

So by 1600 his success was multifarious. He had much to busy himself with besides courtesy. Especially he had to take account of his own reaction to his multifarious success. He found, as Eliot has found, that 'fools' approval stings', and that the sting itself is an incentive to new writing. So came the work which was foreshadowed in the fourth act of *Much Ado*.

The new writing made its powerful impact—and created its own new success—by censuring the world in which he had succeeded, censuring himself, too, for the means of his success. He felt that in winning prestige, prosperity and status, he had exploited beauty and refinement as a mere instrument of ambition. Honesty had been transformed into a bawd. He discerned such indignity in himself that it were 'better my mother had not borne me'. His subject became the imperfection of man, the shortfall from ideals, the disorder of society. In *Hamlet* grace and reason are jangled. In *Othello* the mildness that complements a soldier's courage is baffled and his sword turned from the heathen against a wife who is the very emblem of mildness. In *Julius Caesar* gentleness is wrested awry, the gentleness of Brutus. In *Troilus* gentleness has gone awry. Hector is the figuration of heroic gentleness—strength tempered by mercy, honour tempered by reason, reason tempered by fellowship. But the world is so disjointed that this great gentleness fails. We are told at the outset of the play that it has broken down: 'He chid Andromache and struck his armourer.' On the verge of the final disaster we have to witness the repetition of its symptomatic breaking. Andromache beseeches

> When was my lord so much ungently temper'd,
> To stop his ears against admonishment?

but Hector is offended and offends and drives Andromache away while Cassandra wails his doom, his sun setting in mass brutality, and debonair Troy sinking, and the old chivalric code of courtesy and courageous benignity ending. In these dramas of the human shortfall Shakespeare worked best and most often with gentleness, because gentleness was the ideal he and his age valued most. And above all he worked with it because he had fallen short of it in the very act of becoming a gentleman and a gentle poet; to exploit it was to fall short of it, to succeed by it and in it was to contaminate it.

In the last plays he forgave himself. He even forgave himself for writing plays. Polixenes in *The Winter's Tale* adjures Camillo

> As you are certainly a gentleman, thereto
> Clerk-like experienced, which no less adorns
> Our gentry than our parents' noble names....

Shakespeare's clerk-like experience was his theatre, and he now accepted it, including the plays of gentleness and the plays of protest, as an embellishment of his gentility.

One must not, of course, sanctify the last plays and the man who wrote them. Polixenes' lines witness that at the end there still remained in Shakespeare, amid the clear-seeing, an inexpungable nucleus of that Proustian snobbery with which he started his work; and still, as in the earlier years, Shakespeare metamorphosed that besetting vice into literature. Indeed, it matches the terms of the pardon he offers the world, that this contradiction still remained with him. Hypersensitively aware of the partnership of folly and merit (in Wolsey or you or me or himself), of dream and reality, of violence and gentleness, he implies that the beauty of life is the collision of opposites—and the beauty of art the collation of opposites. So he startlingly uses violence and tenderness in the last scenes of *Pericles* and *Cymbeline*. At the climax of *Pericles* he just failed—supposing our text is correct—in mating violence and tenderness to the illumination of each. The story lent him a perfect opportunity: Pericles struck his unknown daughter before he was united with her. It looks from the text as if Shakespeare could not make up his mind how far to take this situation, so near to his personal difficulties as a father who loved his daughters and suffered from his love. Should he do as he had sometimes done in the past, refine the plot and avoid a shock which might be too painful to the sensibility? Or should he admit the pain which is inseparable from the transport of love? Torn between the two solutions, he blurred the issue. That 'something that glows' upon her cheek appears to be Marina's instinct, not his passionate blow; the violence he does her is not an outright blow but a crazy shaking and a thrust away. The scene has its tenderness, but its most penetrating dramatic possibility has been muffed. Not so with *Cymbeline*. Here he does not flinch. In the superb 'long take' of the last scene Posthumus strikes the unrecognized Imogen. That is a blow to break the heart of the striker, and by the mystery of love it is the completion of love. It is also the completion of a Shakespearian process: the refiner of English drama has become its brutalizer, but in accepting the toughness of the world he has mastered its purest and most ecstatic gentleness.

I promised to consider biography a little but style mainly, and I do not want to finish in terms of Weltanschauung. My last point shall rather be one of theatrical technique, the effect of Shakespeare's concern for the gentle style on the actors of his company. We gather from *Hamlet* that he deplored the railing he found habitual among the actors. And obviously a practitioner of the gentle style would deplore it: his gentle lines would lose their character if they were bombasted. So he urged restraint in elocution and gesture. His suggestions must gradually have trained his company in the command of lower pitches; that in turn must have given more value to ranting when ranting was apposite; and the men must have realized the advantages of a range of light and shade, and have worked to increase it. Thus Shakespeare improved the instrument for which he wrote; and as he heard it improving, he could extend himself further and write lines which challenged the actors to new subtleties of pitch and texture. At length he could write *Antony and Cleopatra*, which is virtuoso scoring for a human orchestra, demanding swift and brilliant shifts of elocution, and culminating, certainly, in a texture of sound, morbid and ravishing, that no poet had previously known how to ask from the human voice. This was an unexpected technical reward for the once ambitious and self-indulgent cultivation of gentleness for gentility's sake.

Gentleness is only one of several Shakespearian styles. We are agreed that not any one element in him, but a plurality, and the blending and re-blending of unlike elements, has given him his claim on the world. But by thinking of his gentleness as Jonson, Heminges, Condell, and Chettle appear to have thought of it, we can see it as a distinctive contribution to the Elizabethan stage; can see how it arose from his problems; how he transformed his problems into an art, and not one art but a changing art; how he subjected his techniques to constant scrutiny and to an experimentalism so lively that not even success checked it. But though he richly developed the gentle style, he did not, of course, invent it. He had received it, with its dynamically conflicting suggestions of the high virtues of an hereditary aristocracy and the recognition that the virtues may be absent in the hereditary aristocrat and present in another man, from his predecessors, especially from Chaucer, for whom 'gentle', or words formed from it, is a touchstone. In one respect Shakespeare was a dangerous writer to assume the responsibility for the tradition: he did overvalue the hereditary element, the Coriolanus element, the blood of the gentleman, whereas the tradition favours the deeds and the virtues; but in the course of living and writing he grew to love the virtues increasingly; and he had moments of clear unanimity with the code and drew and exposed a Bertram. He made two crucial contributions to the tradition. He carried it into the theatre and so to the widest and most impressionable audience. And he established it *definitively*. If we are to illustrate gentleness, we may choose passages from Chaucer or Shakespeare; but if we are to illustrate the tradition we shall do best to choose them from Shakespeare. It is his voice which is echoed whenever, for the next three hundred and fifty years, English writers speak for gentleness, to urge the transplanting of the gentle values from literature into social life and civics, or speak for it by simply speaking with it. Through his example and after his patterns English literature has emphasized: the ideal of modesty, as embodied in understatement, which is part of gentle courtesy; the ideal of mildness as grace, and the practice of mildness as persuasion ('Let gentleness my strong enforcement be'); the ideal of sympathy which grows to active benevolence. In John Milton, that keen reader of Shakespeare and of many late Elizabethans, there are signs of these ideals and of a love for the style that represents them; and though he buries them in magnificence as well as in theology and polemic, they are an active leaven. More overtly and effectively, they reappear in those readers of both Shakespeare and Milton, the eighteenth-century novelists, through whose insistence they permeate the *mores* of the British novel.

MILTON ON SHAKESPEARE

BY

R. K. DAS GUPTA

Commenting on a possible Shakespearian allusion in Milton's 'Elegia Prima' Thomas Warton said that 'seduced by the gentle eloquence of fanaticism, he listened no longer to the "wild and native wood notes of fancy's sweetest child"'. The remark seems too categorical and the evidence that is produced in its support may not appear altogether unquestionable:

> In his ICONOCLASTES he censures King Charles for studying, 'One, whom we well know was the closest-companion of his solitudes, WILLIAM SHAKESPEARE'.... This remonstrance, which not only resulted from his abhorrence of a king, but from his disapprobation of plays, would have come with propriety from Prynne or Hugh Peters.[1]

This observation angered several Miltonists of the nineteenth century: Charles Symmons called it 'perverse imbecility'[2] and J. A. St John called it 'paltry malignity'.[3] The question may be asked if Milton adored Shakespeare as a great poet and if Renaissance poetry as a whole answered to his idea of great poetry. Without comparing Milton with the author of *Histrio-mastix* (1633) it is legitimate to inquire if Milton's judgement on Renaissance literature, so far as it can be ascertained from his writings, was not derived from a conception of poetry not typical of contemporary literary taste. To consider the allusion to Shakespeare in the first chapter of *Eikonoklastes* as a two-fold denigration of a bad prince and of a bad poet may be an unjust inference. But that Shakespeare could be a comforting poet to a deposed monarch might have been consistent with Milton's own estimate of the dramatist. It is significant that the reference to Shakespeare in *Eikonoklastes* is immediately followed by a comment on 'the vain amatorious Poem of *Sr Philip Sidneys Arcadia*; a Book in that kind full of worth and witt, but among religious thoughts, and duties not worthy to be nam'd'.[4] *Arcadia* is 'no serious book...not to be read at any time without good caution'. *The Reason of Church Government* condemns the 'vulgar amorist' and the 'rhyming parasite'.

Is there enough material in Milton's writings to represent his opinion of English literature? Did Milton think it important to state that opinion in his observations on literature and his own literary plans? His first published piece is his sixteen-line epitaph on Shakespeare,[5] and this is Milton's only poem on any poet. How far is this poem an expression of a high enthusiasm for the poetry of Shakespeare? J. H. Hanford certifies that 'Milton's admiration for Shakespeare is sincere, in spite of the implied reservations of other passages in his works'.[6] E. M. W. Tillyard, too, thinks that 'Milton's praise is indeed extremely reverential, far more so than the politeness of a verse tribute absolutely demanded'.[7] In the nineteenth century Mark Pattison called it 'the original and unprompted utterance of the young poet's admiration and sympathy',[8] an estimate which a recent critic has reaffirmed more strongly than either Hanford or Tillyard. 'The lines prove', says Kenneth Muir, 'that he honoured Shakespeare's memory "on this side idolatry as much as any", and they indicate perhaps why it was impossible to imitate his work.'[9] Against his array of unreserved appreciation of a famous poetic homage it seems a critical temerity to present an altogether contrary opinion, yet I must confess that I consider Hurd's criticism of the poem entirely just: 'This is but an ordinary poem to come from Milton, on such a subject.'[10] I think it is not only ordinary, but largely artificial. Its conceits are intricate, too intricate to evoke a powerful feeling. The concluding couplet represents a climax which is rhetorically faultless, but which does not gather up corresponding sentiment into an expression of any lyrical intensity. The poem is certainly a genuine tribute but there is nothing in its diction and rhythm to suggest that it is also an inspired tribute. It is a good judgement in good verse but is much less than a song of adoration. And the argument of the poem shows that Milton did not intend it to be anything more than a set of verses addressed to a writer of high reputation. The theme of monument does not imperceptibly grow into the deeper theme of genius. Expressions like 'unvalu'd Book' and 'Delphick Lines' are even more conventional than 'easie numbers', and the only suggestive phrase, 'wonder and astonishment', does not fulfil its promise in the idea of

> Our fancy of it self bereaving,
> Dost make us Marble with too much conceaving.

Even as a poem in the metaphysical vein it could have had an ending showing greater consistency and depth of imagination. At twenty-two Milton was certainly capable of greater aptness and force of expression than is shown in the last two lines of the poem.[11]

In the compositions of the Cambridge period there is no allusion to Shakespeare or to any English poet; in the apostrophe to his native language in 'At a Vacation Exercise' (1627) there is no mention of any poets who had made that language great in the eye of Europe, although there is a fling at 'our late fantasticks'. Amongst the many literary references in the Prolusions there is none to Shakespeare or to Chaucer or to Spenser. In the pre-Horton period Milton does not voice any enthusiasm for any English writer. The conception of divine poetry embodied in the 'Elegia sexta' did not, so far as we can tell, inspire any high regard for the literature of the Renaissance. Even in the Horton period, when pursuit of polite literature engaged his entire attention and when by way of preparing himself for his literary task he covered the whole field of European literature, his enthusiasm for Shakespeare and his contemporaries was extremely limited. The reference to Shakespeare in 'L'Allegro' does not refer to his tragedies and in 'Il Penseroso' the allusion—

> What (though rare) of later age,
> Ennobled hath the Buskind stage—

is too brief and too qualified an appreciation to indicate a real enthusiasm for Shakespearian tragedy. The passage on literary forms in *The Reason of Church Government* speaks of 'those dramatic constitutions wherein *Sophocles* and *Euripides* raigne' and mentions the Apocalypse of St John as a 'high and stately Tragedy'[12] but is silent about the tragic universe of Shakespeare. And when we consider the still more striking exclusion of Shakespeare from the short essay on tragedy prefixed to *Samson Agonistes*, it indeed seems extremely doubtful if Milton was an admirer of Shakespeare's works in this kind; it is equally unlikely that the adverse criticism of Renaissance tragedy included in this essay excepted the plays of Shakespeare. We may not assume that when Milton wrote of playwrights who 'intermixing Comic stuff with Tragic sadness and gravity; or introducing trivial and vulgar persons, which by all judicious hath bin counted absurd; and brought in without discretion, corruptly to gratify the people',[13] he excluded Shakespeare. The only quotation from Shakespeare in Milton's works occurs in *Eikonoklastes*. There is not even a bare allusion to him in the *Commonplace Book* which mentions Chaucer four times and Spenser twice. And while he quotes from Spenser in relating the story of Greenshield in *The History of Britain*[14] he does not refer to Shakespeare in the passage on Lear and his daughters[15] which follows immediately. We can, therefore, assume that the greatest creative genius of the English Renaissance was not a force in Milton's literary life and that he realized that the older poet represented a moral universe and an order of poetry which were different from his own.

This attitude to Shakespeare is the key to his entire attitude to romantic literature. It is true that Milton speaks with particular regard about Spenser and that his allusions to Chaucer and Gower are also respectful. But the poetic doctrine explained in *The Reason of Church Government* has no room for any of them either in respect of form or content. It is particularly significant that the discussion in that tract on the Christian epic has not even a bare reference to the kind of poetry exemplified in the *Faerie Queene*. While Milton desires to emulate the literary patriotism of Ariosto and 'fix all the industry and art I could unite to the adorning of my native tongue', he seems reluctant to admit that his native tongue had already some adornments. The entire tone of the poetic plan in *The Reason of Church Government* suggests that the ideal poetry of the English nation was yet to be produced and that England was still to achieve the literary eminence of Greece and Rome, of modern Italy and of the Hebrews of old. The whole achievement of the English Renaissance is ignored. When fourteen years earlier he had hailed his native language he had been anxious to discard from it those 'new fangled toys, and triming slight' as unwelcome accumulations. It is not easy to ascertain which particular writers Milton meant when he said that '*England* hath had her noble atchievments made small by the unskillful handling of monks and mechanicks',[16] but it is plain that it was Milton's conviction that England had not yet produced her national poet who 'in new and lofty *Measures* would sing and celebrate thy *divine* Mercies and *marvelous Judgments* in this land throughout all Ages'.[17]

NOTES

1. *Poems* (1791), pp. 425–6.
2. *Life of Milton* (1806), p. 332.
3. *The Prose Works of John Milton* (1872), p. 326.
4. *The Works of John Milton*, ed. F. A. Patterson (*The Columbia Milton*, New York, 1931–8), v, 86.
5. The poem was published on the leaf following sig. A 4 in the Second Folio edition (1632) of Shakespeare where it is entitled 'An Epitaph on the admirable Dramaticke Poet, w. SHAKESPEARE'. In the 1645 edition of Milton' *Poems* the title is 'ON Shakespear. 1630'. For a bibliography of this poem, see Robert Metcalf Smith, *The Variant Issues of Shakespeare's Second Folio and Milton's First Published English Poem* (Lehigh University Publications, 1928) For discussions of the different readings of the poem and of its possible sources see H. W. Garrod, 'Milton's Lines on Shakespeare', *Essays and Studies*, XII (1926); Heinrich Mutschmann, 'Sources of Milton's *On Shakespeare*', *Further Studies Concerning the Origin of Paradise Lost* (1934); and Theodore Spencer, 'Shakespeare and Milton', *Modern Language Notes*, LIII (1938).
6. *A Milton Handbook* (New York, 1946), p. 147.

7. *Milton's Sonnets* (1883), pp. 79–80.

8. *Milton* (1946), p. 50.

9. *John Milton* (1955), p. 22. The second part of this statement echoes E. M. W. Tillyard's shrewd comment on the poem: 'As a model Shakespeare was discouraging; and Milton is interested in setting forth the reason' (*Milton* (1930), p. 51).

10. *Poems* (1791), p. 317.

11. J. H. Hanford thinks that since the poem 'was very probably written to order for the folio, I should assume that Milton's date is, as frequently, a little too early' (*A Milton Handbook* (1946), p. 146). There is, however, no direct evidence to prove that the date was later than 1630.

12. *The Columbia Milton*, III, 237–8.

13. Preface to *Samson Agonistes*. Sir Oliver Elton thought that Milton's reference to the contemporary tragedy in 'Il Penseroso' implied a distinction between Shakespeare whom he admired and 'writers like Webster, so unlike the austerity of form and thought of his favourite Greeks' (*Il Penseroso* (ed. 1894), p. 13).

14. *The Columbia Milton*, X, 18–20.

15. It is believed that Milton made additions and corrections in the work of his nephew Edward Philips, *Theatrum Poetarum*, published in 1675 and Thomas Warton notices a resemblance between the praise of Shakespeare in 'L'Allegro' and the criticism of his tragedies in this book. Edward Philips remarks: 'In tragedy, never any expressed a more lofty and tragic heighth, never any represented nature more purely to the life: and where the polishments of art are most wanting, as probably his learning was not extraordinary, he pleases with a certain wild and native elegance' (p. 104. *Poems* (1791), p. 64). The occurrence of the words 'wild' and 'native' does not necessarily prove that the judgement as a whole was inserted by Milton. It is more likely that Philips used his uncle's words in restating the well-known comment of Ben Jonson.

16. *The Reason of Church Government* (*The Columbia Milton*, III, 237).

17. *Of Reformation* (*The Columbia Milton*, III, 78).

AN UNRECORDED ELIZABETHAN
PERFORMANCE OF *TITUS ANDRONICUS*

BY

GUSTAV UNGERER

The early stage history of *Titus Andronicus* comes within the darkest period in the annals of Shakespearian drama. Little is known when, by whom and for whom the tragedy was performed. There is concrete evidence that it was acted five times in public theatres for London playgoers. Now, further fresh and conclusive evidence is available to prove that by January 1596 it had been produced at a private house in Rutland.

We may well start with the new record itself:

Le Jour de lan fut monstree la liberalité de ces bon[s gens] & principalem^t de Mad: la Contesse [Russell] car depuis le plus [grand] iusques au plus petit elle en donna bon tesmoignage, mesm[e] i'en puis dire quelque chose. Les commediens de Londres son[t] venus icy po^r en auoir leur pt. on les feit iour le soir [de] leur venue & le lendemain on les despecha

On a fait icy vne mascarade de linuention de Sir Edw: wingfild on a aussi ioué la tragedie de Titus Andronicus mais la monstre a plus valeu q̄ le suiect.[1]

This eyewitness report, registered in the terse style of a chronicle, was written down for the ubiquitous and omniscient, though gout-stricken, Anthony Bacon—which accounts for its having been preserved among his papers in Lambeth Palace Library. The body of this collection is made up of Anthony Bacon's correspondence, carried on in his function of secretary to the Earl of Essex. It includes many French, Italian, Spanish and Portuguese letters written by agents in the pay of Essex's secret intelligence service. Even although Thomas Birch utilized some of the material for his *Memoirs of the Reign of Queen Elizabeth*, these papers remain largely unknown and unused. Among them is the letter from which the above quotation has been made—a letter from Bacon's Gascon servant Jacques Petit.

Jacques was an attendant in Bacon's household who could put forth a claim to some university standing. He was, therefore, always called upon when there was need of a French interpreter, and frequently he was singled out for special missions. We first hear of him in the company of Antonio Pérez, the one-time secretary to Philip II, who had arrived as an envoy of Henry IV, and who took refuge in England with a view to inducing the Queen to attempt an invasion of Spain by land and sea. The traitor was disavowed officially out of fear of Spanish retaliation, yet he was approved of underhand. The Queen does not appear to have minded Essex's offering him a key position in his intelligence service. It was in Essex House that the ill-starred Spaniard made the acquaintance of Jacques Petit. The fallen minister and the petty manservant met on common ground over literary issues, for both had some pretension to literature. The Spaniard gave vent to his morbid state of mind in adulatory epistles addressed to his patrons, and the Frenchman curried favour with his social superiors by dedicating doggerel poems to them.[2]

Jacques Petit again emerges from the bulk of the Bacon Papers as a tutor. Sir John Harington had appointed him to his household in succession to M. le Doux, who was also in the service of Essex's secretary of foreign affairs. The pupil whose French studies Petit had to supervise was no less than Harington's three-year-old son and heir, John. This, however, turned out to be a short-term engagement; Petit's duties can be assumed to have commenced with his arrival at Burley-on-the-Hill, Rutland, in the first December week of 1595;[3] they were cancelled at his wish in February 1596[4] because of some rivalry with another tutor employed in the extensive household of Sir John Harington.

Petit's pedagogic mission coincided with the Christmas festivities that were held on a grand scale at Burley-on-the-Hill in 1595/6. The landlord of the Manor was the exponent of a rising gentry family who owed their wealth to office-holding among the Tudor monarchs and to a series of happy marriage settlements. In 1592 Sir John had inherited one of the largest landed fortunes in England. He became the owner of the manors of Exton and Burley and by virtue of his marriage with Anne Kelway he possessed Combe Abbey in Warwickshire.[5] By 1595 Sir John was already renowned as a local Elizabethan worthy who had assumed the conduct of the nobility. His 'port' was that of an aristocrat. In commissioning a Gascon as French tutor to his heir, he gave apparent proof that, though legally he was still a country gentleman, socially he approximated to the state of an influential baron. If Queen Elizabeth was conservative in conferring peerages upon her subjects, he showed that he could afford to keep abreast with the peers in providing his children with the education that befitted a nobleman. Sir John chose the instructors of his children with great circumspection, and from Anthony Bacon, as an authority on French matters and friend of the educationalist and essayist Montaigne, he often sought for advice.

The Christmas revels that were staged at Burley in 1595/6 bear the stamp of Sir John Harington's expanding social policy. Being fully awake to his position as senior representative of the Haringtons, he made up his mind to extend an invitation to all his relatives. By mid-December two hundred guests had made their way to Burley and were lodged in the Manor House. Sir John rose to the requirement of accommodating and diverting this ebullient group eager to ape any social activity sanctioned by the Court of Queen Elizabeth. A series of transformations in his estate management brought about by the marriage in 1594 of his daughter Lucy Harington to Edward Russell, the Earl of Bedford, had proved to be a beneficial measure, and the redevelopment scheme of his demesne in exchange of rents was beginning to show a profit; this was fortunate, for his maintenance costs soared when the Lord of Misrule initiated the ancient twelve days of licence,[6] which extended from Nativity to Epiphany. Up till then, Sir John had been catering merely for his relatives and private guests, but from Christmas Eve to Twelfth Night he had to supply food and amusement to as many as nine hundred visitors. Anybody from the neighbouring county towns and hamlets, regardless of social standing, was admitted to the Manor.

For the literary historian, the most salient feature of these Christmas revels was the intense dramatic activity associated with them. Sir John Harington opened the theatre season some time in December when his two hundred guests had assembled at Burley. Local amateur companies must have provided most of the entertainment, much to the dislike of the academic-minded Jacques Petit. Harington would have been better advised, he argued, not to have spent vain money on superfluous drolleries which had to be acclaimed out of sheer courtesy:

Et encor est on apres a inuenter & brouiller vne confusion de ruine ce Noel faisant beaucoup de vaine despence po^r des tragedies & ieux de M^r le desordre. Mais comme la coustume est po^r tout mauuais ieu on tient bonne mine.[6]

Had Petit conceived a better opinion of the histrionic talents of the local mummers he might not have been so short-spoken in his report to Anthony Bacon. There was, however, one memorable dramatic event which he felt bound to deal with at slightly greater length. The play season at Burley-on-the-Hill culminated on New Year's Day, 1596, with the amateur production of a family masque and a performance by a professional company of players. The pertinent passage written by Petit in Burley and dispatched to his master in London has already been quoted at the beginning of the present article.

The date of the amateur performance of Sir Edward Wingfield's masque and of the professional performance of Shakespeare's *Titus Andronicus* seems, at first reading, to be open to discussion. The account given by Petit was written some time in January, after the first and not later than the sixth. The date has been obliterated by the binding of the manuscript. Bacon's endorsement is not of much help, for he has omitted to state the accurate date of receipt. The text itself points to New Year's Day. The first paragraph is so shaped as to drive home the outstanding events that happened on that day—the profuse generosity of Lady Russell in presenting New Year's gifts to all, from the nobles down to the humble servants, and the spectacular arrival of a professional company of players. What induced Petit to detach the next line from the foregoing paragraph is not clear. Did he mean to convey to the receiver of his letter that the masque and the tragedy were acted on a day other than New Year's Day? Or were the entries made at two different sittings? It would seem most probable that the players said to have arrived on New Year's Day performed *Titus Andronicus* the very night of their arrival. It seems impossible to assume that the professional company acted another play not mentioned by Petit, since this would necessarily mean that an unknown amateur company was commissioned to perform *Titus Andronicus*.

That Sir Edward Wingfield should one day be remembered as the author of an intimate indoor revel peculiar to Christmas rejoicings is due entirely to the fact that he had become related to the Haringtons through his marriage with Mary, one of Sir John's eight sisters known to have contracted marriage. Whether the author was endowed with an unexpected dramatic talent does not concern us here. Suffice it to say that what seems to have been expected from him was the compilation of a conventional piece of circumstance suitable for celebrating this family reunion. Most likely Sir Edward composed the masque by going through the family annals, selecting the doughty deeds of the 'renowned race'—as the Haringtons were called by the poet Sir John Harington, the cousin and namesake of the owner of Burley-on-the-Hill[7]—and couching them in an uninspired metrical form. The actors must have been recruited from among the family members themselves. There is evidence that Sir John's two daughters Lucy and Frances took an active part in the masques written by Ben Jonson for the entertainment of the Jacobean Court.

Which production was given precedence on that memorable night? From Petit's diary-like entry we gather that the professional players were engaged for an evening performance, which, being modelled on court practices, must have begun about ten o'clock and dragged on into the small hours of the next morning. The masque apparently preceded the tragedy as a substitute for the daily dancing and carolling after the evening meal. If this was the case, the Lord of Misrule showed some dramatic sense in retarding the appearance of the professional players until the amateur actors had aroused the keenness of the audience. Whether this was a conventional arrangement we cannot tell.

This performance of Shakespeare's *Titus Andronicus* has escaped attention so far. It is the only private performance that is known to us to have taken place in Elizabethan times and it is also the sole record to prove that the tragedy was put on in the provinces as well as in London. It further corroborates Ben Jonson's statement that the play competed with Kyd's *Spanish Tragedy* for first place in the affection of certain Elizabethan playgoers over a long period. One question of prime importance is whether a London company which happened to be on tour at that time was invited by Sir John Harington to perform *Titus Andronicus* on 1 January 1596, or whether a London company rushed down to Burley especially for this New Year performance. Obviously an attempt to answer this question demands careful sifting of the companies known to have existed at that time, particularly those which emerged after the plague of 1593. The best method here is to proceed by way of elimination. First, there is Petit's own account to be taken into consideration; for all its annoying brevity, it yields a great deal of indispensable information. Petit writes that the 'commediens de Londres son[t] venus icy po^r en auoir leur pt.' Hence the unauthorized patronless road companies, the provincial town companies of legal standing, the country companies under the patronage of some local nobleman or commoner, all can be dismissed without comment. Petit makes it abundantly plain that this was a regular London company of professional players, and there is the suggestion that these professional players had come down to Burley-on-the-Hill to have their share in the Christmas festivities.

The next step clearly is to consider all the London companies known to have been involved in the stage history of *Titus Andronicus*:

1. The title-page of the First Quarto (1594) professes that the play was acted by the 'Earle of Darbie, Earle of Pembrooke, and the Earle of Sussex their Seruants'.

2. 'Titus Andronicus' was produced by Sussex' Men as 'ne' for Henslowe on 24 and 29 January 1594, and for the third and last time on 6 February 1594.

3. 'Titus Andronicus' was produced by the Chamberlain's and/or the Admiral's for Henslowe on 7 and 14 June 1594.

4. The title-page of the Second Quarto (1600) adds the Chamberlain's Men to the companies mentioned in Quarto 1.

5. The title-page of Quarto 3 (1611) excludes all companies except the Chamberlain's, the then King's Company.

The enumeration of the companies in the 1594 edition suggests a chronological order of performance. It implies that the play was first acted by Derby's Men and last by Sussex's Men. The Earl of Sussex's Men had been obliged to travel in the provinces at the outbreak of the plague in 1593. When it subsided in London and the theatres were reopened, this company started their performances again in London on 26 December 1593, but a fresh outbreak of plague soon caused the theatres to close once more. This misfortune must have brought the company to the verge of bankruptcy. *Titus Andronicus*, the only new play of the curtailed season, was entered in the Stationers' Register presumably on the very day of its last performance, 6 February 1594; probably they sold their copy in order to get some ready cash from a publisher. No efforts, however, could remedy their desperate condition. Although they reappeared at the Rose Theatre together with the Queen's Men for another brief season of eight nights, between 1 and 9 April, the company vanished from the stage's annals. W. W. Greg thinks that some of the actors may have found their way to the continent; E. K. Chambers believes it not improbable that they may have been absorbed in the Queen's for travelling purposes. If the latter is right, it is possible that the Queen's–Sussex' merger carried to provincial audiences a tragedy which had proved popular with London playgoers.

The annals of the Pembroke's Men are still more scanty. Like all the other actors, they were compelled to turn to the provinces in 1593. During the course of the summer, they returned to London, pawned their wardrobe and sold several of their plays to rival companies. Thereafter there is a blank in their record, although the fact that they reappeared in London in 1597 perhaps means that they held together in the provinces, where presumably they acted plays from their London repertory.

As for Derby's Men, it stands to reason that, if their inclusion in the title-page of the First Quarto is due to their having played *Titus Andronicus* in a possibly earlier form of 'Titus and Vespasian' (1592–3), they must be eliminated. If, however, we do not endorse the possibility of a chronological order in the list of companies on the title-page, thus associating Derby's Men with the revised version printed in 1594, some members of that group may have taken the play to the provinces.

There remain the two leading Elizabethan companies—the Admiral's and the Chamberlain's. Both of these were linked with the play as early as June 1594. The claim of the Admiral's Men can, however, easily be argued away. They are ruled out by the simple fact that, on the very night *Titus Andronicus* was staged in Burley-on-the-Hill, the Queen had engaged their services at Court. The most likely company to have been concerned is the Chamberlain's; their inclusion in the title-page of the Second Quarto of 1600 might well mean that they had taken over the rights in *Titus Andronicus* after the performances of June 1594.

If, however, the Chamberlain's Men were responsible, we are confronted by a peculiar situation. It is certain that on occasion the London companies toured the provinces either under the pressure of the plague, as they did in 1593, or during the slack summer months. Such off-season tours were relatively long-term ventures, lasting up to some months. Short-term visits to royal palaces and country houses in the immediate neighbourhood of the capital while the winter season was in full swing were also quite regular; so were performances in the London residences of wealthy courtiers. What is surprisingly inconsistent with known Elizabethan practice is to find a prominent company leaving London in the midst of the dramatic season in order to give a single private performance on an out-of-the-way stage a hundred miles from the capital. The actors would have had nine days at their disposal, between 28 December 1595, when they played for the third successive time before the Queen, and 6 January 1596, when they had another court commitment. If we can take it for granted that they left London on 29 December, they must have contrived to achieve the standard speed of twenty-five miles a day, either travelling in coaches or riding on horseback. For the return journey they would have had a comparatively wide margin.[8]

To sum up this intricate problem, there is no conclusive evidence which justifies the assigning of the Burley performance to any one of the above-mentioned companies. Most likely it was one of them, but which it was cannot be determined with certainty. On the other hand, this is the only private production whose record has come down to us. It bridges a wide gap in the stage history of the play, no performance between 1594 and 1660 having so far been known.

It is, indeed, unfortunate that Jacques Petit did not provide us with more information, even although we recognize that a full description of the performance could hardly have been called for in the letter which he addressed to Anthony Bacon. Apart from the fact that he himself was a foreigner rooted in a different dramatic tradition and so was likely to look with sternly critical eyes at such a play as *Titus Andronicus*, his mission in writing to Bacon was merely to provide for his master a summary account of the various festivities organized by Sir John Harington. His single comment, however, 'la monstre a plus valeu q̄ le suiect', raises an interesting question. It may be that Petit himself found *Titus Andronicus* boring because he was not able to follow the English dialogue and because it lacked classical form and that consequently his attention was directed more towards the actors than towards the dramatist's words. On the other hand, we recall that the only contemporary drawing which illustrates a play by Shakespeare is the sketch executed by Henry Peacham in 1595.[9] Do the facts that Peacham chose this play as the subject of his design and that Petit emphasized the quality of 'la monstre' serve to suggest that special attention was given by the actors to the production of this tragic drama? Clearly, no definite answer can be given to such a question, but obviously Petit's brief remark has its own tantalizing interest.

JACQUES PETIT'S LETTER REFERRING TO THE PERFORMANCE OF 'TITUS ANDRONICUS' AT BURLEY-ON-THE-HILL

Apres ces iours vacans pleins daise & passetemps ie prens la hardiesse saluer treshumblem^t vos bonnes graces par la presente laquelle contiendra aussi (s'il vous plaist) l'excellente & magnifique reigle qui s'est tenue en ceste maison auec toute honneste resiouissance ce Noel

L'ordre estoit tel po^r bien reigner & entretenir 8 ou 9 cens voysins qui venoint chasque iour faire leur feste icy

Deux fois le iour il y auoit presche dans lesglise le mat[in] & l'appresdisnee & chasque iour nouueau ministre M^r & Ma[d] la Contesse [Russell] sy trouuoint po^r la plus part

M^r le Comte estoit serui auec tout lhonneur & respect [qui] estoit possible. a disner & souper la musique alloit [&] 30 ou 40 gentilshommes seruans quand ils portoint la viāde deux ou 3 cheualiers & les Dames oultre force gentilhomes [*sic*] & damoiselles estoint a sa table, puis apres le repas ensuiuoit la dance & ieux plaisans po^r donner a rire & seruir de recreation

Sr Jean disnoit a la sale po^r recueillir ses voisins & principaulx fermiers les festoyāt auec vne chere excessive, de toute sorte de mets & de toute sorte de vins.

Son m^e dhostel s'attendoit a regarder que rien ne manquast au[x] aultres faisant garnir 4 ou 5 longues tables de viande po^r quatre vints ou cent personnes a la fois lesq̄ls ayant acheué faisoint place a autant dautres & se retiroint, apres que [tout] estoit fait on portoit aux pooures [*sic*] du pain & de la via[nde] a pleines barriques tellem^t que tous estans contentes [il] en demeuroit beaucoup de reste

Le Jour de lan fut monstree la liberalité de ces bon[s gens] & principalem^t de Mad: la Contesse car depuis le plus [grand] iusques au plus petit elle en donna bon tesmoignage, mesm[e] i'en puis dire quelque chose. Les commediens de Londres son[t] venus icy po^r en auoir leur pt. on les feit iouer le soir [de] leur venue & le lendemain on les despecha

On a fait icy vne mascarade de linuention de Sr Edw: wingfild on a aussi ioué la tragedie de Titus Andronicus mais la monstre a plus valeu q̄ le suiect

Oultre ce q̄ dessus & qui est encore plus a priser cest q̄ sortant des festes on ny fait qu'entrer car la bonne chere & le passetemps sont plus grands & plaisans & rien ne diminue que la foule & trop grand nombre des gens rustiques

Je me resiouirois bien plus si quelqu'un de vos gens me vouloit faire ce bien que de m'aduertir auec vre bon conge si six lres que ie vous ay escriptes sont este rendues a vre seigneurie Car ie m'ennuye de vous ennuyer cognoissant bien que ma methode & mon stile ne valent rien po^r presenter a tel iugem^t que le vre mais la bonne volonte que i'ay de vous seruir & de vous fār cognoistre la deuotion & affection humble & sincere que ie vous ay vouee me fait accepter mon ignorance & lourde confusion po^r vous en monstrer telles q̄lles preuues esperāt gaigner par ma fidelité & diligence vre bonne grace qui excusera le defaut de ceste subtille finesse & astuce desprit qui sert a beaucoup d'autres. Et sur ceste bonne esperance Je baise treshumblem^t vos pouures mains malades auxquelles comme aussi a tout le corps ie prie Dieu

Monseigneur

Qu'il luy plaise enuoyer quelque parfaite & immuable santé auec tout heur honneur & contentem^t a vre esprit

de Januier 1596

> Vostre treshumble tresdeuotionne
> plusfidelle seruiteur
> Petit

[Je] vous [renu]oye auec la presente les deux ganiuets que R. m'enuoya po^r en rauoir s'i[l vous pla]ist vn bon come ie luy auois escript auec prieres.

Addressed to: 'A Mon treshonore
           Seigneur
           Monseigneur de Bacon
           A Londres'

Endorsed: 'De Jaques Petit le mois de
               januier 1596'

Lambeth Palace Library MS. 654, no. 167. Holograph, 2 pp. sealed.

NOTES

1. Lambeth Palace MS. 654, no. 167. Dated: '[?] de Januier 1596.' Endorsed: 'De Jaques Petit le mois de januier 1596.' Holograph, 2 pp. sealed. All MSS. quoted below refer to the Anthony Bacon Papers.

2. MS. 653, no. 48. Endorsed in Bacon's hand: 'Des vers faits par Jaques pour presenter a Segnor Antonyo Perez le iour de son depart le ij me de juillet 1595.' In his *Anglo-Spanish Relations in Tudor Literature* (Berne, 1956), the writer of the present article argues that Don Adriano de Armado, the Spanish braggart in *Love's Labour's Lost*, is a burlesque on Antonio Pérez.

3. MS. 654, no. 47. Dated: 'Le 20 de Decembre 1595.' Endorsed: 'De Jaques le 24 me de Januier 1596.' Holograph, 3 pp.

4. On 20 March 1596 he was appointed to accompany the Baron von Zirotin to Scotland and in October 1596 he was dispatched by Bacon to attend on Lord Rich, who accompanied the ambassador extraordinary, the Earl of Shrewsbury, on his mission to ratify the League Offensive and Defensive with the King of France.

5. Ian Grimble, *The Harington Family* (1957).

6. MS. 652, no. 161. Dated: 'De Burghley ce 14 de 10bre 1595.' Endorsed: 'De Jaques Petit le 19 me de Decembre 1595.' Holograph, 2 pp. sealed.

7. Norman E. McClure, *The Letters and Epigrams of Sir John Harington* (Philadelphia, 1930).

8. An authorized company of players on a prolonged tour through the provinces must have travelled more slowly, but how many miles they made a day cannot be determined. It might prove worth while going through the accessible manuscripts in the county record offices with a view to gleaning minute information on the arrivals and departures of regular companies. Besides the travelling licences and payments, there are bound to be carters' contracts which might reveal some facts. Spanish archives are rich in this kind of document. See Hugo Albert Rennert's *The Spanish Stage in the Time of Lope de Vega* (The Hispanic Society of America, New York, 1909), pp. 154–5 and Henri Mérimée's *Spectacles et comédiens à Valencia 1580–1630* (Toulouse, 1913), pp. 116, 122, 124.

9. See J. Dover Wilson, '*Titus Andronicus* on the Stage in 1595', *Shakespeare Survey*, 1 (1948), 17–22 and plate 1.

STRATFORD-UPON-AVON
A HUNDRED YEARS AGO: EXTRACTS
FROM THE TRAVEL DIARY OF THE
REVEREND WILLIAM HARNESS

The manuscript diary from which these extracts are taken was made by the Rev. William Harness in 1844. Harness, born in 1790, a lifelong friend of Mary Russell Mitford, had a wide acquaintanceship with literary men and actors of his time; and, as his notes show, he was a fervent admirer of Shakespeare, an edition of whose works, in eight volumes, he brought out in 1825. An interesting reference is made in one of his letters to the pious task he carried out in restoring the inscriptions on the Shakespeare tombstones during his visit to Stratford:

I have [he wrote to his sister], had the Epitaph restored to Mrs Hall's tombstone; and am now having the letters refreshed on the stones of Dr Hall her husband, and Mr Nash who was the first husband of Shakespeare's granddaughter, and the heiress of Mrs Hall. Shakespeare and his wife and these three all lie together side by side in front of the altar. This restoration will not cost me more than £3. How strange that it should have been left for me to do; and I'm making a step towards saving the money by leaving off sugar, which Dr Thompson advised me to do, and I find a great improvement in the tea, now I'm used to it.

The extracts are here printed by kind permission of Mrs Caroline M. Duncan-Jones, a great-great-niece of the Rev. W. Harness, and author of *Miss Mitford and Mr Harness* (1955). Professor and Mrs A. E. Duncan-Jones have assisted in editing the text.

1844 Stratford-upon-Avon

August 19th. Left Stratton Lodge at 8 o'clock in Mr Mason's gig, who was to drive me to Bedford to meet the Cambridge and Leamington Coach, which was to be at Bedford by ten. We had a beautiful morning, and ugly as Bedfordshire is generally considered, a very agreeable drive. I found a front place behind the Coachman. The road was agreeable to Northampton, particularly near a place extremely well wooded and with a nice old Elizabethan House, belonging to a Mr Hitchens or Higgins—I could not exactly make out which—and after we left Northampton by Weedon and Daventry on to Leamington it was quite lovely. Just such a country as one would be fond to drive a foreigner through, and only too happy to have a corner of to make one's nest in for the rest of one's life.

As to Leamington itself, except that they seem to be building some pretty churches, the place would to me be detestable; a sort of second Cheltenham, with this difference that, at Cheltenham, you seem to live in a bower and to be domesticated at Vauxhall; at Leamington the trees are only just planted and the bowers are newly planned out and you seem to be living at Vauxhall in a state of preparation. I remained here only a few minutes, as the stage for Stratford was ready to start. It was a most slow coach, for though we left Leamington at five and the distance is about eleven miles, we did not reach Stratford till eight. I took up my abode at the Shakespeare Hotel where after a very comfortable dinner, which not having eaten or drunken anything (two buns excepted at Northampton) since eight o'clock at Stratton Lodge was highly acceptable. I read Wheeler's history of the town till about eleven, and then I betook me to my bed. I ordered them to call me at seven.

Tuesday 20th. As soon as I had breakfasted, which was as quickly as it could be conveniently obtained, I set out to the Church, that I might with my own eyes see the monument of Shakespeare, stand beside the stone that covers him—not for worlds would I have stood upon it—and above all to breathe the air of the Church wherein he was christened and worshipped and was buried.... It is not true as Washington Irving states, that the grave of Shakespeare was opened, and nothing was found there. It since has been opened. In making the vault for Mrs Davenport, the wife of the last Vicar, a hole about the size of a man's hand was broken evidently into the Poet's vault, but nothing could be seen through such an aperture.

I enquired of the clerk, a very intelligent and well-mannered young man whose name was *Kite*, but is as little like a bird of Prey as any one I ever saw, whether he could direct me to any clean and respectable lodging. He told me he would for a week or two accommodate me himself, as the lady who generally occupied his apartments (a Miss Haggard) was at present away travelling. I immediately walked with him to his house to look at the rooms, and found them exactly what I wanted in every respect. I'm to enter them tomorrow after breakfast and pay him 15s. a week for a fortnight, during which time I am to be secure of any interruption from Miss Haggard.

As soon as this important matter was negotiated, I went to the Post Office (letter from Mr Makeham) and then being in Henley Street, the street in which Shakespeare's father lived, I enquired my way over the fields to Shottery, that I might see the house in which he lived and irregularly won the love of his wife Ann Hathaway.

There are some things, thank God, which can't be altered. The march of intellect and improvement, as it is called, has changed the face of the picturesque old town, flattened its pointed gables, smoothed away its old carved wood work and its irregular casement windows and its overhanging upper stories, but still much remains as it must have been when Shakespeare lived here, and when the air of the place was gay with the sunny light of his wit and wisdom, and when he threw off every day jests enough to send all the good people of Stratford who were not confirmed Puritans every night laughing to their beds. The great forms of nature are unchanged. The shapes of the hills are the same, the windings of the Avon are the same, the reeds, the rushes, the meadow sweet, the long grasses that grow upon its banks are the same. The pasture lands on either side are now as they were when he walked musing along them....

As I took the short cut over the fields to Shottery this morning I am as satisfied that I was not only looking to the same hill as he would have had before his eyes, but that I was treading the very path to what was the house of the Hathaways which he would have trod, as if I had seen him hurrying on before me, the limp in his gait become more conspicuous than it was in general from the rapid movement to which he was urged by his impatience to reach his love. Shottery is a short mile over the fields from Stratford. It is a scattered village, consisting of one substantial farm-looking house of red brick and rather recently built, another better kind of house of more gentleman-like appearance, and about a dozen or so of cottages. It has no church, but is a hamlet of Stratford. I walked round the village to see if I could find out which was likely to be the house of the Hathaways—and after I had determined in my own mind which it must be, I enquired of a woman I saw at her cottage door, which it was? She told me I had passed it, and pointed out the one I had conjectured it to be. In talking with me on the subject of the house and the Hathaways, she told me that old Mr Taylor, who now lives in the cottage, inherited it from his grandmother, who was the last of the family of Shakespeare's wife, and that the property had now passed from their descendants altogether as the old man had sold it, without letting anybody know what he was doing, to the Mr Barnes who lives in the red brick farm house. . . .

The house stands at right angles to the road, with a garden in front of it and an orchard on the side opposite the road. It is now divided into two tenements but has evidently been one originally. It was built in firm timber frame work and plaster. Where the plaster has from age given way, the parts between the timber have been filled in with bricks. In the passage is an old wooden seat, with a high back, such as is sometimes seen in farmhouses in the country, and more frequently by the fireside of village inns. It has evidently belonged to the old kitchen or hall adjoining. The name of the 'courting seat' has been given to it, and I should think there is little doubt but Shakespeare and Ann Hathaway may often have sat on it together. The kitchen, though very low and not very large, still retains the traces of its having been the bettermost room of a substantial yeoman's family of those times. It was panelled all over with what appears to be walnut and some of the panelling is remaining; it is handsome of its kind, a good deal worked. Above there is a chamber containing an old-fashioned carved bedstead, certainly coeval with the house, and a chest of no less antiquity. The bed has a carved wooden back and top to it—which I never saw before—and the posts are very massy and highly wrought; this is also of walnut tree. The daughter of Taylor, Mrs Baker, showed me the house, a respectable middle aged woman; she told me her father sold the premises without her knowledge, that he did not get two-thirds of the value of them, but he had married a second wife and she had persuaded him to it, that she might touch the purchase money; when first she heard of the sale it had fretted her a good deal. She pointed out the alterations the new proprietor had made—how he had cut down the yew hedge, and taken the orchard into his own garden; she also showed me as relics of the former dignity of the family of the Hathaways, an old sheet and pillow case, which her grandmother had given her 'because she was sure she would not part with them'. They were of linen, of very old manufacture, and the singularity of them consisted in the very broad, elaborate open work, by which the breadths of the stuff were connected at the seams.

Wednesday 21st. . . . Saw the house Shakespeare was born in. This also had passed from the family. The last Hart who had possessed it sold it in 1806. It was so mortgaged, that he could keep it no longer; it was purchased by the husband of the old woman who now shows it. Her name is Court. It will, she says, at her death be sold again—Government should purchase it and have it kept up in its present state. There are two fine old carved chests, or rather wardrobes, in the house, which she says have always been part of the property. When I observed 'the Corporation of Stratford ought to buy the house of her heirs', she answered, 'The Corporation don't care about Shakespeare. Strangers—Americans, people from the Indies—care much more about him than the people here do'. She said that some time ago an American who came over here got her to lay down a mattress on the floor that he might sleep in the room ! !—She showed me the names of C. Dickens, the King of Saxony and others in the album which is kept—the page with Dickens' name is almost worn out with handling. . . .

Thursday 22nd. Read Merry Wives of Windsor—wrote to Makeham. To the Post Office—no letters—went to Charlecote. A beautiful walk. In the small Church are the monuments of the Lucys, father and mother. . . . But for Sir Thomas Lucy all the vigour of the great Poet's life might have exhausted itself in headlong excursions against his neighbour's deer, and all his wit have wasted in a jovial meeting with his comrades afterwards. Besides, we owe something to the man who was the original of Justice Shallow, though the amusement he afforded us was an involuntary benefit on his part. The monument of the father of Shallow lies in armour at full length, on the entablature of the pedestal that supports his statue are the kneeling figures of his seven sons and seven daughters; and on a cushion beneath kneels the statue of his wife, the mother of Shallow, as large as life. As a proof of the correctness of local and traditionary information, the clerk's wife, who showed me the Church, told me that the Lady Lucy murdered all her fourteen children, and therefore the family ever after were obliged to have a bloody hand painted on the arms of their carriage. This monument is in a little Chapel apart from the Church. The monument of the veritable Shallow is to the south side of the altar; he and his wife recline here at full length. The monument of the son and his wife is very fine, of marble and of Italian workmanship. What a compliment it is to Shakespeare and what a proof of the superiority of genius over everything else, that we should care a farthing about these people. How sad too that their everyday, commonplace natures should be perpetuated in the same line—the name still flourishing, the place still supporting its wealthy appearance, its turrets unbroken, its timber luxuriant, its deer abundant, its property undivided, while of the etherial race of Shakespeare not a being survives—his house is destroyed, his property scattered and the very paternal and humble dwelling in which he was born has passed away from the only family who could have a collateral connexion with his blood! It is all very strange.

Saturday 24th. ...I walked to Shottery, and paid another visit to Mrs Baker in Ann Hathaway's house. She let fall that a great many entries of the births of members of the Hathaway family were made, not in a Bible, but in a copy of *The Whole Duty of Man* which was in the possession of her aunt at a village some five miles from Shottery. I should like to see that book—and will. It is a melancholy thing to see the last of a respectable family like this reduced to wages of 10s. a week—yet such is the case. She is a well behaved most respectable person and her two little children are as clean and well dressed as if they were the children of substantial farmers....Home and wrote a note to Darling, dressed and went to dinner with Mr Sherwood and his son at the Shakespeare. The old man is rather breaking, but he was most agreeable. Our talk was all of poetry. He remembers Garrick and saw him take leave—Mrs Abington, Barry's Jaffier—Mrs Barry—Woodward—Foote: to talk to him is like a return to another age. His recitation, by the by, which is very fine, perfectly easy and natural, is a thorough refutation of a fancy of Dyce's that he should not be able to endure any of the old actors if they were to return, not even Garrick, on account of their having all had a sing-song declamatory tone, for he imitated, and very well too, i.e. with great energy and animation, the concluding bit of the quarrel scene with Don Felix and Violante—Garrick being Don Felix, Mrs Abington Violante—and some of Kitely (Garrick) and it was impossible for anything to be better....

Tuesday 27th. ...Mr Parker called upon me to take me to Mr Wheeler's. We found that gentleman at home and he showed me many most curious law papers which he had come in possession of in the course of his antiquarian researches into the Shakespeare family. He thinks as I do, that Shakespeare's father was both a wool stapler and perhaps a butcher and a glover; this change of occupation is still common in this town, as he gave an instance. There were two John Shakespeares; the other was a shoemaker. There was the deed of sale making over the house at Stratford to him—or rather to Gilbert, William's [brother] for him. The Poet's signature ought to have been attached; but was not. He showed me the signature of Mrs Hall, Susanna the oldest daughter: and the mark of Judith Quiney the youngest: he also showed me the signature of his granddaughter Eliza Nash and, as Eliza Bernard, a fine bold hand. There is a letter from Adrian Quiney, the father of Shakespeare's son-in-law, to Shakespeare borrowing £50. In his collection he has a massive gold seal ring with W.S. engraved on it, which was found near the Church some time ago, and which he believes to have been Shakespeare's—reason why— the workmanship is undoubtedly of that time; it must have belonged to some one of wealth and importance of that time. There was no one else of such a condition in the town at the time whose initials were W.S. The Quineys and others had seals similar to this, as may be seen by the seals attached to other legal papers in Mr Wheeler's possession; Shakespeare had lost his seal. This is evident from the will, in which it was written, according to the usual form (for the right words see the will), signed, sealed, and delivered, but the *sealed* was erased, and a seal is attached....

Thursday 12th. ...Called on Mr Clayton with the purpose of speaking to him about restoring the inscriptions on all the Shakespearian tomb stones. He was from home; and gone to the Church. I followed him and found him with Mr and Mrs Gatty of Doughty Street—he gave me his consent to do all I wished—and orders were immediately given for the same—returned home—finished 'Much ado about Nothing' a little after 12, at which hour I was engaged to take a drive with Dr Thompson through the villages mentioned in Shakespeare's traditionary epigram.... About two the Dr and I set off in the gig on our exploring drive, with a fine threatening stormy sky over our heads and a magnificent gleaming light to illustrate the landscape. We took the Bidford Road, from which we first diverged through some fields to the left to visit Hillborough. This place, if it was a village in Shakespeare's time, consists now of no more than two farmhouses. On leaving this we retraced our steps to the road, and after a short drive we came up with two men, resting from their work at the lime kiln close by, whom Dr Thompson addressed to ask if they knew whereabouts the Shakespearian crab tree stood? The younger of the two, an intelligent fellow, said it was just above on the top of the hill, and he would go and show us the exact spot: this he did. It is in the hedge close to the road, and by a gate leading into a ploughed field. The young man told us that Shakespeare lay down there drunk on Saturday night and slept till Monday morning and that when he awoke on the Monday and saw the labourers at work in the fields, he was so unconscious of the length of time that he had lain there, as to suppose it was Sunday and reproached the men for working on that day. The tree was cut down about 15 years ago, it was not very large but evidently very old; before it was cut down an attempt was made to set fire to it. We now asked our friend if he knew the lines of Shakespeare written at this place—when he immediately began to point them out to us as they were visible from the spot, and repeated—'Piping Petworth, Dancing Marston, Haunted Hilborough, Hungry Grafton, Dodging Exhall, Papist Wexford, Beggarly Broom and Drunken Bidford'. Bidford probably had been the scene of his debauch as the tree stood beside the road between it and Stratford. The Doctor remunerated our friend and we drove on to drunken Bidford, a long straggling village with the Church close to the Avon, and a fine old bridge across it; having driven across the bridge and the length of the town we turned back, enquiring our way of some labouring men whom we saw lounging over a barn door, and saying 'we wished to go to Broom, Grafton and Wexford', they all seemed to be quite *au fait* with Shakespeare's verses. We took a road to our left which led us past the few houses to the left that constitute Beggarly Broom—by a tidy farmhouse—some fine elms and a beautiful hilly country to Papist Wexford. We first stopped to enquire about Grafton and Exhall of a fine looking old man we saw in his cottage garden but he told us 'It was useless to address him as he was as *deaf as the stones*'. We enquired at the next cottage, where we saw a woman and a fine healthy party of children knitting blue worsted stockings—we thought she must be keeping school, but she said they were all her own—she had nine of them. They paid, she said, only chief rent i.e. ground rent, to Sir — Throgmorton for the cottage and garden 10s. a year. Her father and mother lived with them. It was strange that this woman, the only person we attempted to speak to besides the deaf one, was a Papist. There are still many of that persuasion there. It is accounted for by the Throgmortons' having possessed this village and neighbourhood. The country before us looked so pretty that Dr Thompson determined on not going to Grafton and Exhall as we intended, but passing the Avon over the pretty bridge at Wexford and going round by Ragley (the fine deserted place of Lord Hertford) and Alcester home....

Thursday 19th. Went to the Church and had a long talk with the man who is cutting the Shakespearian tombstones; he learnt the verses about the villages round the crab tree from his grandfather; the man is about 40, he remembers them upwards of thirty years and his grandfather he says must have known them at least 70, there is thus traditionary evidence direct for 100 years. Started at 12 by the Worcester coach for Malvern.

INTERNATIONAL NOTES

A selection has been made from the reports received from our correspondents, those which present material of a particularly interesting kind being printed in their entirety, or largely so. It should be emphasized that the choice of countries to be thus represented has depended on the nature of the information presented in the reports, not upon the importance of the countries concerned or upon the character of the reports themselves.

Australia

While the Shakespeare plays most often produced in Australia are still likely to be those set for the annual school examinations in the different States, there was in 1959 a much greater willingness to experiment with the less popular plays.

Among the principal professional productions in 1959 were the J. C. Williamson *King Lear, The Winter's Tale, The Merchant of Venice* and *A Midsummer Night's Dream.* In Melbourne, Adelaide and Perth all four plays were presented by a company led by John Alden and John Laurie. The first three of the plays were also presented in Sydney, where John Alden produced *A Midsummer Night's Dream* for the Independent Theatre. The other main production in Sydney was the Elizabethan Theatre Trust's *Julius Caesar.*

The semi-professional and amateur groups in country towns as well as in the cities probably gave more attention to Shakespeare in 1959 than for many years past. In Victoria, for example, the Warrandyte Arts Association presented *A Midsummer Night's Dream,* produced by Harold Bargent; the Adult Education Association, *A Comedy of Errors;* the Mt Gambier Theatre Group, *Othello* (produced by Gavin Dyer); the Swan Hill, *Henry VIII,* during its Drama Festival. In Sydney, the Genesians produced *Julius Caesar* and the St Paul's College Mummers, *Troilus and Cressida.* In Western Australia a production of *A Midsummer Night's Dream* by the Kalgoorlie Repertory Club in the park at Kalgoorlie won so much praise that the performance was repeated by invitation at the Festival of Perth. (The producer was Senator Seddon Vincent of the Commonwealth Parliament.) The Adelaide University Footlights Club presented *Hamlet* and the Independent Repertory

Theatre *Julius Caesar;* and in Brisbane a cast drawn from the students and staff of the University and its colleges acted *Love's Labour's Lost* (produced by Eunice Hanger), while the Brisbane Repertory Theatre gave ten performances of *The Merchant of Venice* (produced by Babette Stephens).

Mention must also be made of the first 'live' television productions of Shakespeare in Australia: in June 1959, the Australian Broadcasting Commission presented *Hamlet* (produced by Royston Morley) and *Antony and Cleopatra* (produced by Christopher Muir).

H. J. OLIVER

Austria

Shakespeare productions in 1959 were incomparably smaller in number than in previous years. Some of them were also problematical in quality, and many a theatre-goer may have asked himself whether or not these productions were based upon a knowledge of the original text or any profound understanding of Shakespeare's art.

Much Ado About Nothing was produced by Leonard Steckel in the 'Theater in der Josefstadt', Vienna. The translator (or should one say the adapter?) of the text remained anonymous. He succeeded in alarming many critics by his numerous cuts in the text and by his introduction of farcical elements over long stretches of the play.

The critics were almost unanimous in their condemnation of Leon Epp's production of *Macbeth* at the 'Volkstheater', Vienna. It was felt that the text used was one of the most inadequate translations available—Karl Kraus' version, which had already been shown up as inadequate. Its inadequacy of language, the critics stated, was coupled here with an abstract setting whose main feature was darkness, so that the 1959 Vienna *Macbeth* became a gigantic though meaningless affair.

Only three other plays were produced during the year—*Twelfth Night* (the Stadttheater, Klagenfurt, the Landesbühne, Burgenland, and the Reinhardtseminar, Vienna); *As You Like It* (Landestheater, Linz) and *The Taming of the Shrew* (Friesach Festival).

SIEGFRIED KORNINGER

Belgium

Shakespearian activities in Belgium have this year been limited to the Flemish-speaking theatre, with the production of *As You Like It* and *The Winter's Tale* at the National Toneel, and *Much Ado About Nothing* at the Flemish Theatre in Brussels. All these productions have been presented for the usual limited run and occasional one-night stands in the provinces. Poetical flavour was rare in Arden, a cloud of heavy academism hung over Sicilia and much low comedy was apparent in Bohemia. This summer's season at Rubens House and Court-Yard will present a production of *The Tempest* by the Reizend Volksteater. The gardens of this princely mansion will serve as a superb acting area for the Masque in Act IV.

The value and quality of some of the Netherlands translations of Shakespeare's work will always be a matter of opinion. However 'clever' some of the more recent translations may be, it remains a fact that the time-honoured translation of A. L. Burgersdyk (highly praised by J. T. Grein) is still the most honest and loyal rendering of the original text.   DOM. DE GRUYTER

Canada

Shakespeare in Canada now means the Shakespearian Festival Foundation at Stratford, Ontario. Mr Earle Grey, who for ten years ran his own less professional festival in the Quandrangle of Trinity College, Toronto, has returned to England.

At this Canadian Stratford, the 1960 season was particularly interesting since all three festival plays were from Shakespeare's early period. Douglas Seale came over from England to direct *King John*, Douglas Campbell, a former Old Vic man now a Canadian citizen, directed *A Midsummer Night's Dream* and Michael Langham directed *Romeo and Juliet*.

A Midsummer Night's Dream was a good tourist performance, in that it concentrated on making the play rambunctious and jolly at the expense of the poetry. Indeed, Jake Dengle, though wonderfully muscular as Puck, had no idea how to speak verse and Deborah Cass almost succeeded in making a tragic heroine out of Titania. The lovers, instead of being courtly-mad became hoydenish and at one place even mocked the poetry they were supposed to be speaking. The rude mechanicals, of course, were superb and the Pyramus and Thisbe scene was well conceived, well played and vastly enjoyed.

King John grew in stature through the Festival and both Douglas Rain, as King John, and Christopher Plummer, as the Bastard, emerged as very good Shakespearian actors. (Plummer is due to play at England's Stratford in 1961.) Rain was able to give real authority to John in the first two acts, which made his final downfall and death more pathetic and moving than it often is. Plummer, whose gifts as an actor include a superb sense of timing, showed us clearly that the Bastard is a good first sketch of Thersites. The women, however, were disappointing.

Romeo and Juliet was the great success of the season, since Langham's concept of the play was clear and he used the peculiar capabilities of the Guthrie-Moiseiwitsch Stratford stage to their fullest. On three levels and through five or six exits—two of them through the audience—the play flowed in passionate intensity from the initial brawl to the final death.

Miss Julie Harris, a noted Broadway star, brought a freshness to the role of Juliet and a gift for projecting her personality which overcame her real vocal limitations, and Bruno Gerussi, a Vancouver actor who has learned all his technique at Stratford in the past six or seven seasons, made a thoroughly believable character out of Romeo.

The production would not be well received in England (the North American accent would see to that), but it was triumphantly received in Canada—which proves that there is emerging at Stratford a Canadian theatrical style (especially for Shakespearian productions) which, though it cannot yet travel, is still a satisfying domestic product.

Two innovations are now trying to get the Stratford Festival out into the rest of the country. One has already happened, one is still in the planning stage.

The first was a Shakespeare Seminar designed for all those interested in seeing and discussing Shakespeare's plays. Professor C. J. Sisson came out to give three lectures and the directors and actors of the company (together with professional critics) participated in the discussion groups. This Seminar, attended by nearly two hundred people, many of them teachers, was sponsored by the universities of Canada and will probably lead to a better understanding between scholar and actor —an understanding which the Seminar discussions themselves showed is not yet in existence.

The second is a tour now being arranged, which will

take the 1961 productions (with their original casts) to the campus of every major university in the country. This is an expensive undertaking in a country so vast as Canada, but the costs will be underwritten to a large extent by the Canada Council, a national cultural foundation, which will match what the universities themselves can put up.　　　ARNOLD EDINBOROUGH

Czechoslovakia

This year I should like to concentrate on three different Shakespearian productions currently to be seen in Prague.

First comes Ota Ornest's adaptation of the *Comedy of Errors*, played by the Comedy Theatre with music by Jan O. Fischer. The producer, Rudolf Hrušínský, together with the adapter, have stressed the farcical element and more or less subdued all the more serious aspects of the play. Thus it is only Aegeon and his wife who are played as 'straight characters', the rest being good-humouredly caricatured. Shakespeare's text, in a new translation by Jaroslav Kraus, was cut, spiced with songs, and a dozen of lines in prose added. The result was in places hilariously funny.

The second, and more important, production was that of *Hamlet*, which opened in the National Theatre on the same night that *Coriolanus* was first performed in the Army Theatre. Since for a long time *Hamlet* had not been played by a Prague professional company, the new production was eagerly anticipated. The director was Jaromir Pleskot, young and talented, with several Shakespearian presentations to his credit. A new translation by Zdeněk Urbánek was used, specially commissioned by the National Theatre for this production. English readers can hardly realize what liberties are sometimes taken by translators with Shakespeare's originals: Urbánek's text, though in verse, somehow reduced Shakespeare's language to a bare statement of facts voiced in modern, colloquial phrases, sometimes slightly smacking of newspaper jargon, and all the purple patches were consistently rendered 'in a different way from before'. The reason for all of this was that the producer wanted to show *Hamlet* as a modern play, dealing with modern problems. The costumes were in keeping, combining 'modern dress' with the rudiments of traditional dress. Notwithstanding these peculiarities, this is a thrilling performance, and Radovan Lukavský in the title-part gives a very intelligent and intellectual rendering of a lonesome, betrayed prince. The impersonality which—perhaps unintentionally—is stressed in this production is enhanced by the *décor* of Josef Svoboda, which clearly follows Craig's ideas: high black marble

slabs, minimum of furniture, and lights, The best scene, curiously enough, is the scene on the Plain which has a unique atmosphere of doom: the drums of Fortinbras' army suddenly acquire a new meaning, as Hamlet, heavily escorted, is led away.

Last there is the Army Theatre production of *Coriolanus* in a new translation by Eric Adolf Saudek, laureate of the Klement Gottwald state prize, produced by Jan Škoda. The reading of the characters was interesting. Novel was the interpretation of the tribunes: we saw them as wise, honest, sincere, deep-thinking, class-conscious. On the other hand, Menenius Agrippa was interpreted as a rather nasty old loquacious fox of a politician, extremely derisive, who almost seemed to be the villain of the piece. Unfortunately this interesting production was badly set back by a blurred, though ranted, speaking of the lines by some of the actors.

As for other Shakespearian events: Jiří Trnka has finished his puppet-film version of *A Midsummer Night's Dream*, and the first two volumes of Josef Václav Sládek's translations from Shakespeare, comprising all the comedies, edited by Otakar Vočadlo, have been published by the State Publishing House KLHU.

BŘETISLAV HODEK

France

The Théâtre National Populaire presented *A Midsummer Night's Dream*, in a translation by Jules and Jean-Louis Supervielle, at the Avignon Festival, July 1959, and in Paris, at the Palais de Chaillot, during the following winter. The name of Jean Vilar is associated with Shakespeare's history and tragedy rather than with his fairyland, and this venture in the realm of comedy was awaited with some curiosity. Actually Vilar conceived in a solemn and dramatic way the conflict of Oberon and Titania, which brings disturbance in nature and confusion in the heart of man, and the quarrels of the lovers reached, at times, a degree of violence which seems justified by the text but is seldom seen in the interpretation. By pitching the performance rather high it became possible to suggest the cosmic hierarchy which underlies the play and to indicate the various levels of action: kingdom of spirits and monarchy of men, mortal couples, elves and clowns. The façade of the palace in Avignon provided a noble and austere background for *Richard II* and *Macbeth*, but could not so easily conjure up the atmosphere of the enchanted woods, Léon Gischia's settings acquired, on the Chaillot stage, a depth and mystery which it lacked in the open air, and midsummer magic came to life better, perhaps, by artifice than under the stars of a Provençal night.

The production, by Maurice Jacquemont, of *Othello* among the ruins of the castle of Vaujours, in Touraine (July 1959), suffered from hasty preparation and a poor level of acting: Jacquemont's Iago alone came to life, as a cunning valet of French comedy rather than as the mixture of Malcontent, Vice and Machiavellian villain we know. And the audience seemed to believe that the repetition of 'Put money in your purse' was just a verbal trick, like Moliere's 'Que diable allait-il faire ?', to make people laugh. The ruins, overgrown with vegetation, which served for a stage, bore no relation whatever with Venice or Cyprus, though the architectural vestiges were used, more often than not, in a way which aimed at being realistic. Jacquemont, like many other producers, could have done better work with adequate financial means. His *Othello* was given, the same summer, at the Festival of Sarlat. And his *Hamlet*, which was performed there some years ago, was presented the following winter at the Comédie des Champs-Elysées. The interest of the experiment lay in the use, without any cuts, of the translation by Jacques Copeau and Suzanne Bing. A stage structure reminiscent of the 'dispositif' at the Vieux-Colombier in Copeau's days was meant as a further tribute to the master. A young film star, Jean-Louis Trintignant, took the part of the Prince, giving him the appearance of a being too beautiful and innocent for this world.

Shakespeare's lighter comedy, presenting affinities of plot and character with French comedy in the Latin and Italian tradition, has a special attraction for our young companies. *The Taming of the Shrew* is still a favourite. It was presented by Michel de Ré during the Festival of Angers (June 1959) and quite recently (July 1960) by Michel-Eugène Ferrand in Autun, with Catherine Sauvage, a music-hall actress with a difference who recently took a part in Claudel's *L'Échange*, and whose name at any rate suited admirably the characters of the Shrew. A third 'Mégère' within the space of a year was produced by René Lafforgue for the Comédie de Provence. It made capital out of the 'coloration méditerranéenne' of the play, with some Provençal spices thrown in.

I shall give an account of recent productions of *Romeo and Juliet* in Lyon-Charbonnières, *Hamlet* in Carcassonne, and Marlowe's *Edward II* in Orange, in my notes for the next issue.

Information collected in recent years for the preparation for these notes was used with earlier material, for an exhibition of Shakespearian and Elizabethan production in France since the days of Antoine (Institut Pédagogique National, Paris, May to October 1960). It brought out the fact that for Antoine, Gémier, Copeau, Pitoeff, Dullin, Baty, Barrault and Vilar, the producing and acting of Shakespearian drama became a crucial experience, introducing a new stage in their artistic development.

As usual, Mlle Rose-Marie Moudouès must be thanked for her assistance in the preparation of these notes.

JEAN JACQUOT

Germany

Even in the festival year of Schiller's bicentenary, Shakespeare remained the most popular playwright with twenty-two plays produced in seventy-four theatres, 2224 performances altogether. This year *Twelfth Night* scored the highest number of performances with eleven new productions on 289 nights. Of the tragedies, *Hamlet* again has been the most frequently produced and performed; 184 performances at eleven different theatres are recorded, this being almost a third of the total number of performances of Shakespearian tragedies. Most of the new productions, however, were of comedies, the rapidly rising interest for *The Two Gentlemen of Verona* being a notable feature of this vogue. Most of the *Hamlet* productions, of which those at Meiningen, Göttingen and Bonn may be mentioned, appear to have emphasized in Hamlet's role the aspect of courageous desire for revenge and the determination to defy and break down the rotten state of affairs, rather than his brooding melancholy and hesitation. A quite unusual and extraordinary event in the stage-history of *Hamlet* was a performance at the 'Gehörlosen-theater' (Theatre for the Deaf) at Dortmund, where every scene was put into pantomime, explanatory texts being projected on a screen to indicate the progress of the action. The murder of King Hamlet was performed on the stage, the scene of the players turned into a ballet. Although only amateur actors took part in this performance, its artistic achievement and its effect on the audience appear to have been quite remarkable. An interesting and striking version of *Macbeth* was presented at Bochum by Hans Schalla, who used Eschenburg's prose translation of 1777, which considerably tones down Shakespeare's poetical language and brings into relief the factual aspect of the action.

A number of Shakespeare productions showed a remarkable tendency towards experiment. Thus Paul Mundorf (Aachen) inserted passages from the sonnets in his production of the *Tempest* and Erich Engel (Landesbühne Schleswig-Holstein), abandoning the five-act structure of that drama, produced it in nine separate scenes. This innovation, of course, involved various short cuttings and other alterations. There was also a new approach to the *Taming of the Shrew* in Halle (W. Böttcher). In this production Kate's quarrelsomeness is interpreted as the expression of her distrust; similarly it is suggested that the lovers' fights and arguments are only make-believe.

Of events connected with Shakespeare, the performance of Helmuth Käutner's modernized film version of *Hamlet*, 'Der Rest ist Schweigen' ('The Rest is Silence'), drew perhaps the largest audience. Most of the ideas and themes of the original Shakespeare drama are transferred to a twentieth-century setting. The industrial magnate Paul Claudius, his wife and his nephew, John Hamlet, who suspects that his father was killed by his uncle during an air-raid, are the essential characters. John Hamlet, however, turns out to be little more than an amateur detective who, at the critical point, hands over the 'case' to the police. The revenge motive is omitted, and Hamlet's character is considerably altered, being deprived of its tendency towards melancholy and philosophizing, so that, as a result, this *Hamlet* version is more of a thriller than an adequate adaptation of Shakespeare's play.   KARL BRINKMANN

                                      WOLFGANG CLEMEN

Hungary

The 1959–60 theatrical season has been one of the most successful in the recent history of the Hungarian stage so far as Shakespeare is concerned. Nine of the plays had each a run of twenty to thirty performances in seven towns of the country.

The lively rhythm introduced into the new production by K. Nádasdy, in the National Theatre of Budapest, of *Richard III* (in the translation of I. Vas) was an improvement on earlier productions of the tragedy there. T. Major gave a considerably mellower and, at the same time, more colourful rendering of the usurper than he did in the same role several years ago. *Othello* has held the stage at the same theatre, as reported in earlier volumes of *Survey*. This year it was also presented by the stock company of Szolnok. R. Nógrádi's production, in the realistic settings of T. Upor, emphasized the extremes of the Moor's despair. E. Tallós' Iago was a remarkable amalgam of Renaissance and modern villainy. *Macbeth* likewise had two productions, at Debrecen and Pécs. The latter, with its atmosphere of doom and gloom was especially notable. It was ably directed by Antal Németh, with Otto Szabó as Macbeth and E. Spányik as his Lady. In the good workmanlike Debrecen performance of the same tragedy, directed by J. Szendró, music and *décor* were rather too much in evidence. At Kaposvár Gy. Kamarás directed a finely

emotional *Hamlet* with the young P. Somogyvári as a very good Prince and Adrienne Jancsó a memorable Queen.

One of the most successful performances of the season was that of *Antony and Cleopatra* in the National Theatre in Budapest. This was the fourth production of the tragedy in Hungary during our century. The play was given in its entirety, with all the forty-two changes of scene, one half of the stage being Rome, the other half Egypt—the two being separated by diagonally-set curtains. The ingenious *décor* of M. Varga gave the director, T. Major, a good opportunity to stage a practically uncut text with rapid alternation of the scenes. It must be said, however, that some of the actors, though occasionally very good, did not always succeed in conveying the emotional and intellectual many-sidedness of the tragedy. Next to M. Lukács' Cleopatra (albeit in places uneven), F. Kállai's Enobarbus, T. Bitskey's Octavius and G. Raksányi's Mardian came nearest to being truly Shakespearian figures.

Among the comedies, *Twelfth Night* was presented in Miskolc and *A Midsummer Night's Dream* in Szeged. In Budapest the Madách Theatre had a successful run of *The Tempest* with Tibor Uray as a balanced and wise Prospero. The success of the year was *Much Ado About Nothing* in the National Theatre of Budapest. The direction of T. Major emphasized the strong contrasts and the fairytale-like elements of the comedy. Ági Mészáros' brilliant Beatrice has been one of the most memorable theatrical events of the year.

In the field of scholarship mention must be made of L. Kéry's slim volume which manages to give a carefully balanced and clear analysis of all the tragedies of Shakespeare.   LADISLAS ORSZÁGH

India

A noteworthy production was presented by the Shakespeare Society of St Stephen's College, Delhi, which started its histrionic career with the trial scene of *The Merchant of Venice* in 1924, and which has staged the full play twice, once in 1934 and now again, a quarter of a century later, in November 1959. The play was produced by William Jarvis and directed by Rajan Chetsingh.

Another Hindi translation of *Othello* has appeared in print. This is by H. R. Bachchan, and extracts from it were relayed on 26 February this year by the All India Radio, Delhi.   H. MITHAL

Israel

The Chamber Theatre has given our audiences a new *Twelfth Night* under Shmuel Bunim's directorship, with

Orna Porath as Viola, Hanna Meron as Maria, Yosef Yadin as Sir Toby, and Zalman Leviush as Malvolio. The Hebrew version of the play was prepared by Raphael Eliaz and published by the Hakkibbutz Hameuchad Publishing House with sketches by the scene-designer, Arie Navon.

The publication of Shakespeare's Tragedies in one volume by the Am Hassefer Publishing Company is an event which the Hebrew reader has welcomed very warmly, as it is considered an event worthy of note in the realm of the publication of Hebrew books in general and of Hebrew translations of classic writers in particular. This is a luxurious octavo-form volume of close to six hundred double-column pages. The volume was edited by Reuben Avinoam and Israel Efros, and contains, apart from an essay on the life and work of Shakespeare (by Reuben Avinoam), Hebrew versions of nine tragedies, with introductions and explanatory notes to each.   REUBEN AVINOAM

Italy

The season at the Ostia Roman theatre was inaugurated in June 1959 with the *Sogno d'una notte di mezza estate*, translated and adapted by Gerrado Guerrieri; the producer, Mario Ferrere, utilized the open-air setting with great adroitness, the ancient columns aptly providing the classical element; Titania was impersonated by Rossella Falk, Oberon by Franco Graziosi, Puck by Vittorio Congia, Hermia by Anna Maria Guarnieri, Helena by Anna Brandimarte, Bottom by Glauco Mauri; Mendelssohn's music accompanied part of the performance, which had a moderate success. Scenes from *Hamlet* were staged at the Taormina theatre in July on the occasion of the *Trial of Orestes* (*Processo ad Oreste*), a medley (including also passages from Aeschylus and Sartre) within the frame of a proper trial in which actual lawyers took part. Vittorio Gassman impersonated Hamlet. In March 1960 the Italian Television made one of its most ambitious efforts in producing *Re Lear* (the producer was Sandro Bolchi) with Salvo Randone as Lear and Wandisa Guida as Cordelia. But the event of the year has been the series of recitals given by Sir John Gielgud in various towns, particularly at the 'Festival dei due Mondi' at Spoleto in July 1959 and at the charming Teatro della Cometa (a little theatre opened by the munificence of Countess Anna Laetitia Pecci-Blunt) in Rome in March 1960. Sir John had an enormous success with his anthology of Shakespearian passages illustrating various moods of youth, virility and old age: his magical voice and the perfect taste of his delivery carried the audiences off their feet. In the field of scholarship,

Professor Benvenuto Cellini has produced a notable edition of Shakespeare's *Sonnets*, with a commentary (Milan, 1960).   MARIO PRAZ

Japan

The English Literary Society of Japan celebrated Shakespeare's three hundred and ninety-fifth anniversary by presenting a Japanese version of *Twelfth Night* by Jiro Ozu at Aoyama Gakuin University Hall. It was produced by 'Gekidan Nakama' (The Companions' Theatre) directed by Shunichi Nakamura. Though the physical condition of the hall was far from ideal, it was very much appreciated by nine-hundred visitors. Another *Twelfth Night*, translated by Isao Mikami, was produced by 'Haiyuza' (The Actors' Theatre). The director was Bitaro Ozawa, a veteran actor who visited the Old Vic and the Memorial Theatre in 1958. It has now become a fashion in this country that a dramatist or an actor who has recently returned from England produces a Shakespearian play in Tokyo. The performances by Haiyuza were particularly heavily booked; starting in October, they drew full houses every Sunday evening until the end of the year.   JIRO OZU

Kenya

During 1959 there was a production of *Othello* given by the Makerere College Players in the newly opened Uganda National Theatre, Kampala. In Kenya the African Alliance High School gave a performance of *Macbeth* cast entirely from the African tribesmen studying there. At the Coast the newly formed Shakespeare Group held monthly readings and discussions and presented *A Midsummer Night's Dream* at the Mombasa Little Theatre, when they repeated the success they had achieved with their initial production of *Macbeth* the previous year. For the 1960 Birthday they arranged an Elizabethan Feast in one of Mombasa's hotels, with the singing of rounds and catches and other Shakespearian songs. This active group is now planning a production of *Twelfth Night* in a newly laid-out open-air theatre within sound of the breakers of the Indian Ocean. At the East African Shakespeare Festival there was a production of *The Winter's Tale* in the Kenya National Theatre. Special performances were given for schoolchildren of all races.   A. J. R. MASTER

The Netherlands

This year, apart from productions by Dutch repertory companies, a number of guest performances were offered to Shakespeare lovers in the Netherlands by the 'Nationaal Toneel van België'. Thus, in January, *The*

Merchant was put on at Middelburg—thereby confronting theatre-goers with the third production of this comedy in the 1958/9 season (see *Shakespeare Survey*, 12) —once more in the translation by Voeten. In the same month the Philips theatre at Eindhoven was gladdened by a delightful *Shrew*, produced by Michael Warre with the 'Ensemble' company, in a translation by O. van den Berg. The Belgians, again, by the end of the month came to Udenhout with *Othello* in the 'classical' Burgersdijk translation.

Until June no new Shakespeare productions graced Dutch theatre bills. By then, however, the 'Nationaal Toneel van België' gave a rousing performance of *As You Like It* at Goes, also in the Burgersdijk translation, and three weeks later the Holland Festival at the Hague started a run of *Troilus and Cressida*, directed by Johan de Meester in a new translation by Voeten.

This production, which was also taken to Paris in order to represent Dutch theatre-craft at the 'Théâtre des Nations', was intended as the showpiece of the season. In colourful presentation it certainly was, and the set-designer, Wim Vesseur, deserves to be mentioned together with the director for the forceful restraint of the conception—a conception marked by the use of no more than one or two stylized token properties on an octagonal blood-red dais built out into the pit across the orchestra, with brilliantly hued curtains behind the black-and-scarlet Greeks over against the grey-and-blue Trojans, a white-and-gold Cressida, a flaming Helen and a purple Cassandra. The final scene, where Pandar is rejected by Troilus, was transferred to v, iii, and Pandar's concluding speech was compressed into a four-line epigram. The play ended, accordingly, with Troilus' appeal to the Trojans to live in hope of revenge. The production clearly aimed at stressing the 'modernity' of the play's satire; Pandar, played by the late lamented Cees Laseur, was a gem of an aged charmer, completely disarming in his lack of morals and natural lechery, yet suggesting every now and again the steel underneath the picturesque patina of his character's corrosion. The lovers were watered-down 'Romeo and Juliet', with the spiritedness and poetry cut out. The most prominent performance was Bob de Lange's Ulysses.

After this more than gallant effort, the Arnhem company, 'Puck', put on the *Midsummer Night's Dream* in October to commemorate the tenth anniversary of their foundation. Directed by Egbert van Paridon in a decidedly over-popularized re-hash of Burgersdyk's translation by Gerard den Brabander, the production was hardly a success.

The most brilliant venture of the season was the *Comedy of Errors* presented in settings and costumes of about 1910 by the Rotterdam company under the direction of Ton Lutz.
A. G. H. BACHRACH

Norway

Three plays have been staged in 1959: *Hamlet*, *The Tempest* and *Twelfth Night*. *Hamlet* appeared in April at the National Theatre in Oslo, and in September at Rogaland Theatre in Stavanger. Both these productions profited by a new and superb translation done by the poet André Bjerke. This translation, in fact, is of such a superior quality that one has the impression of listening to an original version—as if Shakespeare himself had written *Hamlet* in Norwegian. André Bjerke had for many years trained his hand on rendering lyrical poetry from English, French and German and on preparing a version of the *Midsummer Night's Dream*. In Oslo Hamlet was taken by Knut Wigert, an actor of ideal physical stature, a beautiful voice and a very expressive face. He created a Hamlet entirely convincing, genuine, without one false note, a young mind deeply wounded, and a prince. Pelle Christensen was the first Hamlet to appear in Stavanger. He gave us a clearcut figure, the idealist deeply shaken by the inconceivable amount of evil in the world, the young avenger pursuing his aim with firmness and decision.

The Tempest was given at the Norwegian Theatre in Oslo in March. This proved an interesting performance, with all the leading parts in good hands: Harald Heide Steen as Prospero, Rut Tellefsen as Miranda, Urda Arneberg as Ariel and Lasse Kolstad as Caliban.

Twelfth Night at Trondelag Theatre, Trondhjem, in December, was particularly notable for Carsten Winger's Malvolio and Jens Ek's fool, merry but with a tragic undertone.
LORENTZ ECKHOFF

Poland

1958 brought a rich harvest in the field of Shakespearian studies. New versions of *The Two Gentlemen of Verona*, translated by Zygmunt Kubiak (State Publishing Institute, Warsaw), *Measure for Measure*, translated by Witold Chwalewik (issued by the same publishers) and *The Tempest*, translated by Władysław Tarnawski and edited with an introduction and commentaries by Stanisław Helsztyński (Ossolineum, Wrocław) have all appeared within the year. In addition, the *Complete Works* of Shakespeare, the fifth venture of this kind in Poland, has been brought before the public. This edition consists of earlier versions of Shakespeare's plays executed by Stanisław Koźmian, Józef Paszkowski and Leon

Ulrich. Since all these translators achieved a high standard in their renderings, there was good reason for bringing them once more to light.

Perhaps the most remarkable publication in this area is *Shakespeare in Poland* (Ossolineum, Wrocław), a vast bibliography, prepared by Wiktor Hahn, running to nearly 400 pages, and containing nearly 2500 entries. It covers all Shakespearian activities in Poland from the beginnings down to the present—translations of Shakespeare's works, performances of his plays on the stage, and Polish studies of Shakespeare and his work. Unquestionably the book will prove helpful both for Polish and for other scholars.

A survey of performances during 1959 proves that popularity of Shakespeare on the Polish stage is undiminished.

We had twelve new productions—three in Warsaw (*A Midsummer Night's Dream, The Two Gentlemen of Verona* and *Hamlet*) and the rest in provincial centres— in Bydgoszcz *The Winter's Tale* and *Romeo and Juliet*; in Gdańsk *The Taming of the Shrew*; in Kraków *Love's Labour's Lost*; in Nowa Huta *The Tempest*; in Olsztyn *Romeo and Juliet*; in Opole *Twelfth Night*; the same play in Wrocław; in Zielona Góra *The Tempest*.

Five plays produced in 1958 continued to hold the stage—in Warsaw *The Taming of the Shrew*, in Częstochowa *Romeo and Juliet*, in Koszalin *Twelfth Night*, in Lódź *Measure for Measure*, in Rzeszów *Othello*. Other productions prepared in 1959 for opening in 1960 were *King Richard the Third* and *The Tempest* in Warsaw, *The Taming of the Shrew* in Białystok, *A Midsummer Night's Dream* in Częstochowa, *Antony and Cleopatra* in Katowice, *Romeo and Juliet* in Szczecin.

In all, twenty-four Polish centres were engaged in producing Shakespearian plays during 1959.

STANISŁAW HELSZTYŃSKI

Sweden

A rich harvest of Shakespeare performances can be reported from the last season. Comedies and romances have been very popular.

Fragments from the comedies have been presented by the Riksteatern, with Inga Tidblad in the title-roles. The Riksteatern has also been travelling with *The Taming of the Shrew*, produced by Sandro Malmquist. *The Merchant of Venice*, as staged at the Göteborg Stadsteater, was directed by Keve Hjelm. The scenic pictures were drawn with a firm hand by Carl Johan Ström, and Bertil Anderberg made a good Shylock.

The repertory of the Hälsingborg Stadsteater included *As You Like It*, produced by Frank Sundström. The

performance was characterized by very lively acting. Marianne Aminoff, lithe and slim and an experienced actress, was a particularly fine Rosalind.

The Winter's Tale, very popular in the provinces at the end of the last century, but since then almost forgotten, has resumed its popularity with the performances at the Malmö Stadsteater. Many suggestive details were conjured forth by the skilful producer, Sandro Malmquist. Fabulous beasts, dancers, vehicles and processions thronged the spacious stage which reached far into the auditorium.

After the reconstruction of the building and the stage of the K. Dramatiska Teatern had been completed, the theatre was reopened with *Hamlet* on 25 March 1960. The producer, Alf Sjöberg, and the designer, Lennart Mörk, made a happy combination whose skill had already been exhibited in last year's *Measure for Measure*. Hagberg's classical translation was used, without any shortening of the text. Ulf Palme was the new Hamlet. Inga Tidblad took the part of the Queen, Anders Henrikson that of Polonius and the young Christina Schollin that of Ophelia. All the critics found praise for Palme's unsentimental, unromantic Prince.

New translations of *Cymbeline*, by Nils Molin, *Romeo and Juliet* and *Julius Caesar*, by Björn Collinder, have been published in the series of classics 'Levande Litteratur' (Natur och Kultur, Stockholm).

NILS MOLIN

Switzerland

Five of the plays were produced in the course of the year. At the Berne Stadttheater there was in May a competent, pleasant, but not otherwise remarkable production of *The Taming of the Shrew* in Schlegel's translation. Geneva had the privilege of seeing, in the summer and early autumn, two of the comedies. In an open-air theatre the Carouge company in August gave *Twelfth Night* in F. M. V. Hugo's translation, repeating their success of 1958 (see *Shakespeare Survey*, 12, 116). In October the 'Comédie' opened its season with a spirited performance of *The Merry Wives* in R.-L. Piachaud's translation which, once again, proved its eminent virtues. *Much Ado* was produced at Basle by H. Hilpert.

GEORGES A. BONNARD

Turkey

Five Shakespearian productions in four outstanding theatres during the last twelve months prove to be a record in this country.

Hamlet, produced by Yildiz Kenter (formerly Mrs Y. Akçan), opened at the National Conservatoire of Ankara on 7 April 1959, with Üner Ilsever and Kartal

Tibet alternating the parts of Hamlet and Laertes, Bozhurt Kuruc and Oguz Karaali alternating those of Claudius and the First Grave-digger and Ergin Orbay and Ali C. Çelenk alternating those of Polonius and the Second Grave-digger.

Since the performance of *Romeo and Juliet* at the antique theatre of Aspendus in 1953, Shakespeare has become a favourite of the Festival spectators at various ancient theatres all over western Turkey. In April *Hamlet* was carried to the Greek theatre of Hierapolis and some twenty thousand people (mostly peasants) filled the enormous amphitheatre.

For the first time, in May, a night performance under limelights was given at the Roman theatre of Aspendus by the National Theatre. *Twelfth Night* proved to be a good vehicle for an outdoor romance under these conditions, and here, too, the audience numbered twenty thousand. Cüneyt Gökçer, who is the Director General of the National Theatre with four playhouses in Ankara and two out of town, was responsible for the production and the part of Malvolio. His tall and slim body in dark tight suit pacing across the wide orchestra area measuring 160 feet in diameter gave a particular colour to the performance.

Muhsin Ertugrul, after a short interval, returned to his old work at the Municipal Theatre of Istanbul and re-established the long tradition of opening the season with a Shakespearian production. This was his seventh adventure in *Hamlet*, the first being in 1911 when he enacted Laertes as a young debutant of nineteen. The Turkish version of *Hamlet* was by Orhan Burian.

Othello opened in February 1960 at the National Conservatoire of Ankara and is still playing. This is Mahin Canova's second production of the play, the first being at the National Theatre several years ago, and here, too, the translation was by Orhan Burian.

NUREDDIN SEVIN

U.S.A.

The dynamic stage being what it is, the problem of translating Shakespeare from text to stage is precisely that which faces a translator of the text into a foreign language. Should he remain faithful to the Renaissance language, idiom, and poetry, should he modernize the text into the language current in his own country, or should he make a combination of both? And when he has done what he has chosen to do, has he been faithful to Shakespeare? Does he not say that all his changes are made *only* because he is being faithful to Shakespeare?

In 1959 a 'Texan version' of *A Midsummer Night's Dream*—produced by Alex Reeve, British-born and

trained—made Lysander and Demetrius carry guns and almost draw them in their quarrel; Puck wore a coon-skin cap and lassoed fairies. In similar vein the widely toured Players, Inc. version of *Twelfth Night* introduced a cigar-smoking Maria and a Santa Claus Sir Toby (how could such a disparate pair marry at the end?). Every shred of sympathy for Malvolio was removed and Orsino's loud groans of love made him ridiculous. Another production toured by this same group was *The Comedy of Errors*. It too was 'produced' rather than presented. Like *Julius Caesar*, it begins with a mob scene in which Ephesian placards inscribed 'Ephesus for Ephesians', 'Syracusans Go Home', 'We like Duke Solinus', are waved wildly as some demagogue recites lines announcing the edict against Syracusans. At the wildest moment, in strolls Aegeon with an over-sized carpet bag and immediately becomes the butt of the mob. The mob wails loudly as Aegeon's tale is unfolded, but they will do nothing to save him. And so it goes on with farce added to farce—Ossa on Pelion—as a frowsy Nell cavorts madly around the stage after a scampering Dromio much to the delight of an adolescent audience.

The Canadian Players who tour widely in the United States also adhere to the Comedy-as-Farce school. Petruchio's coming to his wedding as a barbary pirate is a little too much—especially as he has been described differently a few moments before. When he arrives home with his bride, his servants exhibit signs proclaiming 'Welcome home, boss!' and then, wearing fezes, execute a ludicrous dance. The director of this production, having imbibed some scholarship relating to the 'whistle boy', infuses one of the characters in the play with this function, so that at half a dozen scene-endings his shrill whistle calls for attendants who push props and flats around in a manner to make the audience laugh.

These productions have been selected because they have been widely seen, but not as widely seen as the television *Hamlet* presented to a nationwide audience by the Old Vic Company on 24 February 1959. I cannot tell whether English audiences were treated to the same production, but in this one the director decided to emphasize 'melodrama and action'. When he was asked why, he declared, 'Frankly, to get a bigger rating. While it's fine to stimulate interest among the Shakespearian societies, the schools and colleges, I believe our big guns should be trained on the larger audience, the people who are afraid of longhair, egghead and Shakespeare, and who associate these things with everything dull.' And there's the rub. There was action from the beginning until the end when Hamlet hurled his poisoned sword to spear Claudius. The murder and revenge and readiness was all. Snow fell at the opening scene—an innovation easily possible on television. Although late-nineteenth-century costume was worn, yet the Ghost was seen to wear his 'beaver up'.

For the hundreds of thousands of readers of the *TV Guide*, Old Vic director Ralph Nelson had an even bigger treat; he wrote a brief western version of the play to show how modern it *could* be. Unfortunately it was not done on television. It might have been the be-all and end-all of such productions.

The U.S. festivals continue unabated. Hofstra on its 'replica' Globe presented the *Merry Wives*. Oregon for forty days presented *Twelfth Night*, *King John*, *Measure for Measure*, and *Antony and Cleopatra*. Colorado offered *Macbeth* and the *Dream* to the growing western audience. The New York City Festival, after much bickering with the Department of Parks over the funds for park improvement, managed to gather money enough for a three-week run of *Julius Caesar*. Arrangements have now been made for a permanent festival amphitheatre in 1960. The American Shakespeare Festival at Stratford, Connecticut, offered a seventeen-week season of *Romeo and Juliet*, *The Merry Wives*, *All's Well*, and *A Midsummer Night's Dream*. In the far west the San Diego Festival offered *Romeo and Juliet*, *Love's Labour's Lost* and *Henry IV*. A venture to stage a Shakespeare Festival in a tent in San Francisco failed in a few days, but a new Festival on the porch of a 'Tudor' mansion in Akron, Ohio, was successful with an unusual production of *Romeo and Juliet* which reinstated the eighteenth-century funeral procession.

LOUIS MARDER

SHAKESPEARE PRODUCTIONS IN THE UNITED KINGDOM: 1959

A List Compiled from its Records by the
Shakespeare Memorial Library, Birmingham

JANUARY

14 *Othello:* The Little Theatre, Ilford. *Producer:* GRAEME WRIGHT.

26 *Love's Labour's Lost:* The Playhouse, Sheffield. *Producer:* GEOFFREY OST.

FEBRUARY

10 *Hamlet:* Birmingham Repertory Theatre. *Producer:* BERNARD HEPTON.

12 *Julius Caesar:* The Library Theatre, Manchester. *Producer:* DAVID SCASE.

16 *The Merchant of Venice:* The Century Theatre, Wolverhampton. *Producer:* ERIC SALMON.

23 *Twelfth Night:* The Arts Theatre, Salisbury. *Producer:* RONALD MAGILL.

24 *The Taming of the Shrew:* Bristol Old Vic Company, at the Theatre Royal, Bristol. *Producer:* FRANK DUNLOP.

24 *Julius Caesar:* The Curtain Theatre, Rochdale. Producer not known.

MARCH

1 *Coriolanus:* The Oxford University Dramatic Society at the Playhouse, Oxford. *Producer:* ANTHONY PAGE.

2 *The Merchant of Venice:* Guildford Repertory Theatre. *Producer:* RICHARD HAYTER.

3 *Julius Caesar:* The Belgrade Theatre, Coventry. *Producer:* BRIAN BAILEY.

3 *Hamlet:* Nottingham Repertory Theatre. *Producer:* VAL MAY.

9 *Henry IV, Part I:* The Marlowe Society, at the Arts Theatre, Cambridge. Producer is anonymous.

10 *Henry IV, Part II:* The Marlowe Society, at the Arts Theatre, Cambridge. Producer is anonymous.

24 *Macbeth:* The Playhouse, Liverpool. *Producer:* WILLARD STOKER.

APRIL

7 *Othello:* Shakespeare Memorial Theatre, Stratford-upon-Avon. *Producer:* TONY RICHARDSON.

21 *All's Well that Ends Well:* Shakespeare Memorial Theatre, Stratford-upon-Avon. *Producer:* TYRONE GUTHRIE.

22 *Hamlet:* The National Youth Theatre, at the Barn Theatre, Dartington Hall. Later at the Queen's Theatre, London. *Producer:* MICHAEL CROFT.

22 *Twelfth Night:* Castle Theatre, Farnham. *Producer:* PETER JACKSON.

MAY

4   *The Merchant of Venice:* Bromley Repertory Theatre. *Producer:* TONY BECKLEY.

5   *Twelfth Night:* Northampton Repertory Theatre. *Producer:* LIONEL HAMILTON.

25   *A Midsummer Night's Dream:* Oldham Repertory Theatre Club, at the Coliseum, Oldham. *Producers:* HARRY LOMAX and DAVID BROOMFIELD.

26   *Twelfth Night:* The Playhouse, Oxford. Later at the Lisbon Trade Fair. *Producer:* FRANK HAUSER.

JUNE

2   *A Midsummer Night's Dream:* Shakespeare Memorial Theatre, Stratford-upon-Avon. *Producer:* PETER HALL.

5   *Antony and Cleopatra:* Harrow School. *Producer:* RONALD WATKINS.

9   *The Tempest, or, The Enchanted Island* (Dryden, Davenant-Purcell opera): The Old Vic Company, at the Old Vic Theatre, London. *Producer:* DOUGLAS SEALE.

16   *Twelfth Night:* The Bankside Players, at the Open-Air Theatre, Regent's Park, London. *Producer:* ROBERT ATKINS.

19   *King John:* The Norwich Players, The Maddermarket Theatre, Norwich. *Producer:* IAN EMMERSON.

JULY

7   *Coriolanus:* Shakespeare Memorial Theatre, Stratford-upon-Avon. *Producer:* PETER HALL.

13   *A Midsummer Night's Dream:* The Bankside Players, at the Open-Air Theatre, Regent's Park, London. *Producer:* ROBERT ATKINS.

21   *The Merry Wives of Windsor:* The Cambridge Theatre Group, in the Fellows' Garden, Trinity Hall, Cambridge. *Producers:* RAYMOND TUNMER and CAMILLE PRIOR.

24   *Richard II:* Stowe School. *Producers:* W. L. MCELWEE, L. A. W. EVANS and C. J. W. GAUVAIN.

AUGUST

18   *Henry VI, Part I:* The Hovenden Theatre Club, London. *Producer:* VALERY HOVENDEN.

18   *King Lear:* Shakespeare Memorial Theatre, Stratford-upon-Avon. *Producer:* GLEN BYAM SHAW.

SEPTEMBER

3   *As You Like It:* The Old Vic Company, at the Old Vic Theatre, London. *Producer:* WENDY TOYE.

22   *Romeo and Juliet:* Bristol Old Vic Company, at the Theatre Royal, Bristol. *Producer:* JOHN HALE.

28   *The Winter's Tale:* The Arts Council at the Little Theatre, Middlesbrough and later on tour in North-west England and Wales. *Producer:* TOBY ROBERTSON.

OCTOBER

13   *The Merchant of Venice:* The Marlowe Theatre, Canterbury. *Producer:* DONALD BAIN.

13   *A Midsummer Night's Dream:* Nottingham Repertory Theatre. *Producer:* VAL MAY.

20   *Othello:* The Citizens' Theatre, Glasgow. *Producer:* PETER DUGUID.

NOVEMBER

3 *Henry IV, Part I:* The Library Theatre, Manchester. *Producer:* DAVID SCASE.

9 *Macbeth:* Theatre Royal, Lincoln. *Producer:* K. V. MOORE.

16 *Twelfth Night:* Theatre in the Round, Pembroke Theatre, Croydon. *Producer:* ROBERT ATKINS.

17 *Richard II:* The Old Vic Company, at the Old Vic Theatre, London. *Producer:* VAL MAY.

20 *Julius Caesar:* The Norwich Players, The Maddermarket Theatre, Norwich. *Producer:* IAN EMMERSON.

23 *Othello:* Guildford Repertory Theatre. *Producer:* ERIC JONES.

DECEMBER

2 *The Merchant of Venice:* Fylde College Theatre, Tower Circus, Blackpool. *Producer:* FRANK WINFIELD.

7 *Hamlet:* University College, London. *Producer:* ROY BATTERSBY.

11 *Julius Caesar:* The People's Theatre, Newcastle-upon-Tyne. *Producer:* TOM EMERSON.

22 *The Merry Wives of Windsor:* The Old Vic Company, at the Old Vic Theatre, London. *Producer:* JOHN HALE.

PLATE I

A. Silvia and Valentine   B. Launce and Crab

'THE TWO GENTLEMEN OF VERONA', SHAKESPEARE MEMORIAL THEATRE, 1960
Directed by Peter Hall, designed by Lila de Nobili

C. The Greek Council; Ulysses speaking   D. The death of Hector

'TROILUS AND CRESSIDA', SHAKESPEARE MEMORIAL THEATRE, 1960
Directed by Peter Hall and John Barton, designed by Leslie Hurry

PLATE II

A. Cressida, Pandarus and Troilus
'TROILUS AND CRESSIDA'

B. 'O God, thine arm is here'
'HENRY V', OLD VIC THEATRE, 1960
Directed by John Neville, designed by John and Margaret Bury

PLATE III

Shylock
'THE MERCHANT OF VENICE', SHAKESPEARE MEMORIAL THEATRE, 1960
Directed by Michael Langham, designed by Desmond Heeley

PLATE IV

A. 'If you do love me, you will find me out'

B. The trial-scene

'THE MERCHANT OF VENICE'

THREE DIRECTORS: A REVIEW OF
RECENT PRODUCTIONS

BY

JOHN RUSSELL BROWN

> ...And the production most remarkable: it only needed a few rehearsals by
> Barker and myself to be perfect.[1]

The task of a theatre director is so complicated that it is tempting to treat the matter as one
of personal taste, as did Bernard Shaw writing to Mrs Patrick Campbell, to give 'no other
but a woman's reason', but think it so because we think it so. And normal difficulties are
increased when Shakespeare's plays are discussed, for everyone has different recollections of
earlier productions and probably their own views on how to translate the plays into modern
terms and adapt them for modern theatres. Yet while it is hard to formulate general rules, we
may describe individual methods and compare them. The summer of 1960, for instance,
showed the work of three directors of Shakespeare, each with clearly divergent training
and abilities, and so by lining up their achievements it is possible to assess a wide range of
currently accepted techniques.

I

Peter Hall had the fullest showing at the Memorial Theatre, Stratford-upon-Avon, with a
Two Gentlemen of Verona, a *Troilus and Cressida* (in which he had the assistance of John Barton)
and a revival of a *Twelfth Night* from two years earlier.[2] This director came to Shakespeare after
staging twentieth-century plays, and the experience is mirrored in his work. It is most obvious
in his attitude to speaking Shakespeare's verse and prose: he is determined to avoid stuffiness,
or solemn staginess, and seeks instead liveliness, humour and point—in a word, vitality. He has
had an apron built over the orchestra pit and uses it for direct and forceful contact with the
audience. The clear gains of this policy are in certain comic passages where the actors have
sufficient skill to sustain the size of their delivery without crudeness. Patrick Wymark as Launce
animated his repetitive speeches by a variety of timing and emphasis, and based all on a sympathetic understanding of the large-minded, stubborn character who is yet at the mercy of
circumstance. He made the audience wait for words, when he could do so without slowing up
his performance, and so invited them to enter his view of the world of the play: correcting
Speed for counting 'slow of speech' among his maid's vices, he then looked in blank wonder at
the audience so that the following line, 'To be slow in words is a woman's only virtue', was the
necessary statement they had been waiting for, an exaggeration which satisfied where it might
have fallen dead with its stale wit. Such acting is well served by Peter Hall's quest for vitality.
And so is the quick, restless art of Max Adrian. As Pandarus he sometimes spoke with a running
laugh or simper, or invented excited gestures to indicate the prurience and childishness of an

impotent *voyeur*; short phrasing, over-emphasis, repetitions, proverbs, images—'she fetches her breath as short as a new-ta'en sparrow'—were explained, illustrated, heightened, made to seem inevitable by the actor's invention and performance; he could point his lines, standing right down stage, and bear any scrutiny. Although Pandarus has direct address to the audience, he did not involve them in his thoughts; rather they watched him among others, and at the end were given a spectacle of self-pity and purposeless anger, not a demand for sympathy. As Feste, Max Adrian's performance lacked perhaps a continuous line, or an openness requisite for the professional fooling; but his moments of isolation were bitter and compellingly realized.

Among the rest of the Stratford Company, Dorothy Tutin gained most by Peter Hall's treatment of the dialogue. Visually her Cressida may have been too obviously or too early a seductress from an exotic film—would it not explain Troilus' talk of 'purity' if for a time she were successful in keeping her vow, 'nothing of that shall from my eyes appear'?—but the liveliness and humour she found in the part—the vitality her director seeks—was finely judged and enacted with control and intensity: 'he will weep you, an't were a man born in April', promises Pandarus, and Cressida momentarily stills the mockery with, 'And I'll spring up in his tears', and then releases it with, 'an't were a nettle against May'. A Shakespearian heroine thus becomes a creature of impulse and quick intelligence; the value of this was shown in Hall's production of *Twelfth Night* where Miss Tutin was over-emphatic in the early scene with the Sea Captain but, as Cesario, indicated Viola's feelings half-hidden beneath her disguise with both subtlety and strength; this gave an emotional centre to the entire production.

Equally clear is Peter Hall's pursuit of visual elaboration. He gave *Twelfth Night* a series of detailed settings and costumes in brown, gold, plum and mulberry colours, and hung the stage with gauze to give mellow lighting effects. *The Two Gentlemen* had a large revolving stage, on which were set small but detailed trees and buildings—a tower, gatehouse, chimney-piece and so forth—much of it in careful, picturesque ruin. The colours here were dark blues and greens and, again, dull golds and browns, and in the background there was a painted cloth of high, bosky hills and a stormy sky. It is difficult to guess the motives for choosing to imitate Irving or Tree in this manner, for the simulated jet of water in a fountain and the stuffed doves on the gatehouse were artless enough, to modern eyes, to destroy any simple 'belief' in the 'picture'. Moreover, the whole cumbersome effort seemed at variance with the pursuit of vitality in diction.

For *Troilus*, however, the policy was apparently reversed. This play was set on an irregular, raised and raked octagon, covered with pale sand. By itself this would have suggested a play-pit or a tray from a bird-cage. But behind it stretched a vast abstract backcloth designed by Leslie Hurry in copper-reds with black hieroglyphic markings; it suggested a furnace, a volcanic cliff, an ancient palace hung with undecipherable trophies, a storm, a dragon's wing. In front of this the sanded platform seemed a torrid desert or an arena for gladiatorial combat. Peter Hall had modified, not changed his policy: so far as the structure of Stratford's theatre would permit he had provided a simple platform stage, but placed it within a wide, emotive setting. He even repeated his interest in small visual details by the eye-catching novelty of the sand: Cressida langorously made it flow through her fingers and the action traced changing patterns across it as in a bull-ring. Moreover banners, stools, a high throne, carpets and one of the director's favourite potted trees were used to 'dress' the arena, controlled by a hand practised in more obviously elaborate settings. So the stage was capable of varied emphases: after Æneas had gone off with Troilus to meet Diomede for the first time, Pandarus was suddenly alone on a stage of desert-like emptiness; when Achilles at last spoke to Hector after the duel with Ajax, he did so from beside a tall, black standard to the back and right of the stage, a position of ominous emphasis created for this moment. The most spectacular effects were in the last battle-scenes where smoke hung low around a darkened stage, illuminated with sulphurous and glaring lights; the simplest mechanisms had been used for the detailed pictorial quality which is one of this director's most evident marks.

A further one is a constant pursuit of business. Sir Toby eats a slice of melon, Achilles and Thersites share a chicken leg, Orsino is served with coffee. These inventions are often in character, as when Agamemnon, who is said to speak 'like a chime a'mending', rises between two discourses from Ulysses as if to speak himself, but instead crosses in front of Ulysses to drink from a goblet, conveniently placed on the floor. But however well this fits the character it is questionable whether it serves the scene as a whole; the primary task at this moment is to interest the audience in what Ulysses is saying. This aspect of Peter Hall's direction can be distracting, especially when business is allowed to obliterate the connexions, contrasts and emphases suggested by the text of a play. For example, in *The Two Gentlemen*, the song, 'Who is Silvia?', gives a moment of rest and impersonal harmony as the course of love goes out of tune and harsh, but in Hall's production it did not sound with unprecedented ease, for immediately before the outlaws had been presented as a boyish troop, harmonizing a song from *As You Like It*.

But any director's achievements must be judged by his handling of complete plays. *The Two Gentlemen* was the least well received, failing to sustain interest. Pictorial lavishness was much to blame, for invented business as the stage revolved—a beggar, a gatehouse-keeper, a singer, dances, hide-and-seek, and the duke taking his shoes off before a fire—slowed down the narrative by awaking an idle curiosity. The transitions of the play are clear and quick—ironically so at times, as when Julia's leave-taking, silent because of her 'true love', is followed immediately by Launce's complaint that his dog at parting 'sheds not a tear nor speaks a word'. This production consistently dissipated such effects. Moreover, the director's insistence on vitality in speaking made the 'straight' scenes far too slow. Their language is clear and bright, with rapid turns of thought, needing a light and graceful delivery; but here it sounded laboured, as when Proteus, with clenched fist, emphasized, 'I cannot leave to love, and YET I DO'. Juxtaposed with Speed's garrulity, Valentine's 'I would it were no worse' and 'I have dined' (II, i, 169 and 177) do not need to be made large, with embarrassed movement and kissing of his letter; such underlining loses the speedy economy of the musical and sentimental contrast. Silvia's

> Well, I guess the sequel;
> And yet I will not name it; and yet I care not;
> And yet take this again; and yet I thank you,
> Meaning henceforth to trouble you no more. (II, i, 122–5)

needs a nimble grace, not ejaculatory point; there is too much of this kind of writing for that treatment. Besides slowing down the play, the search for vitality and business cheapened it: between the speeches in the letter-scene Julia chased Lucetta until she cried 'Owh!', and as she entrusted her reputation to her maid's keeping she tickled her nose and laughed; there was a special pause after Proteus had promised to serve Silvia so that the lady could giggle with pleasure. Peter Hall is to be praised for seeing point and humour in much of the dialogue, but not for stressing it so broadly. Occasionally soft lyrical utterance was encouraged, but this, which can modulate from a delivery as stylish and mannered as the writing, here sounded odd and studied. Pictorially and vocally the production was too heavy and unsophisticated: the lovers seemed like pampered children, overgrown and playing in rich and glowing clothes. Vitality and sumptuous stage-pictures did not serve the grace, clarity, wit, sentiment, excitement and fluency of the early romantic Shakespeare—the poet whom his contemporaries called 'gentle' and 'honey-tongued'. Only Launce and Speed could grow to proper stature, and their humanity seemed unrelated to anything else in the play.

In missing its style and tempo, the director also missed the romantic climax of the play. The last scene was dominated by laughter—at Silvia's 'Oooh!' as Proteus unblindfolded her (an interpolated incident), at the trotting Julia's comic faint, at Proteus' high-pitched 'were man But constant, he were perfect', at the outlaws' routine pranks, and at the fuddled duke and his roguish laugh as he saw through Julia's disguise. The threatened rape of Silvia was a broad joke: Valentine's embarrassing, impossible, generous, 'All that was mine in Silvia I give thee', was spoken so that it was hardly noticed; Proteus' repentance was a sentiment to laugh at. Much work went into sustaining a romping conclusion, but the conflict of love and friendship, and the manifestation of generosity, faithfulness and truth went unheeded. In this slow-moving production no other course was possible; the director had been too busy with other matters to attend to the development of these issues, and the style of delivery was incapable of presenting them in the dialogue Shakespeare has provided, for pauses and emphasis had already been used too lavishly; the economy and the main-spring of the comedy had been forfeit.

Twelfth Night was better received. It was less of a game. Unbounded vitality gave way here to the creation of mellow-toned pictures, and the acting was altogether more subtle: Viola, Sir Toby and Feste were played with distinction; Derek Godfrey suggested soldier-like qualities beneath Orsino's affectation, and Eric Porter's Malvolio was unusually consistent, a well-observed portrait of a steward. The production was occasionally slowed down by intrusive business, some of it vulgar (as the priest's smirk when he turned away from Olivia and Sebastian) and some of it distracting from the main issues. But brash over-emphasis was mostly confined to Fabian, Maria and Olivia—especially the lady, who seemed encouraged to appear both cock-sure and inexperienced. Peter Hall's procedure had not radically changed; rather it had been refined by well-judged acting and his happy (if somewhat inexplicable) belief that the play needed a mellow tone. This production had a kind of ease that could contain a fair measure of both humour and sentiment; its most noticeable lack was, perhaps, the airy excitement suggested by the text.

Troilus and Cressida had the advantage of a far less fussy and more appropriate setting, and the liveliness, humour and point of the speaking served the satirical elements well, and the vaunting encounters of the soldiers. The two difficult council-scenes failed, however, to hold a close attention. The Greek was slow and too uniformly stressed; in particular, Ulysses spoke too weightily for a man of his acute (or fox-like) intelligence. In Troy the princes seemed to try too hard to sustain the longer speeches and two opportunities for variety were lost by giving Priam to a small actor placed on a rickety throne and by allowing Cassandra to look and sound uncomfortable rather than terrible and commanding; the scene lacked a shape and a centre. Yet generally, the fire and the absurdity of love and warlike preparations were clearly delineated, and this play, unlike the other two, seemed to sweep forward, broadening and defining its scope, finding its energy from within the characters and situations, rather than from the director's hand. Pandarus and Paul Hardwick's Ajax were comic performances, and Derek Godfrey's Hector and Patrick Allen's Achilles heroic, which had vitality appropriate to their language and their characters. And Miss Tutin's Cressida, particularly when she had parted from Troilus, showed her complaisance to be her 'plague', her will and memory unable to change her desires; silence among the Greeks and then the mocking of Menelaus became eloquent of her 'quick sense', and the last scene with Diomede showed her to be both cunning and helpless.

Yet the end of the play was disappointing. First Troilus (Denholm Elliott) did not sustain interest after Cressida's last appearance. Throughout he had been striving for an impression of energy—he even tried to endow 'a strange soul upon the Stygian banks' with a kind of brightness. A more tender Troilus, with a more pitiable Cressida, would have been well within this actor's powers, but in the vital idiom of the production his voice seemed lacking in size and range, his movements consistently nervous. He had no reserve of power to transform himself into a cold, resolved 'savage' for the last scenes; he could only become tense and shout his anger. The second disappointment was caused by the director giving way to his love of detail: every fight was prolonged; an extra entry was invented for Ajax; Achilles had a long pause in his last short speech to turn over Hector's body with his foot; the final departure of the Greeks was delayed while some of them picked up Hector's cloak and looked at it. After the early forcefulness the battles needed to be rapid, if they were not to disperse the charged interests; Hall's were fine pictures, but too often a dumb deflation of the drama, especially when the stage-smoke was allowed to obscure the fighters.

Added to Hall's marks of vitality, with its dependence on fine acting to avoid coarseness, of elaborate settings and of a pursuit of business, must be a slack grasp of form. All three plays were over-slow at the end, but it is probably more than a question of tempo and style. In *The Two Gentlemen* there was lack of trust in the main-spring of the romance plot; by refusing to accept sentiment and authority as a source of excitement, Hall allowed the last scene to become farcical and without a firm centre in the duke. Something of the same difficulty was involved by the treatment of Olivia in *Twelfth Night* and the weak Priam of the council-scene of *Troilus*. And in recollection these productions suggest that Hall's sense of form is weak because he is insufficiently responsive to unifying ideas behind the plays, the treatment of love and friendship in the romance *and* comedy of *The Two Gentlemen*, and of time and fate in *Troilus* among soldiers, politicians and lovers. In *Troilus*, men and women, by satisfying their own appetites and desires, find that in time they are forced to do what they 'would not'; they learn that time has a 'robber's haste'; they foresee fate and defy fate; they swear by Diana in their licentiousness; their minds become like fountains 'troubled' of which they cannot see the bottom, and, finally, there is 'no more to say' except to triumph in an act of butchery or cover an 'inward woe' with hope of revenge. This train of actions and sentiments relating to the changes time enforces might easily have been more emphasized, by giving stature to Cassandra, by making the pledges to the future shared by Troilus, Cressida and Pandarus as boldly formal as the writing of that incident, by more relentless pressure in the battle-scenes (broken for the inevitable encounters of Achilles and Hector), by a modified style of utterance which could make isolated emphasis where the issues seem to demand it. It is possible that such attention to an idea would give a more compelling form to the plays as well as greater eloquence and fuller interest.

II

At the Old Vic *Henry the Fifth* was directed by John Neville, comparatively new to production but experienced as a Shakespearian actor. The play started freshly with a bare stage and the Chorus dressed in casual modern clothes and speaking without splendour or showmanship; he gained a new hearing for his lines, but this was an actor's innovation, something for one man to implement and not a new presentation of the play as it first seemed to promise. In fact, the production was all too full of theatrical clichés. As the first Chorus finished, the two prelates spoke their scene in front of a drop curtain with showy gusto: on 'It must be thought on', Canterbury wagged his head in emphasis and moved smartly in front of Ely. This behaviour seemed all the more unnecessary after the lithe enunciation and simple movements of the Chorus. For the announcement of Falstaff's death, Mistress Quickly sat down and, as if they were posing for a photograph, the others crouched round about her; so she was able to speak it on a still stage, straight out to the audience. Theatrical effectiveness too easily took the place of the interplay of characters in action. So the stage emptied slowly after the reckoning of Agincourt: the English, soldiers and dukes, sang 'Non nobis Domine' and with bowed heads walked in single file round the stage and off; Pistol solemnly covered a boy's corpse with a cloak and then followed; and the king, having stood alone and silent, brought up the tail of the procession. Meanwhile lights were lowered on stage and cyclorama so that the curtain fell slowly on an empty and darkened world. To the complaint that soldiers do not sing in this pious manner nor take such circuitous routes, the director could answer that they were acting in accordance with a stage convention to sustain a pictorial and aural effect; Pistol's uncharacteristic deed might be said to serve the same purpose, and the unlikely and unceremonious movements of the king. But the trouble is not that this is a convention, but that it is a tired one and used so that it destroys the proper relationship of the characters and the requisite emphasis and tempo. One evening as the house-lights came up, a lady was heard to remark to her neighbour, 'Is that the end? I thought there were two intervals.'

The merits of the production lay where its director's knowledge of acting could be of most help: the return of the glove, the French lesson and the wooing scene were all played easily, without forcing. And more rare today, there were attempts to give size and full significance to crucial points by sheer acting—for example, Henry's anger on being told that the Dauphin's gift was tennis-balls. Here the king rose quickly from his seat, then held himself back forcibly, and after a very long pause spoke coolly with obvious control; from this he worked towards a climax and finished with a curt, 'Fare you well'. This and similar ideas were imperfectly realized perhaps, but they showed a director willing and able to work towards histrionic effects. The scale of acting is usually kept smaller.

Yet despite this occasional interest Neville's production remained too full of clichés and, therefore, slight. And, again, contrasts suggested by the text were often disregarded, as when the boy punched across the words of his soliloquy after Pistol's departure with his prisoner, almost in the bragging manner of his master. The wooing scene passed without the sober attestation of a good heart, a phrase which echoes, and draws strength and meaning from, the extended scene with the traitors, the prayer before Agincourt, and William's assurance that all 'offences come from the heart'. As well as losing contrasts and variety, the wholly comic playing of the wooing belittles one of the themes of the play and loses something of its formal strength.

III

By one stroke Michael Langham in directing *The Merchant of Venice* at Stratford-upon-Avon showed that he was concerned to give meaning and form to the production: in the trial-scene, after Shylock has said that he is 'content' and Gratiano that he would have had him hanged, a crowd circles round the Jew jeering at him, and he stumbles to the ground; Portia moves across, the crowd falls back silent, and Shylock rises face to face with the boy-like lawyer who has spoken of mercy and of fines. There were no words for them to speak, but the point of the moment was to show that all had been done, that the two were irreconcilable. Possibly such an emphasis would have been better made earlier, where Shakespeare directed the two to confront each other, but, together with other details, it ensured that the trial was as exciting as it usually is and more clearly the necessary centre of both the Venetian and Belmont strands of the plot.

The merriment of the fifth act at Belmont often seems detached and irrelevant after the drama of the fourth, and here again Langham's resource was to emphasize a theme, that of friendship. This was long prepared for: for example, Antonio's 'Fie, fie' in the first scene, when Salerio accuses him of being in love, was forcefully spoken and followed by an emphasizing moment of embarrassed silence, and the description of the parting of Antonio and Bassanio was listened to in such a way that the answering 'I think he only loves the world for him' sounded no less than a measured truth. By such means Langham was able to present Antonio's silent figure in Act v as the merchant of Venice who had just given all his wealth in love to Portia; at the end he was left alone on the stage, seated and idly playing with the piece of paper which had given him the irrelevant news that all his argosies were 'richly come to harbour'. This silent, isolated drama had something of the force of the silent, isolated drama as the other merchant of Venice departed from the court of law without the 'means by which *he* lived'. While the confrontation of Shylock and Portia gave meaning to a moment, the treatment of Antonio throughout the play allowed the end to draw strength from the whole.

Nevertheless, the outstanding aspect of the production was Peter O'Toole's Shylock. The reprieve from a persistent quest of vitality, which enabled individual points to be emphasized, also allowed one performance to tower above the others. This was less through the longer speeches than in short phrases, snatches or bites at single words: 'I *hate* him...If I can *catch* him.... Even on *me*...I have an oath in *heaven*...Is *that* the law?' Sometimes this effect was delayed or reversed, as when he waited for the third 'let him *look* to his bond' before fully realizing and uttering his hatred, slowly and quietly. Occasionally the sudden snarl seemed irrational or perverse, as in '...who *then* conceiving'. His was not a pathetic Jew: 'no tears but of my shedding' was not said for sympathy, but with ritualistic beating on his breast. He expressed pain here and at the memory of Leah by showing his effort to bear it himself, with clenched control. After this the trial disappointed at first, for Shylock had not the intellectuality to carry off the long, quietly taunting speeches; these were broken with movement and self-regarding feeling, as when 'If every ducat...' was said with quiet voice and almost closed eyes. But as Portia drew the trial towards an issue, the shorter phrases—a shouted 'I stand for judgement...' stilled an angry court—and the intense sharpening of the knife had full power. After the collapse of his 'rights' Shylock regained some of his strength with his dignity; he laughed at the sparing of his life and prided himself still on his sense of right—'send the deed after me, And I *will* sign it'.

All along O'Toole was aided by his director. The tripping music of a masque off-stage gave strength by contrast to his farewell to Jessica. His costume was more dignified than usual, so that when he returned after his daughter's flight with his gown torn and muddied the audience was at once aware of a great reversal. Neither director nor actor stressed the 'inhumanity' of Shylock: his rapaciousness was not evident, for he was dressed too well for a miser; he walked too upright to suggest cunning or unbridled hatred; in the savagery of the court scene he was controlled. Moreover, this 'magnificent Shylock', as one review called him, was opposed by a gushing, nervous, trivial band of Christians.

Presumably this was another of the director's ideas for the play, for it was consistently maintained. Antonio, who was given considerable prominence, was a sombre figure, with little joy in his generosity. The others were light. Lorenzo was brisk and Jessica unaccommodating. The crowd in the trial-scene was callow, mechanical in its reactions, and cheaply exultant. The first two casket scenes were played for the comedy that could be extracted from, or given to, the wooers, while Portia's predicament and desires were almost lost to sight. The caskets did not stand still and mysterious, but were carried around by three pretty girls. Lest the audience took the Bassanio casket scene too intently, Portia was dressed in swirling pink, moved about and often spoke loudly across the stage to Bassanio. While Bassanio was 'commenting on the caskets' and the song was sung, a collapsible arbour was carried across the stage to encircle Portia. During the soliloquy, 'How all the other passions fleet to air', attention was drawn away from the speaker to a crowd of servants moving around stage to encircle Bassanio. There was little opportunity for warm intimacy, modesty, deep intelligence. In Act v there was such emphasis on gaiety, with chasing round in circles and patronizing Antonio, that Portia's underlying confidence and pleasure in Bassanio, and her good sense, could scarcely show through. Fortunately Miss Tutin played the role, and through the ebullience managed to suggest a star-eyed eagerness, and in the trial scene, without the dignity of the usual robes, spoke the mercy speech with clarity and a solemnity that seemed to come from beyond Portia's own powers or consciousness.

In all this Langham directed consistently and with an intellectual grasp of the basic conflicts of the play. While the Shylock was not cunning, rapacious or inhuman in pursuit of revenge and the Portia did not appear wise in love, by pointing the form of the play, its crises, contrasts, repetitions, developments, the director ensured that the audience was involved in the play as a whole; under this condition, false emphasis and wayward characterization cannot destroy its holding power.

For the last five years Michael Langham has directed plays at Stratford, Ontario, and this has probably influenced some details of his work. His choice of a low, dark setting, changing little except in lighting and furniture as the action moves from Venice to Belmont, might be explained by his familiarity with Ontario's open, basically unchanging stage. At the Memorial Theatre, the single set gave fluency, as did Hall's for *Troilus*, but lacked emotive, visual appropriateness—a considerable loss on a picture-frame stage. The eighteenth-century costumes are more difficult to explain; they may have been chosen to give elegance to the gaiety of this Belmont, or possibly the example of Tyrone Guthrie, his predecessor as Director of the Canadian Festival, encouraged Langham to experiment in this way. Indeed Guthrie, who directed *The Merchant of Venice* in Ontario's Stratford in 1955, often seemed to be behind this production: he had directed the caskets to be carried by three maids who moved about 'freely'; his Aragon was accompanied by 'three black-clad tutors' (Langham's had one and a mother); for cutting the pound of flesh, his Antonio was tied to a 'sort of frame' which seemed 'symbolical of crucifixion' (Langham used a simpler pillory); his crowd indulged itself in 'jeering and jostling and even spitting' at the trial; his Antonio was left 'lonely and dispirited' at the close of the play.[3] In both productions a 'choir' sang on stage for Portia's pleasure and the lovers 'wreathed' around during the ring-jests of Act v.[4] If these details represent direct indebtedness, it is still quite clear that in total effect, especially in their Shylocks and the oppositions of the trial scene, the two productions were wholly disparate. Besides giving strong and embracing form to his production, Langham had learned and assimilated the experience of another director and of the opportunity of working on another kind of stage.

NOTES

1. *George Bernard Shaw and Mrs Patrick Campbell: their Correspondence* (1952), p. 126.
2. Reviewed in *Shakespeare Survey*, 12 (1959).   3. *Ottawa Citizen* (30 June 1955).
4. *Toronto Globe* (1 July 1955).

THE YEAR'S CONTRIBUTIONS TO
SHAKESPEARIAN STUDY

1. CRITICAL STUDIES

reviewed by BERNARD HARRIS

'The work of Shakespeare is like life itself', T. S. Eliot once wrote, 'something to be lived through', and the words are used by Rudolf Germer[1] to introduce his brief account of the significance of Shakespeare in Eliot's poetry. This influence has been constantly reciprocated, of course, for although Eliot has produced no substantial body of Shakespearian criticism some of his incidental observations, not in themselves original, have achieved a currency akin to the proverbial. One of the most celebrated statements is that upon the essential unity of Shakespeare's work:

We do not understand Shakespeare from a single reading, and certainly not from a single play. There is a relation between the various plays of Shakespeare, taken in order; and it is a work of years to venture even one individual interpretation of the pattern in Shakespeare's carpet.

The very ease of the notion, the strong wish that an artistic life as rich, and diverse, as Shakespeare's should be comprehensible as a whole, brings with it all kinds of complexities for criticism. Critical studies which range over the whole field of Shakespeare's work inevitably concentrate, by necessity, upon some essential but single attribute—the development of language, of imagery, of ethical concern; studies devoted to a single play are forced to take stock of so many different factors that a view of the whole is difficult to preserve; and studies of relationships between different plays depend upon certain suppositions of chronology—'taken in order' is an excellent idea; what order?

Such platitudes occur to one frequently, and are prompted this year in particular because the second quotation from Eliot above is set down as an adage before L. C. Knights' latest book,[2] which is acknowledgedly 'based on the belief that Shakespeare's plays form a coherent whole'. If this view has gained wide acceptance it is not because Eliot and others have repeated it at the level of assertion, but because critics as independent as Wilson Knight, Tillyard or L. C. Knights have undertaken the demonstration. It is a work of years—parts of the present book have become familiar in earlier publication and have therein been reviewed—but it remains to attest that the kind of coherence sought in the plays is present in this book. It opens with brief reflexions 'On some contemporary trends in Shakespeare criticism', and observes that

Conceptions of the nature and function of poetic drama have been radically revised; the essential structure of the plays has been sought in the poetry rather than in the more easily extractable elements of 'plot' and 'character'; and our whole conception of Shakespeare's relation to his work, of the kind of thing he was trying to do as an artist whilst simultaneously satisfying the demands of the Elizabethan theatre—this conception has undergone a revolutionary change.

[1] 'Die Bedeutung Shakespeares für T. S. Eliot', *Shakespeare Jahrbuch*, 95 (1959), 112–32.
[2] *Some Shakespearean Themes* (Chatto and Windus, 1959).

The 'new' Shakespeare, Knights believes, is less impersonal than the old, is much more 'immediately engaged in the action he puts before us'. Furthermore, 'the verse has moved well into the centre of the picture' and linguistic vitality 'is now felt as the chief clue to the urgent personal themes that not only shape the poetic-dramatic structure of each play but form the figure in the carpet of the canon as a whole'. He defends attention to imagery against superficial attack, and against superficial employment, and confirms that imagery, 'or any other component that may be momentarily isolated' takes on its full significance only when properly related to the larger meaning 'determined by the "plain sense" of what is said, and by its overtones, by the dramatic situation and the progress of the action, by symbols and by the interplay of different attitudes embodied in the different persons of the drama'. Knights draws authority from Elizabethan proficiency in verbal and musical training, and enjoyment of both, to emphasize that the conventions of Elizabethan drama encouraged concentration on poetry; such conventions were neither coherent nor explicit, 'but some degree of convention other than the naturalistic convention with which we are most familiar there was bound to be': and the advantage of a non-naturalistic convention lay precisely in the opportunity for a great artist to achieve 'the depth and activity of response at which art may be said to aim'. To claim that the 'essential structure of Shakespearean tragedy is poetic' is to 'do no violence to Shakespeare the Elizabethan dramatist', for we are not concerned with 'statement poetically embellished...but with a poetry that is profoundly exploratory'.

These are important reminders of what Knights and others have said before, because the recovery of a sense of the dramatic activity of poetic drama is of equal and related importance as the recovery of the sense that Elizabethan drama is poetic. Knights' exposition of such matters is of exceptional clarity, and throughout the book there is a nicely judged relationship of tone and matter. 'A book of criticism is an offer of conversation', he remarks, and his comments upon Shakespeare in discussing *Henry IV, Part II* may suitably be used to reflect the reader's reaction to the conversation:

we know we are dealing with a free mind—one that is neither driven, nor bent on driving, an 'idea'; the sombre preoccupations are not obsessions.

The preoccupations, not ultimately sombre, of this book 'can be indicated by such words as: time and change, appearance and reality, the fear of death and the fear of life, the meanings of nature, the meanings of relationship'. The works selected for treatment, after a preliminary examination of the theme of the public world in a number of plays, are the Sonnets, *Henry IV, Part II, Troilus and Cressida, King Lear, Macbeth, Antony and Cleopatra* and *Coriolanus*. Many of the judgements on these plays are already a part of our experience of them, in particular, perhaps, the analysis of *Lear*, which, from the point of view of this book is placed as 'the great central masterpiece, the great exploratory allegory to which so many of the earlier plays lead and on which the later plays depend'.

Naturally, there are objections to this point of view, and they are of a fundamental kind. Kenneth Muir[1] chose as his theme for the annual lecture on Shakespeare at the British Academy in 1958 that of the dramatist's tragic pattern, and touched on 'nearly all of Shakespeare's tragedies so as to show that each play is unique and *sui generis*', believing that 'the differences between one

[1] 'Shakespeare and the Tragic Pattern' (Oxford University Press, 1959).

play and another are more significant than the resemblances'. The lecture adopts the proposition, *contra* Bradley, that 'There is no such thing as Shakespearian Tragedy: there are only Shakespearian tragedies', and the point is developed through a personal focusing of such diverse approaches as those provided by source reference, Elizabethan opinion, literary models, and historical and contemporary criticism. The result is a feat of adroit compression and concise illumination, exemplified in the brief remark, in comparing Hamlet's situation to that of the man between two worlds in Arnold's poem, that the place of Hamlet's wandering 'was the blank page between the Old and New Testaments'.

Hamlet, not uncharacteristically, acquires more than an equal share of the discussion in Muir's lecture, and is the only play this year to command a book to itself. H. Levin[1] derives his principles of approach from the familiar observation that Hamlet, the character, 'loses no opportunity to display or discuss the conditions and standards of Shakespeare's craft'. Accordingly, the book attempts to follow a critical procedure in close relationship to the dramatic action perceived in the play. The three main chapters are entitled Interrogation, Doubt and Irony, a rhetorical correspondence to what Levin argues are the three phases of thesis, antithesis and synthesis in the dramatic action. What follows is a tightly packed commentary on the course of the whole play, drawing upon three principal areas of reference defined in an introductory chapter of 'Presuppositions': these are, that since drama depends upon physical conditions we try to restage a play as we read it, that since a play is a vehicle of ideas we must have recourse to the history of ideas, and that 'since it is primarily and finally a verbal structure, our scrutiny is most concretely rewarded at the level of phrase and emphasis'. The intentions are excellent, their execution formidable. It is at the level of phrase and emphasis within the book itself that the reader is most taxed. The comments on stagecraft are not concentrated upon any personally developed perceptions, but are rather interspersions of theatre history, such as what Mrs Siddons made of Ophelia, or Tommaso Salvini of Hamlet, even that the backstage nicknames of Rosencrantz and Guildenstern are 'the Knife and Fork, partly because they are inseparable, and partly because it is their task to feed Hamlet his lines'. The history of ideas is resorted to only on the most expected of occasions, such as Hamlet's oration on Man, when the great chain of being is rattled once more and Erasmus is called upon to testify 'to the conception of man as a two-faced biped'. The poetry is quoted as a series of starting points for debates which lead on and off but rarely back into the poetic activity. It is as a stimulus to critical dissension that the book has real merits, though even here its value would have been improved by some annotation of the critical judgements cited in the text. There are three useful supplementary studies of 'The Antic Disposition', 'The Tragic Ethos' and 'An Explication of the Player's Speech', the latter especially suggestive. There are also three charts of illustrative figures. In fact, the book has an obsession with three-fold correspondences, which are teased out with constant ingenuity; so much so that in a comment such as that 'The drama might almost be described as a triangle-play with a vengeance' one is not sure just how much intended irony the last word conveys.

Shorter critical contributions on *Hamlet* include Fredson Bowers'[2] conduct of a legal inquiry into the situation at 'The death of Hamlet', in which it is argued that 'the actual killing of the

---

[1] *The Question of Hamlet* (New York: Oxford University Press, 1959).

[2] *Studies in the English Renaissance Drama, in memory of K. J. Holzknecht* (New York University Press, 1959), pp. 28–42.

king would come under the head of manslaughter since the fruition of the revenge was in fact only secondary', and that Shakespeare's 'exact arrangement of the final action to remove guilt, must have seemed to him both warranted and necessary'. Robert Ornstein[1] discusses Hamlet's murder of Polonius as one instance of a crucial issue for decision on Shakespeare's moral attitudes: these have been defined too much by recourse to the history of ideas, whereas we should attend rather to the manner and extent of Shakespeare's poetic and dramatic art in shaping our moral responses. Thus, Ornstein argues, 'the murder of Polonius does not disturb us because it does not disturb Hamlet; it is not near our conscience because it is not near his'. David R. Cheney[2] employs historical criticism to interpret Hamlet's cloud speech to Polonius in the light of Elizabethan concepts of the curious and bodeful attributes of the camel, the weasel and the whale. Gordon Worth O'Brien[3] explains Laertes' speech 'O heat, dry up my brains' by reference to Renaissance medical texts. T. Hawkes[4] brings critical support to the Second Quarto punctuation of Hamlet's discourse on Man, not on negative grounds that the comparison of human action and angelic makes Hamlet talk nonsense, but, positively, that 'to compare human "apprehension" to that of an angel is to make him talk a great deal of sense'.

The probable proximity of *Hamlet* and *Troilus and Cressida* make it suitable to turn next to some considerations of that play, especially as its tragic aspects have been emphasized. B. R. Morris[5] argues that 'Though neither Quarto nor Folio text has Act and Scene divisions, there can be no doubt of the antithetical and cumulative nature of the construction'. Tracing the distinct patterns of the generals' plot and the progress of the lovers' passion, Morris finds that the betrayal scene of v, ii 'is intended to be the climax of the play', that Troilus is rescued from his involvement in 'a great but misguided love', and from the general denigration of the heroic and romantic stories, to discover 'his true identity as the champion of Troy'. R. C. Harrier,[6] writing on 'Troilus Divided' in the Holzknecht memorial volume, would also 'like to propose that Troilus is intended to evoke as much admiration as disapproval, as much sympathy as pity', and thinks there is special significance in Aeneas as the authority for Ulysses' comments on Troilus to Agamemnon, and the brief associations of Troilus with Aeneas, 'the single Trojan figure whose virtue and magnificence were unquestionable to an Elizabethan audience'. A. S. Knowland[7] questions specifically the concept of the Greeks and Trojans as 'opposing terms in a central symbolic conflict', and also the isolation of the 'time theme' by critics of this play, when the references to time should be more fully related to those upon fate, fortune, accident, chance, and the Gods. Knowland suggests that our 'total dramatic experience of the play as a whole' must be put in terms of men's attempts 'to transcend the flux of events and the attitudes they give rise to by finding among them something of abiding significance'. Trojans and Greeks alike set up values of love, chivalry and order; and though the collapse of all three is 'comprehended in Troilus' experience', it is argued that Troilus (who is compared with Ellie Dunne) is 'strong enough to survive the shock', and that the play's final effect is to convey a sense that 'The achievements themselves are transient, the impulse to erect them endures'. Discussions on

---

[1] 'Historical Criticism and the Interpretation of Shakespeare', *Shakespeare Quarterly*, x (1959), 3–9.
[2] 'The Meaning of the Cloud in *Hamlet*', ibid. pp. 446–7.　　[3] '*Hamlet* IV, v, 156–7', ibid. pp. 249–51.
[4] 'Hamlet's "Apprehension"', *Modern Language Review*, LV (1960), 238–41.
[5] 'The Tragic Structure of *Troilus and Cressida*', *Shakespeare Quarterly*, x (1959), 481–91.
[6] Op. cit. pp. 142–56.　　　　[7] '*Troilus and Cressida*', *Shakespeare Quarterly*, x (1959), 353–65.

Troilus and Cressida are commonly inconclusive. And even so simple and emphatic a phrase as the 'knot, five-finger-tied' with which Cressida sealed her pledge to Diomed, and which seemed to Dr Johnson, and to most of us, just a handshake, is unravelled by T. M. Pearce[1] from Guillaume Peraldus' *A Treatise of the Seven Deadly Sins*, translated in Chaucer's *Parson's Tale*, where 'that other hand of the devel' has for its fifth finger 'Lecherie', and the knot is that tied by the senses.

By comparison with writers on *Troilus and Cressida*, who have an initial task of definition, critics of generally accepted tragedies are free to range in more settled territory. Among studies in Shakespeare's other classical plays H. J. Oliver[2] stresses 'an important similarity of pattern in *Timon*, *Antony and Cleopatra* and *Coriolanus*: in all three a hero of greater soul suffers but the mere man of action survives'. Oliver (who believes that '*Coriolanus* is perhaps the least "dated" of all Shakespeare's plays') is concerned to present a favourable interpretation of Coriolanus' character, and conducts a rearguard action against historical and contemporary critical sniping at its hero. The issue is larger than the interpretation of this particular hero's character, and the discussion offers a general suggestion that 'If no villain is needed to precipitate the action of the last three tragedies, it is not because the evil is already present in the hero himself but because Shakespeare is developing the special theme that it is part of the tragedy of the world that there are certain kinds of goodness which can themselves lead to tragedy'. The disturbance of a general reading of the three late classical plays as satirical tragedies may be salutary; there are further shocks in the sensitive analysis by Winifred M. T. Nowottny[3] of Acts IV and V of *Timon of Athens*. In part she finds that 'one continuous imaginative process shapes the sequence of Timon's encounters and speeches': what she finds less clear is 'what relation obtains between this process and the ensuing encounters with the steward and with the poet and the painter'. The ground suddenly yawns open when we find that she thinks *Timon* to be the work of two hands: could they not both, one wonders, have been Shakespeare's? Stylistic observations on the Roman plays of an associative rather than disintegrating tendency have included a comparative study by M. Charney[4] of 'Shakespeare's Style in *Julius Caesar* and *Antony and Cleopatra*', and some shrewd employment by Michael Lloyd[5] of the suggestion that in *Antony and Cleopatra* 'The Romans, great and small, speak with a single tongue', that their comments stand 'in disagreeable contrast to the lighter tone of Egyptian conversation', and that Shakespeare uses the isolated language of the Romans to represent, among other matters, their capacity for misrepresentation. The Romans, elsewhere, continue to meet with their historical fate of being misliked. Gordon Ross Smith[6] discusses again the view that Brutus' will, not his virtue, is 'the chief constant of his behaviour'. Virtue is seen as Brutus' preoccupation, his self-justification and the cloak of a 'thoroughly egotistical wilfulness'. Smith itemizes fourteen occasions in which 'Brutus proceeds to dominate or to domineer over his fellows': some occasions seem rather trivial—for instance, no. 7, 'When Ligarius appears, Brutus does not say, "Come with me"; he says, "Follow me"', and no. 8, that when Caesar asks the time 'There are nine other persons present who might have answered, but it is Brutus who does so'. Smith agrees, of course, that Brutus is chosen as leader and spokesman, but resents him accepting the role and seeks to reduce it to something nearer the

---

[1] *Notes & Queries* (January 1960), pp. 18–19.
[2] 'Coriolanus as Tragic Hero', *Shakespeare Quarterly*, X (1959), 53–60.   [3] *Ibid.* pp. 493–7.
[4] *English Literary History*, XXVI (1959), 355–67.
[5] 'The Roman Tongue', *Shakespeare Quarterly*, X (1959), 461–8.   [6] 'Brutus, Virtue and Will', *ibid.* pp. 367–79.

concept of an organization-man, and the presentation of his character from that of a poetic creation to that of 'the surface of a recurrent personality type'. By contrast, Norman Nathan[1] finds a distinct new significance for Caius Ligarius, taking on trust the references in the play that Caesar has wronged him, and concluding that the absence of Ligarius from the scene in the Capitol is meant to give us a standard of conduct by which to judge the actions of the conspirators. It may be difficult, in the theatre, to measure a problem so immediate as murder against a standard of conduct apparently being maintained by a minor character in his unremarked absence.

Theatrical presentations of more central importance are traced by Dorothy C. Hockey[2] in the trial patterns of *Lear*. The patterns are by no means complete (Kent, for instance, is neglected), though few will dissent from the statement that 'The movement of the plot, the character of Lear's mind, and above all, the larger meaning of the play have been dramatized with incredible aptness as trials'. What is missed, perhaps, is that dimension of the larger meaning to which the staged trials correspond, that purgatorial wheel of fire beyond the rack of this tough world. Nor is the outcome of the successive trials conveyed very clearly in the decision that 'Justice has capitulated to love', when it is rather the complex relationship of such concepts that has been the ground of the whole action. A useful note on the word '"Love" in King Lear' has been provided by T. Hawkes,[3] who suggests that the probing of the nature of love in the play's first scene may reach as deep as linguistic ambiguity, 'the almost opposite meanings which this word could have at the time when Shakespeare was writing', namely, love as appraisal, estimation or valuation, and as affection. The conflicts of this opening scene, and of others, are taken up by E. A. Block[4] in some reflexions on the ways in which Shakespeare chose to deviate from his source material to create 'a series of equilibriums which can only have been deliberately intended and contrived'. It seems insufficient, however, to attribute to these deviations the 'continuous suspense' which is described as permeating the play and as not appearing 'to have been adequately recognized'. A similar conviction that the dramaturgy of *Lear* still needs defence has prompted Carolyn S. French[5] to protest that 'there *is* a rationale behind the dramatic structure of *Lear*, a rationale which gives intellectual significance to actions incredible by our modern standards of probability': the rationale is, of course, the paradox of wisdom and folly, and St Paul (apparently under a preaching licence from Tillyard), Lactantius, Erasmus, Hooker and Tourneur are invoked to illuminate the adage. There are some questionable usages of words in the statements that Lear's Fool is 'a true innocent—a "natural"', that Lear at Dover is 'a real lunatic', and that 'worldly playgoers' of today find 'fast-paced, uncut performances of *Lear*' failing to offer a moving and significant experience.

Perhaps it is a similar disappointment with the nature of poetic drama which has led Thomas D. Borman[6] to write a colourful account of Desdemona's death in terms of lurid rather than learned journalism. She is seen as 'gaily anticipating a night of love rather than death', with the

---

[1] *Notes & Queries* (January 1960), pp. 16–17.
[2] 'The Trial Pattern of *King Lear*', *Shakespeare Quarterly*, X (1959), 389–95.
[3] *Review of English Studies*, X (1959), 178–81.
[4] '*King Lear*: a Study of Balanced and Shifting Sympathies', *Shakespeare Quarterly*, X (1959), 499–512.
[5] 'Shakespeare's "Folly": *King Lear*', *ibid.* pp. 523–9.
[6] 'Desdemona's Last Moments', *Philological Quarterly*, XXXIX (1960), 114–18.

wholly extraordinary claim that 'the predominance of textual evidence' indicates this. We are told that Desdemona's reply 'I will, my lord!' is 'uttered with joyful surprise' in answer to his instructions 'to be in bed alone'. Apart from the curious qualifying adjective, the real objection is that her reply is directly to his second instruction to dismiss the servants. The critical reading which follows is conducted in a spirit of bantering perversity, and the notion that Desdemona's 'fight for life in bed is an instance of Senecan horror that no director of our day has had the temerity to reproduce' is simply wrong: one has seen it often enough, and as recently as Margaret Johnston's performance at Stratford-upon-Avon in 1956, when it seemed, for a moment, that she might win. One can only endorse a recent comment by Paul Jorgensen[1] that some of our best Shakespearian criticism is to be found in reviews of performances, and regret that theatrical sensitivity so poorly, at times, informs 'scholarly' writing.

Othello has been freshly reconsidered by J. K. Walton.[2] Distinguishing two main trends in the criticism of this play, 'the view that Othello meets his doom on account of some weakness in himself; the other that he is not doomed through any fault of his own', Walton cautions against acceptance of Iago as the prime mover in the tragedy, 'This is to be found in the strength, rather than the weakness, of Othello and Desdemona' and Walton proceeds to show how this is 'brought out in a rich variety of ways throughout the play'. Generosity and modesty contribute to Desdemona's downfall, and it would be truer to say of Othello, it is argued, that 'he falls through modesty' rather than through pride. 'How decisive is Iago's victory?' asks Walton, and concludes that it is never complete, for 'In the scene where Desdemona is killed, the old Othello is already reappearing, brought to life by a sense of the solemnity of the deed he is to perform, which he sees as a sacrifice'. Of the last speech, and the difficulty it has proved in criticism, Walton observes that it must be understood as 'a part of the entire dramatic movement of the play', and concludes: 'Far from Othello's self-inflicted death and his speech leading up to it indicating a self-dramatizing attitude of mind, they are the result of a process of internal development central to his being. Like all tragic heroes, he is consumed by that which nourishes him.' The essay is a subtle and imaginative addition to criticism of this play, which has also prompted a lively and all too brief inquiry by Peter Alexander,[3] who observes that the collusion between Tolstoy and T. S. Eliot in their judgements of the final scene in *Othello* 'opens up most important critical questions'. Alexander asks 'what a man in Othello's position should have done to escape the charge of weakness or of adopting an *aesthetic* pose'. After a daring excursion into comparative studies with Calderón's *El médico de su honra*, and a neat use of Scott's *The Two Drovers*, we reach a further question, 'From what do Shakespeare's protagonists shrink at the end?'; not from their fate, is the answer, but from critical misjudgements such as those of Eliot on Hamlet dying 'fairly well pleased with himself': 'what Othello fears is not death but the name of having acted, as Dr Leavis and others have not hesitated to declare, from "an obtuse and brutal egotism"'. There are many large issues contained in the concluding comments upon the insistence of Tolstoy and Eliot in making 'an understanding of the moral sense of the dramatist the basis of their interpretation', and in the observation that 'the novelist and the poet as they

---

[1] *Shakespeare Quarterly*, X (1959), 116.

[2] '"Strength's Abundance": a view of *Othello*', *Review of English Studies*, XI (1960), 8–17.

[3] '"Under which king, Bezonian?"', contributed to *Elizabethan and Jacobean Studies presented to F. P. Wilson* (Oxford: Clarendon Press, 1959).

survey the dramatist's world come on what they pronounce to be "theatrical utility" rather than moral sense'.

Such problems of the relationship of art and morality are perhaps too easily assumed in Irving Ribner's[1] account of *Macbeth* as 'a closely knit, unified construction, every element of which is designed to support an intellectual statement, to which action, character, and poetry all contribute'. For Ribner 'The idea which governs the play is primarily explicit in the action of the central character, Macbeth himself; his role is cast into a symbolic pattern which is a reflection of Shakespeare's view of evil's operation in the world. The other characters serve dramatic functions designed to set off the particular intellectual problems implicit in the action of the central figure.' Feats of intellectual synthesis have their appropriate justification but they rarely generate much imaginative enthusiasm. William Blissett[2] is more content to make an exploration in depth of the ideas and images of blood, air, seed and time in *Macbeth*. He is sensitive to the need for 'the fullest possible response of a historically informed modern sensibility to the play in the theatre', speaks of his four analyses as 'digressions' and realizes that he risks 'losing altogether the sweep of the dramatic action'. But, in fact, this study clings close to the movement of the play, and such wide references as those to the four elements, or the analogy of the witches with the 'blood-begotten spirits' of Yeats' *Byzantium*, are relevantly used in the exposition of one dimension in the play's dramatic irony.

Attention to the tragedies[3] has been the predominant interest in this year's work, and must claim most space; criticism of the poems and histories has been infrequent, though not negligible.

A treatment by J. B. Leishman[4] of 'Variations on a Theme in Shakespeare's Sonnets' is a valuable addition to literature on the poetry: the theme is the high and resonant·one of Shakespeare's expression of Poetry as Immortalization, with comparisons of its handling by other poets from Pindar to Daniel, and the theme is matched with learning and eloquence. In an essay 'On *Venus and Adonis*' Don Cameron Allen[5] notes that we must read Shakespeare's poem 'for its difference from its predecessors to learn what it is about', and proceeds to do so with wit and scholarly assurance. Sam Hynes[6] comments on the siege of Troy as a metaphor used of Tarquin's soul (though the points he makes were anticipated by C. Devlin in *The Month*, September 1950). J. M. Davis and J. E. Grant[7] exchange some close criticism of Shakespeare's Sonnet 71, though the editors of a little magazine have decided on 'The necessity of rejecting a Shakespeare Sonnet'[8] for reasons of poetic exhaustion. The sonnet turns out to be 'The expense

---

[1] '*Macbeth*: the Pattern of Idea and Action', *Shakespeare Quarterly*, X (1959), 147–59.

[2] '"The Secret'st Man of Blood"', *ibid*. pp. 397–408.

[3] Here may be noted three items on *Romeo and Juliet*: I. Ribner's 'Then I Denie You Starres', in the Holzknecht memorial volume, pp. 269–86; H. McArthur's essay on Mercutio, 'Romeo's Loquacious Friend', *Shakespeare Quarterly*, X (1959), 35–44; and T. Culbert's 'A Note on *Romeo and Juliet*, I, iii, 89–90', *ibid*. pp. 129–32. C. C. Clarke has 'A Note on "To be or not to be"', *Essays in Criticism*, X (1960), 1823; H. W. Donner has commented on '"She Should Have Died Hereafter"', *English Studies*, XL (1959), 385–9; and R. F. Gleckner writes briefly on 'Eliot's "Hollow Men" and Shakespeare's *Julius Caesar*', *Modern Language Notes*, LXXV (1960), 26–8. Beatrice White has a note on 'Claudius and Fortune', *Anglia*, LXXXVII (1959).

[4] Contributed to F. P. Wilson's 70th Birthday tribute, cited above, pp. 112–49.   [5] *Ibid*. pp. 100–11.

[6] 'The Rape of Tarquin', *Shakespeare Quarterly*, X (1959), 451–3.

[7] *Texas Studies in Language and Literature*, I, 214–32.

[8] *The Fifties*, 3, 20–1.

of spirit in a waste of shame'. This is printed, none the less, in a pleasant short anthology edited by A. Guidi,[1] who selects pieces from Wyatt, Surrey, Sidney, Spenser, Shakespeare, Campion, Daniel, Drayton and Jonson. (The texts are in English, the scholarly introduction and notes in Italian.)

The few offerings of elucidation concerning Shakespeare's history plays include Michael Quinn's[2] full and well reasoned analysis of *Richard II*, and a valuable, if too brief, scrutiny of 'Providence in Shakespeare's Yorkist Plays'.[3] Quinn notes that 'The story of the Wars of the Roses, as Shakespeare found it in Hall and Holinshed, was already shaped into a rough demonstration of the truth of a general providence'. Shakespeare's conception of particular providence in these plays is 'nothing like so clear-cut and absolute as that of general providence', and irony results from this awareness of both kinds of providence. 'Irony is not tragedy', Quinn remarks in his conclusion, and a similar phrase 'history is not tragedy' is used by Anne M. McNamara[4] in attacking commentators who 'examine the Shakespearian history in the patently irrelevant terms of tragedy or of a strange hybrid genre that can only be designated as "history-comedy"'. In seeking to incorporate the unity of *Henry IV* in the person of the monarch, however, she seems rather unnecessarily scornful of other critics, who have not failed to notice the title of the play but have sought the unifying element in the dramatization of the theme of sovereignty rather than in the King. The common view that Shakespeare changed his mind during the composition of *Henry IV* is extended by S. Musgrove[5] in an enjoyable note seeking to determine the very moment when Shakespeare decided to let loose Pistol's histrionic armoury. G. K. Hunter[6] has made a short survey of critical approaches to the history plays, which concludes with a timely insistence on the need for an 'undogmatic subtlety of approach' required to hold together 'the multifarious perceptions of the English History Plays'.

The equally strongly felt need to find some acceptable frame of reference for the discussion of Shakespearian comedy has resulted in a book by C. L. Barber[7] which seeks to relate the dramatic form of some of the comedies to Elizabethan social custom. Here unity is sought for much Shakespearian comedy through an understanding of its dramatic development of festive elements in rustic and aristocratic entertainment. Difficulties arise, however, which have been suggested by the book's opening sentence, 'Much comedy is festive—all comedy, if the word festive is pressed far enough'. For though Barber is careful to stress that he is concerned only with certain comedies which are 'festive in a quite special way' this speciality is easily overlaid by the kind of merry generalities to which the spirit of misrule always beckons us. The unity sought for Shakespearian comedy largely eludes the present book, which is curiously uneven in construction. Preliminary chapters on saturnalia and English holiday games are followed by a lengthy rehearsal of the Talboys Dymoke episode of 1601 which might easily have been relegated to an appendix. Then come two of the best chapters in the work, on Nashe's *Summer's Last Will and Testament* as a prototype of festive comedy, and on the folly of wit and masquerade in *Love's*

---

[1] *Lirica Elisabettiana* (Collana di Letterature Moderne, Naples, 1960).
[2] *Studies in Philology*, LVI (1959), 169–86.   [3] *Shakespeare Quarterly*, X (1959), 45–52.
[4] Ibid. pp. 423–31.
[5] 'The Birth of Pistol', *Review of English Studies*, X (1959), 56–8.
[6] 'Shakespeare's Politics and the Rejection of Falstaff', *Critical Quarterly*, I (1959), 229–36.
[7] *Shakespeare's Festive Comedy* (Princeton University Press, 1959).

Labour's Lost. (It is strange to find *The Taming of the Shrew* ignored completely, since one of the maxims of this study is that a characteristic comic movement proceeds 'through release to clarification' and that this 'Release, in the idyllic comedies, is expressed by making the whole experience of the play like that of a revel': *The Shrew* may not be idyllic but it could be shown to work in the same fashion.) Barber notes how hard it is 'to avoid talking as though Shakespeare were a primitive who began with nothing but festival custom and invented a comedy to express it. Actually, of course, he started work with theatrical and literary resources already highly developed.' It is precisely when the author comes to deal with Shakespeare's own further development of festive elements in the mature comedies and in *Henry IV* that those other theatrical and literary resources need consideration; such a basic and traditional theatrical element as disguise itself is insufficiently treated, or literary modes such as the pastoral and masque which demand much more attention in the understanding of *As You Like It* as a festive comedy. Such criticisms of emphasis are complaints against the book's construction rather than against the nature of its approach, for if this has brought out the equal strength of the festive element, alongside the romantic and satiric, then the book will largely succeed in bringing some serious colour and carnival back into the criticism of Shakespeare's comedies. Meanwhile, considerable pleasure is to be derived from the very nature of the attractive and vivifying material with which the book deals.

The unfestive comedies have not gone unnoticed. S. Nagarajan[1] has made another effort to interpret 'The Structure of *All's Well That Ends Well*', and Walter N. King[2] thinks that in that play we find Shakespeare saying '"This is what life is, a mingled yarn. Women like Helena do fall in love with men like Bertram, though why I don't know"'. F. G. Schoff[3] has come to the incensed defence of Claudio and Bertram, protesting that 'We wreck Shakespeare's work if we fling mud at Claudio'. Shylock, on the other hand, has been further traduced: Dorothy C. Hockey[4] argues that the encounter between the two Gobbos burlesques the Jacob-Isaac deception and that since Shylock and Jacob were associated in Shakespeare's mind we can hardly take Shylock tragically; Ralph Nash[5] discovers that Shylock is beset by four of the Seven Deadly Sins and that three of them, Avarice, Envy and Wrath, could be symbolized for the Renaissance mind by the wolf. Opinions such as that 'Shylock no doubt strikes us as the Envious Man', whereas he is apparently 'the Malicious Man', reveal that emblematic concepts still appeal to the modern mind.

Comment on the early romantic comedies seems to have produced only an extended essay by Friedrich Knorr[6] on *The Two Gentlemen*, and a discursive, though well documented, survey of Shakespeare's dramatic interest in change and transformation throughout the comedies, attempted by Ernst Th. Sehrt.[7] A similar lecture by Wolfgang Clemen[8] on the related theme of appearance and reality is both a scholarly compilation (with extremely interesting annotation)

---

[1] *Essays in Criticism*, x (1960), 24–31.
[2] 'Shakespeare's "Mingled Yarn"', *Modern Language Quarterly*, XXI (1959), 33–44.
[3] *Shakespeare Quarterly*, x (1959), 11–23.   [4] *Ibid.* pp. 448–50.
[5] *Ibid.* pp. 125–8.
[6] *Shakespeares Die Beiden Veroneser* (Coburg: Rosenwirth, 1959).
[7] 'Wandlungen der Shakespeareschen Komödie', *Shakespeare Jahrbuch*, 95 (1959), 10–46.
[8] *Schein und Sein bei Shakespeare* (Munich: Bayerische Akademie der Wissenschaften, 1959).

and, for all its brevity, a piece of refined criticism; the images of reality and seeming from Bassanio's reflexions, through the musings of Viola or Sebastian, or the more urgent questionings of Hamlet, are set against each other with developing and multiple response most skilfully presented in the examination of *Lear*.

Shakespeare's late romances have, for once, drawn less attention than usual. Carol Gesner[1] discerns in Longus 'an ultimate influence on *The Tempest*', though the analogies of characters, storms and wedding festivities scarcely suggest that 'Shakespeare was familiar with Longus at first hand'; these are elements not only of stock pastoral, as she grants, but of life as it is lived, and the masque of *The Tempest* scarcely needs elucidation from the country wedding of Daphnis and Chloe. Augusto Guidi[2] has written an introductory book on the last plays, sensibly informed by recent critical opinions, and from Italy, too, has come a new translation of *The Tempest*,[3] with that evocative opening cry of 'Nostromo!'

Though little new published translation has appeared this year James Trainer[4] has gathered 'Some Unpublished Shakespeare Notes of Ludwig Tieck' which make interesting reading. Historically, too, the fortunes of Shakespeare in Georgia have been considerable, and two volumes by Nico Kiasashvili suggest both that these will be extended during coming years and that earlier Shakespearian activities in that country will be more fully documented. The first of these books is a biographical-critical study (Tbilissi, 1959) which surveys the dramatist's career and achievements; the other, *Georgian Shakespeariana* (Tbilissi, 1959), reproduces some previously published essays, and includes some new material. Kiasashvili himself writes on Falstaff, G. Gachechiladze on the democratic tendency in Shakespeare's works, and M. Matadze on some of his stylistic traits. The greater part of the volume, however, is devoted to studies relating to Georgian translations and productions, particularly valuable material being provided on the recent ballet version of *Othello*. Plans are being made for the preparation of later volumes in this welcome series.

Finally a work of general criticism must be noted[5] since it contains a chapter on 'William Shakespeare. Ironist'. Robert Boies Sharpe, holding that 'Drama is impersonation' and that irony involves the simultaneous 'perception of the two concepts *art* and *nature* as at the same time contradictory and harmonious, untrue and true', has been led to attempt a synthesis for Shakespeare's artistic career in terms of the development of a total irony. The chapter on Shakespeare can be recommended to all readers possessed of a similar faculty: it ends

Caliban is all flesh (or is it fish?) except a touch of wistful poetry like that we imagine into a dog's eyes, and lacks the bit of spirit to raise him to man's level from the beast's.

As Montaigne observed 'Men (saith an ancient Greeke sentence) are tormented by the opinions they have of things, and not by things themselves'.[6]

---

[1] '*The Tempest* as Pastoral Romance', *Shakespeare Quarterly*, x, 531–9.
[2] *L'Ultimo Shakespeare* (Padua, 1958).
[3] A. Obertello, *La Tempesta* (Biblioteca Moderna Mondadori, 1959).
[4] *Modern Language Review*, LIV (1959), 368–77.
[5] *Irony in the Drama* (Chapel Hill: University of North Carolina Press, 1959).
[6] Quoted by Clemen, *loc. cit.* p. 46.

2. SHAKESPEARE'S LIFE, TIMES AND STAGE

reviewed by W. MOELWYN MERCHANT

Leslie Hotson's latest work[1] persuasively—and in his usual provocative manner—condenses a mass of new scholarship; at the same time (though this is not his intention) it crystallizes much of our disquiet at the overwhelming preoccupation today with the 'open', 'platform', or 'arena' stage. After an unhappily 'tuppence coloured' opening ('Scandal Packs the Globe') we are given a cumulative argument on Shakespeare's 'theatre in the round' which turns upon the analysis of the earlier pageant theatre, the textual and pictorial evidence for the form of the Elizabethan theatre, and the analogies with the stage methods of private performances at court and in university halls and chapels. This suggests familiar ground but it is reinterpreted in revolutionary manner. The 'De Witt' drawing is read to demonstrate that the important 'Lords' room' (with the 'stage sitters' beneath) is located 'at the back of' the platform, producing a performance totally in the round; the 'tiring-house' is beneath the stage, to which there is access through traps; particular locations, 'discoveries', 'throne of state', 'righteous heaven and sinister hell', all are to be found in the permanent skeletal structures on either side of the platform, which may be of two shallow stories and curtained or uncurtained at need—an arrangement strikingly anticipated by Giotto in his Santa Croce fresco, 'The Ascension of St John' (Plate 114 in Berenson's *The Italian Painters of the Renaissance*, Phaidon Press, 1952). But though this latter device had a venerable and continuous history in painting, and resembles the impermanent booths assumed by G. F. Reynolds, permanent structures would appear to inconvenience a greater number of spectators than Hotson admits.

Furthermore, though there is brilliantly illuminating detail in examination of text, there are general objections which must here be confined to two matters. The sixth chapter, 'In the Round', describes the stage erected in the nave of King's College Chapel, Cambridge, in 1564; it is detailed and circumstantial but, for Hotson's general argument, it proves too much. For this is not theatre 'in the round' but 'on two sides', with delicate matters of production not covered by Hotson's treatment. In the second instance, the 'De Witt' drawing also perhaps proves too much, if it is to be accepted as a demonstration of an important focus of attention upon the audience in the place we have always tended to call the tiring-house. For the vivid little grouping of actors faces away from Hotson's main—or at least socially significant—audience. And so the argument could and will proceed on every matter of detail. Meanwhile it is high time that we agreed on a precise delimitation of the form or forms of the platform stage we are talking about. In the strong emotional pressures against the proscenium stage, the advocates of a Shakespearian orthodoxy against the eccentricities of the actor-managers appear torn between a platform stage backed by a façade strongly disputed in form, an arena theatre poised between academic plays and the baroque, theatre in the round, the half-round or on two sides. So strongly has theatre in the round now become an 'O.K. response', that the London *Times*, in addition to some dozen discussions of arena performances in this last year, headlined on 15 July the archaeological discovery that 'Romans Built A "Wooden O" at Chester', while even

---

[1] *Shakespeare's Wooden O* (Rupert Hart-Davis, 1959).

liturgical specialists now involve our church architects in similar patterns of 'participation'. This multifariousness is a reasonable indication that we are for the moment on safer ground, in default of precise definitions, in exploring limited areas of scholarship. *Shakespeare Survey*, 12 (1959) did exactly this, and it was salutary to have George R. Kernodle reopen the theoretical argument with the question, 'The Open Stage: Elizabethan or Existentialist?',[1] which begins with the warning that 'the Shakespearian stage was not a blank open platform, in which a lonely soul was spotlighted in an empty, insubstantial universe. We have not returned to the Shakespearian stage, but have invented a new form of stage. We use a new form of stage because we want to say something quite different.' Where the classical hero took a central place in 'a cosmos of dignity and order', the platform stage makes of him 'a modern existentialist character'. C. Walter Hodges[2] wittily traces the vagaries in the history of re-creating the Elizabethan theatre, concluding astringently: 'which, if any, of these expressions of taste has the right to claim the centre of the picture, it is still for the unstable judgment of Taste itself to decide.' W. F. Rothwell's question, 'Was There a Typical Elizabethan Stage?',[3] expects and receives the answer No, and his concluding paragraphs are a necessary statement of common-sense principles.

Richard Southern's essay[4] derives its greatest value from his unrivalled knowledge of building materials, methods and blueprints; even when a painting, a Breughel or an unascribed canvas at Drottningholm, is invoked, his conjectures are rarely unbacked by a builder's specification. Equally precise is Richard Hosley's 'Discovery-space in Shakespeare's Globe',[5] demonstrating that 'discoveries' were comparatively rare, involved few props and little movement within the discovery-space. Allardyce Nicoll[6] examines those scenes where the theatre yard was brought into dramatic service, commenting closely on the prepositions in the stage directions, 'on', 'about' and 'over' the stage. Nicoll's interpretations of these directions appear to exclude many of the assumptions of Hotson's skeletal side-structures. The title of J. L. Styan's article, 'The Actor at the Foot of the Platform'[7] assumes that Shakespeare's stage was precisely a platform and not a free-standing structure surrounded by spectators. His use of 'upstage' and 'downstage' begs the very question which Hotson answers in the opposite sense, for in Hotson's theatre all four edges of the stage are necessarily 'downstage'.

Turning to the private theatres, W. A. Armstrong[8] keeps strictly to the precision of his subtitle, 'facts and problems', though he may be considered venturesome by certain scholars in describing the 'obvious structural affinities' of private theatres with the 'open air theatres like the Globe' in having 'stage doors, inner stage, upper stage, and windows'. But this is a valuable addition to the pamphlet series of the Society for Theatre Research, particularly in the care with which it lists and describes the 'four scenic methods' used in the private theatres between 1575 and 1642.

[1] *Shakespeare Survey*, 12 (1959), 1–7.   [2] 'The Lantern of Taste', *ibid.* pp. 8–14.

[3] *Ibid.* pp. 15–21.

[4] 'On Reconstructing a Practicable Elizabethan Playhouse', *ibid.* pp. 22–34 (with figures and plates).

[5] *Ibid.* pp. 25–46.   [6] 'Passing over the Stage', *ibid.* pp. 47–55.

[7] *Ibid.* pp. 56–63.

[8] *The Elizabethan Private Theatres: Facts and Problems* (Society for Theatre Research Pamphlet Series: no. 6, 1957–58).

The audiences for the Elizabethan drama have received some attention. Martin Holmes brings to his study[1] the *expertise* of the professional historian and the enthusiasm of an amateur of letters. His book proceeds chronologically through the plays and the successive fortunes of the theatres and, while he appears to lay too much stress on the contrasting influence of the north- and south-bank sites of the theatres on the techniques of the plays, there are grateful insights into individual scenes and characters. King John, Shylock, and Bassanio are freshly seen in contemporary light; the excellent illustrations deepen conceptions of both stage business and character (the technique of changing rapiers from Saint-Didier's treatise on fencing focuses in a clear woodcut two closely descriptive pages of the duel between Hamlet and Laertes). W. A. Armstrong extends his examination of the private theatres into a more detailed consideration of their audiences,[2] proceeding on the assumption that 'they were mainly drawn from those parts of London adjacent to the theatres' and finding links in behaviour and attitudes between these audiences and those of the Restoration. J. H. P. Pafford[3] reconsiders the notes of one member of the Jacobean audience, Simon Forman's 'Bocke of Plaies' of 1611; he concludes (with the concurrence of Giles Dawson and Sir Walter Greg) that the notes are authentic.

In an important study of *The Tragic Actor*[4] Bertram Joseph extends his earlier arguments concerning the formal qualities of Elizabethan acting to cover the history of tragic acting in England from Burbage and Alleyn to Irving and Forbes-Robertson. The latter is the closing hero of what is for Joseph an essentially unhappy story of the decline into the 'prose drama of naturalism', for he 'was unique in his perfection'. In view of this judgement it is a pity that the book appeared too early to include an account of the recently discovered silent film of Forbes-Robertson's *Hamlet* (of 1913; closely described in *The Times*, 25 April 1960). Much graver is the poor reproduction of the plates and figures and their total lack of documentation, so that they are useless to anyone who is not already sufficiently in command of the material to make them unnecessary. But the text is full of detail which makes it essential reading in this subject. We are again indebted to the Society for Theatre Research for their annual volume for 1959,[5] which reprints in facsimile of very high quality Edmund Kean's text for his performance of Richard III. Alan S. Downer's editing is discreet and his introduction tersely interpretative of a text which Miss St Clare Byrne describes in her introduction as 'the most detailed account in existence of Edmund Kean's moves, business and rhetorical delivery and gesture'. With the excellent frontispieces, realization of the performance becomes a vivid possibility. Successive numbers of *Shakespeare Quarterly* provide studies of illuminating contrasts in acting styles and traditions, as Daniel Seltzer reconstructs with critical documentation 'Elizabethan Acting in *Othello*'[6] and L. F. McNamee describes with the aid of contemporary accounts 'The First Production of *Julius Caesar* on the German Stage'[7] in Dalberg's adaptation of Wieland's translation in 1785. Nearer the heart of things for us, Nugent Monck wrote one of his last reminiscences of his

[1] *Shakespeare's Public* (John Murray, 1960).
[2] 'The Audience of the Elizabethan Private Theatres', *Review of English Studies* (1959), X, 234–49.
[3] 'Simon Forman's "Bocke of Plaies"', *ibid.* pp. 289–91.
[4] (Routledge and Kegan Paul, 1959.)
[5] *Oxberry's 1822 Edition of 'King Richard III' with the Descriptive Notes Recording Edmund Kean's Performance* (Society for Theatre Research, 1959).
[6] *Shakespeare Quarterly*, X (1959), 201–10.
[7] *Ibid.* pp. 409–22.

method and ideals, for the Shakespeare Conference of 1957, an account of the genesis of the Maddermarket Theatre.[1]

This year again has been notable for important work on the music of the Elizabethan theatre, in particular the admirable volume of the music of the King's Men, collected and edited by John P. Cutts for the Centre National de la Recherche Scientifique.[2] Cutts' sensitive introduction includes detailed lists of performances, supplemented by analytical lists of the plays and settings, forming in all an index to the surviving music of the Jacobean players. The music itself (frequently including the lute tablature with its modern transcriptions) is laid out with clarity for performance; but the most valuable section to the Shakespearian may be the lengthy critical notes appended, which cover texts, manuscripts, editions and analysis of variants, with a full criticism of the form and temper of the works. Since this is only part of a larger work which examines the practice and the symbolic use of music by Shakespeare's company, it is greatly to be hoped that the remainder may also be published soon. J. H. P. Pafford examines in extended detail the 'Music, and the Songs in *The Winter's Tale*',[3] reprinting manuscript versions not included in Cutts, and giving a brief account of later music for the play. Richard Flatter reconsiders the complex question of 'Hecate, "The other Three Witches" and their Songs'[4] and Peter J. Seng examines the textual cruces and the 'needless critical speculation' concerning 'The Foresters' Song in *As You Like It*'.[5] Tommy Ruth Waldo and T. W. Herbert[6] argue from close analysis of musical terms, their use and frequency in *The Taming of the Shrew*, that 'their quantity and their degree of complexity in allusion appears to have some validity in discriminating the Shakespearian from the non-Shakespearian hand'. Fernand Corin contributes a 'Note on the Dirge in *Cymbeline*'[7] and John Russell Brown[8] qualifies P. J. Seng's note (*Notes and Queries*, pp. 203, 191–3) in which Seng rehearsed the arguments for believing that Portia influences Bassanio's choice of the casket in the 'Riddle Song'. Brown concludes that 'the song prevents a third recital of twicetold facts, dignifies and heightens the dramatic context...and prepares the audience for Bassanio's following speech in such a way that the sentiments are given a more immediate and wider application'. K. H. Ruppel's 'Shakespeare und die Oper'[9] will be considered in *Shakespeare Survey*, 15, in relation to Benjamin Britten's recent opera, *A Midsummer Night's Dream*.

Candidates for the 'true authorship' of Shakespeare's plays increase in number each year and we are grateful to Frank W. Wadsworth[10] for providing us with a digest of cases put forward on behalf of the claimants. 'Our revels now are ended', he declares in his last chapter, probably too hopefully, for he has traversed strange ways; of those who deny 'the poacher' authorship on account of humble birth, of those who plead on behalf of their own forebears (one of them would also include St Francis and Charlemagne among his kin) and of serious if febrile workers,

[1] 'The Maddermarket Theatre and the Playing of Shakespeare', *Shakespeare Survey*, 12 (1959), 71–5.
[2] *La Musique de Scène de la Troupe de Shakespeare: The King's Men sous le règne de Jaques Ier* (Paris, Centre National de la Recherche Scientifique, 1959): for detailed corrections, see *Music and Letters* (July 1960).
[3] *Shakespeare Quarterly*, x (1959), 161–76. [4] *Shakespeare Jahrbuch*, 95 (1959), 225–37.
[5] *Shakespeare Quarterly*, x (1959), 240–9. [6] *Ibid.* pp. 185–99.
[7] *English Studies*, xl (June 1959), 173–9.
[8] 'The Riddle Song in *The Merchant of Venice*', *Notes and Queries* (June 1959), p. 235.
[9] *Shakespeare Jahrbuch*, 95 (1959), 178–92.
[10] *The Poacher from Stratford* (University of California Press; London, Cambridge University Press, 1959).

such as Delia Bacon, whose life has been narrated by Vivian C. Hopkins.[1] This is a curiously moving account of the 'prodigal puritan' who numbered Emerson, Carlyle and Nathaniel Hawthorne among her friends; though tragic monomania informed her attack on the man from Stratford, her critical insights into the plays themselves were frequently remarkable for her day. Leaving this country of fantasy for the facts of Shakespeare's life, C. J. Sisson extends with precision and grace our knowledge of Shakespeare's friends in the environs of Stratford[2] in his examination of the evidence before a Chancery Commission at Stratford in 1584 and the subsequent very lively story of the suit in question.

There has been the usual crop of sources and analogues to consider, many of them illuminating, some rather Alexandrian in approach. A good general introduction is provided to these notes by Rudolf Stamm, in exploring 'Elizabethan Stage-practice and the Transmutation of Source Material by the Dramatists';[3] concentrating mainly on the Roman Plays and Plutarch, Stamm relates a 'play's physiognomy' to the quality and degree of source-mutation. In the same field but with less general intention, E. A. J. Honigmann[4] penetratingly follows Shakespeare's use of Plutarch, to conclude that he pored over and rearranged 'three major lives, drawing on others occasionally, and perhaps on Appian's *Civil Wars*, a feat impossible without infinite patience and skill and a tireless memory'. Kenneth Muir examines more immediate sources for *Coriolanus*[5] and shows Shakespeare's dependence on *Foure Paradoxes, or politique Discourses* by Thomas and Dudley Digges (1604), with their relation of war to internal dissension and the diseases of the commonwealth, putting the play in a wider context than the Midlands insurrection of 1607. Muir's examination of Shakespeare's indebtedness to compilations of commonplaces[6] leads him to the conclusion that the coalescence of source material in the plays was effective 'only because he had forgotten what he had read', an extension to Shakespearian sources of Lowes' methods with Coleridge. René Pruvost traces the mutual relationships between *The Two Gentlemen*, *Twelfth Night* and *Gl'Ingannati* and the work of Montemayor, Gonzaga, and Secchi, extending some suggestions by Miss H. A. Kaufmann in *Shakespeare Quarterly*, v, 271–80.[7] E. Schanzer considers Shakespeare's indebtedness to Heywood's *Ages*[8] and an earlier sententious tradition; John W. Shroeder usefully considers distinctions between sources and analogues and illuminates one aspect of the relation between *A Shrew* and *The Shrew* in relating them to Caxton's tale of Queen Vastis.[9]

G. Blakemore Evans[10] adds to his collection of 'the surprisingly large number of echoes of Nashe' which he printed in the *Supplement* to *1 Henry IV* in the New Variorum series. Robert J. Lordi[11] points out that Holinshed gives only a hint for Henry's speech at Harfleur but suggests

[1] *Prodigal Puritan: A Life of Delia Bacon* (Harvard University Press; London, Oxford University Press, 1959).

[2] 'Shakespeare's Friends: Hathaways and Burmans at Shottery', *Shakespeare Survey*, 12 (1959), 95–106.

[3] *Shakespeare Survey*, 12 (1959), 64–70.

[4] 'Shakespeare's Plutarch', *Shakespeare Quarterly*, x (1959), 25–33.

[5] 'The Background of *Coriolanus*', *ibid.* pp. 137–46.

[6] 'Shakespeare among the Commonplaces', *Review of English Studies*, x (August 1959), 283–9.

[7] 'The Two Gentlemen of Verona, Twelfth Night et Gl'Ingannati', *Études Anglaises*, XIII (janvier–mars 1960), 1–9.

[8] 'Heywood's *Ages* and Shakespeare', *Review of English Studies*, XI (February 1960), 18–28.

[9] 'A New Analogue and Possible Source for *The Taming of a Shrew*', *Shakespeare Quarterly*, x, 2 (1959), 251–5.

[10] 'Shakespeare's *1 Henry IV* and Nashe', *Notes & Queries* (July–August 1959), p. 250.

[11] 'A Source of Henry V's speech at Harfleur', *ibid.* (June 1959), pp. 219–20.

recollection of Richmond's speech before Bosworth. Two notes explore Chaucerian echoes in Shakespeare: R. K. Presson[1] finds reflexions of *The Parliament of Fowls* in *Love's Labour's Lost*, in the postponement of the marriage and in the roundel of the seasons. J. C. Maxwell[2] also finds *The Parliament of Fowls* to be at least the proximate source of the Queen Mab speech (*Romeo and Juliet*, I, iv), preferring it to the passage in Claudian frequently adduced as the immediate source and even finding it unnecessary to suppose any reference to Claudian in the passage. Joan Rees[3] examines the interdependence of Samuel Daniel's *Civil Wars* and *Letter from Octavia to Marcus Antonius* with Shakespeare's *Julius Caesar* and *Antony and Cleopatra*, demonstrating the extent to which Shakespeare 'deepens and subtilizes' a borrowed dramatic idea. Plutarch, this time in conjunction with Apuleius, provides an intriguing suggestion towards the interpretation of Cleopatra's centrality in the tragedy;[4] Michael Lloyd concludes: 'If we see Antony's tragedy as the centrepiece of the play, its structure is faulty. The fifth act falls, on the contrary, into place as the necessary final stage in the evolution of the play's values, if we see as its subject the statement of the divine humanity which is common to Isis and Cleopatra.'

After a rather daunting opening ('There is no dispute that Shakespeare was a well-read man') Sir Arthur Salusbury MacNalty proceeds to draw some interesting parallels between 'Shakespeare and Sir Thomas More'[5] and in the same volume of *Essays and Studies* Martin Holmes, in 'The Shadow of the Swan',[6] has a pleasant excursion with the young characters in the plays who have been over-subdued by Shakespeare's genius.

Going to Aquinas for definitions of 'appetite' and 'will', 'sense' and 'reason', S. Nagarajan[7] proposes the illuminating suggestion that 'self-deception as it manifests itself in love is the source of the comedy [in *Twelfth Night*] and that the title "What You Will" declares the "actual final cause" of the play'. By this reading of the play there is no room for a 'tragic' interpretation of Malvolio, who should rather be compared with Molière's single-trait characters. John M. Major points to the recurring theme of Dido's tragic love in Shakespeare[8] and suggests that Virgil's legend influences the tragedy of Desdemona. John M. Steadman examines a continuous dualism in renaissance Platonism as it was mediated by the writings of Ficino and as it emerges in Shakespeare's Sonnets and plays,[9] and in a substantial and very suggestive essay, 'The Machiavel and the Moor',[10] Laurence Lerner re-examines the relations within *Othello* as a crucial moment in the shift from moral abstractions to individuals as units of characterization. Finally, one of the subtlest treatments of source criticism is found in R. P. Miller's 'The Myth of Mar's Hot Minion in Venus and Adonis'.[11] Miller examines Shakespeare's creative departure from Ovid (*Met.* x) in his handling of the fable of Venus and Mars. By manipulating the assumptions traditionally

[1] 'The Conclusion of *Love's Labour's Lost*', *Notes & Queries* (January 1960), pp. 17–18.
[2] 'Chaucer in the Queen Mab Speech', *ibid.* (January 1960), p. 16.
[3] 'Shakespeare's Use of Daniel', *Modern Language Review*, LV (January 1960), 79–82.
[4] 'Cleopatra as Isis', *Shakespeare Survey*, 12 (1959), 88–94.
[5] *Essays and Studies* (1959) (John Murray; The English Association), pp. 36–57.
[6] *Ibid.* pp. 58–72.
[7] 'What You Will: A Suggestion', *Shakespeare Quarterly*, x (1959), 61–7.
[8] 'Desdemona and Dido', *ibid.* 123–5.
[9] '"Like two Spirits": Shakespeare and Ficino', *ibid.* x (1959), 244–6.
[10] *Essays in Criticism*, IX (October 1959), 339–60.
[11] *English Literary History*, XXVI (December 1959), 470–81.

associated in his day with the fable, Shakespeare 'reveals a special quality of "wit"'; while Shakespeare's own view of the fable is indicated 'by his exclusion of "Mars's hot minion" from the proper marriage celebrated by the epithalamium masque in *The Tempest*'.

A Midsummer Night's Dream has attracted more attention than usual and Miss K. M. Briggs' *The Anatomy of Puck*[1] constitutes a detailed background to these studies (an admirable and extensive bibliography extends the value of this book beyond Shakespeare to his contemporaries, of whom Jonson receives considerable treatment). Popular and learned beliefs are explored, the serious speculations and the meaner credulities, and there is an appendix of four long notes with original documentation; the dozen illustrations round off a work of the utmost value. The discussions of the supernatural in *Hamlet* and *Macbeth* take the material beyond the bounds of the fairy world as conventionally understood, and *The Dream* is very fully annotated. The ambiguous magic of Midsummer Night/St John's Eve is carried into the sphere of medicine in an article[2] which concentrates on the four attendant fairies, giving a fascinating explanation for the absence of a greeting from Bottom to the fourth fairy, Moth. 'If the abiding friendliness of this wood and the benevolence of the night are to be preserved, no mention must be made of the medicinal use of the moth', who had to be sacrificed before used. Robert R. Reed[3] questions the assumption that Bottom's ass-head is owed specifically to Scot's *Discoverie of Witchcraft* (1584) or even more generally to English superstitions about witch activities; he prefers the parallel episode of the ass's head in *The Damnable Life...of John Faustus* as the immediate source, since it is nearer *The Dream* in date (1592) and more congruous in tone with the 'casual want of ceremony' in Shakespeare's play and 'the joyous mood of the victim', Nick Bottom. To close this group Karl Hammerle examines German versions of the play and the Spenserian echoes in the English text.[4]

Jaroslav Pokorny's *Shakespeares Zeit und das Theater*[5] is a useful handbook, socially orientated, and fully illustrated both with plates and time-charts. After an economic and social introduction to the age and two sections on Shakespeare's theatre and life, the plays are considered in four groups: 'Die Frühzeit, Der Optimismus der Renaissance, Die Tragödie der Renaissance, Versöhnlicher Epilog'; the fresh acuteness of some of the individual judgements belies the apparent political prejudice in the scheme. René Pruvost answers the question, 'Robert Greene a-t-il accusé Shakespeare de plagiat?'[6] by giving a verdict of 'not proven', in response to Dover Wilson's reopening the question in *Shakespeare Survey*, 4, and in the New Cambridge *2 Henry VI*. David L. Stevenson conducts a brilliant examination of 'The Role of James I in Shakespeare's *Measure for Measure*',[7] arguing closely from the political works of the king to the personal qualities he showed in his rule, and this without neglecting wider matters of tone and contemporary belief. J. W. Lever considers[8] one of the less happy manifestations of James' make-

---

[1] (Routledge and Kegan Paul, 1959.)

[2] Lou A. Reynolds and P. Sawyer, 'Folk Medicine and the Four Fairies of *A Midsummer-Night's Dream*', *Shakespeare Quarterly*, X (1959), 513–22.

[3] 'Nick Bottom, Dr Faustus, and the Ass's Head', *Notes & Queries* (July–August 1959), pp. 252–4.

[4] 'Ein Muttermal des deutschen Pyramus und die Spenserechos in *A Midsummer-Night's Dream*', *Anglistische Studien* (Festschrift zum 70. Geburtstag von Professor Friedrich Wild. Wiener Beiträge LXVI, Wilhelm Braumüller, 1958).

[5] (Henschelverlag, Berlin, 1959.) [6] *Études Anglaises*, XII (July–September 1959), pp. 198–204.

[7] *English Literary History* (June 1959), 188–208.

[8] 'The Date of *Measure for Measure*', *Shakespeare Quarterly*, X (1959), 381–8.

up also treated by Stevenson, his dislike of crowds and resentment at invasions upon his privacy, to arrive at a dating of *Measure for Measure* (early in June 1604). Paul G. Brewster[1] compiles a useful handlist of Shakespearian references to games and sports but without relating them in a critical or expository manner to the plays themselves.

Largely owing to the specialized interest of *Shakespeare Jahrbuch*, 95, this year has seen an unusual number of studies of Shakespeare's influence upon later literary figures, movements and ages. Cardinal Frings considers his relevance to the wider matters of belief and doubt in our own day;[2] there are two studies, by Robert Fricker and E. Genast-Merian, of Shakespeare's influence upon English and French Romantic drama;[3] Ludwig Borinski explores sensibility and sentimentality in the successors of Shakespeare;[4] and questions of translation and adaptation are argued in an adversely critical symposium on Rothe.[5] Individual writers examined include Kleist,[6] Hofmannsthal[7] and Byron,[8] and elsewhere[9] Karl S. Guthke gives a valuable analysis of the history of Shakespearian influences on German literature in the eighteenth and early nineteenth century, by way of the criticism of Gerstenberg. D. B. Green finds an allusion to *The Two Gentlemen* in *Far from the Madding Crowd*.[10] Winfred Overholzer, from his wide experience as superintendent of St Elizabeth's Hospital, Washington (where Ezra Pound was confined for thirteen years), gives a lucid account of the beliefs concerning mental disorder among Shakespeare's contemporaries and a sober assessment of Shakespeare's apparent attitudes.[11] His account in modern technical terms of the theories of humours is invaluable, but there is no recognition, in the discussion of demonic possession, that exorcism is still considered a valid and valuable adjunct to psychiatric treatment.

The German artist Josef Hegenbarth makes our most considerable contribution to visual interpretation of Shakespeare[12] in his mordant illustrations of *The Taming of the Shrew*, *Richard III*, *A Midsummer Night's Dream*, *Macbeth* and *The Tempest*. In this folio, with the barest references to the text, Hegenbarth pursues the central thread of the plot in a temper which ranges between a tender cynicism (a dottily arrogant Bottom in a world of hapless fairies) and cruel simplification (Richard posturing to his shadow, Macbeth's vision of the sea of blood, Prospero's exercise of magic are all uncomfortably related in Hegenbarth's line). In a more classical manner Thomas Sommer[13] relates the art of Shakespeare and Caravaggio, parallel studies in *chiaroscuro*. Studies of this kind are valuable in setting up analogies between the arts but they need close critical control.

---

[1] *Games and Sports in Shakespeare* (F F Communications, Helsinki 1959).

[2] Josef Frings, 'Zweifel und Glaube: Shakespeare in unseren Zeit', *Shakespeare Jahrbuch*, 95, 7–9.

[3] 'Shakespeare und das Englische romantische Drama' and 'Der Einfluß Shakespeares auf das französische romantische Drama', *ibid*. pp. 63–81 and pp. 166–77.

[4] 'Der empfindsame Stil in englische Drama nach Shakespeare', *ibid*. pp. 47–62.

[5] Simons, Schröder, Heuer, Clemen, Schücking and Stamm, *ibid*. pp. 238–61.

[6] Max Luthi, 'Kleist und Shakespeare', *ibid*. pp. 133–42.

[7] Max Proske, 'Shakespeare und Hofmannsthal', *ibid*. pp. 143–65.

[8] G. Wilson Knight, 'Shakespeare and Byron's Plays', *ibid*. pp. 82–97.

[9] 'Gerstenberg und die Shakespearedeutung der deutschen Klassik und Romantik', *J.E.G.P.* LVIII (January 1959), 91–108.

[10] 'A Shakespeare Allusion in *Far From the Madding Crowd*', *Shakespeare Quarterly*, X (1959), 129.

[11] 'Shakespeare's Psychiatry—And After', *ibid*. X (1959), 335–52.

[12] *Zeichnungen zu fünf Shakespeare-Dramen* (Berlin, 1957; Köln, Hoffman, 1959).

[13] 'Licht und Finsternis: Studien zu Caravaggio und Shakespeare', *Shakespeare Jahrbuch*, 95 (1959), 193–215.

3. TEXTUAL STUDIES

reviewed by JAMES G. McMANAWAY

There has never been a time, even during the war against Walker by Tonson and the rest of the Proprietors, when Shakespeare was so frequently published or widely read. There would seem to be an edition to suit every purse and every taste. Yet never have editors been so self-critical. A sort of revolution began in 1921, with the statement of principles by the editors of the first volume of the New Cambridge Shakespeare. Sixteen years later, the first of the Penguin paperbacks came from press[1] with an easy text and minimal apparatus. Upon the completion of the last Penguin, the editor still bristles at the mention of 'scientific bibliography', which he seems to equate with the palaeographical attack upon textual problems. Meanwhile, many school texts continued to reprint the Globe text, with or without modification, and scholars began to debate the theory of editing. McKerrow's *Prolegomena* led to Greg's *Editorial Problem*, which was followed by essays and monographs on special problems. Peter Alexander's independent text was followed by C. J. Sisson's, and that in turn by John Munro's. The New Arden volumes, in which special editors are given wide leeway, have raised again the question of modernized punctuation and spelling and—by contrast with the new severely scholarly edition of Dekker— have confronted publishers and reviewers with the problem of what to give the serious reader. It is not without significance that in the land where variorum editions are supposed to be anathema, the New Arden retains many variorum features.

There can be no question of the need of more kinds of text than one. Some of the criteria of a critical old-spelling text were stated by F. T. Bowers in his lecture before the Bibliographical Society in 1958.[2] He gives special attention to the methods of the editor and to the typographical disposition of the apparatus. The general controversy becomes direct and pointed in contiguous essays by John Russell Brown and Arthur Brown,[3] which describe the relative merits of photographic facsimiles, type facsimiles, diplomatic reprints, old-spelling critical editions, and partly or wholly modernized texts, and also their shortcomings. How will editions of plays in manuscript differ from those of printed texts? What shall an editor do about obsolete spellings that lend flavour or occur in rhyme words or, worse yet, convey a double meaning that is partly lost in any modern form? What is wanted or needed in respect of the retention of original punctuation, capitals, type-variations, and layout? Are the answers of fifty years ago (such as, for example, were embodied in the rules of the Malone Society), valid today? Have new techniques of printing or copying changed the picture or given promise of a helpful change? There are no easy answers. Few of the editions of the Elizabethans now in progress or preparation are soundly planned or consistently executed. With every passing year it becomes more imperative that these

[1] See G. B. Harrison's 'An Epilogue' at the end of the concluding volume, *The Narrative Poems* (Harmondsworth, 1959).

[2] 'Principles and Practice in the Editing of Early Dramatic Texts', in *Textual and Literary Criticism* (Cambridge University Press, 1960), pp. 117–50, 171–86.

[3] John Russell Brown, 'The Rationale of Old-Spelling Editions of the Plays of Shakespeare and his Contemporaries', *Studies in Bibliography*, XIII (1960), 49–67. Arthur Brown, 'The Rationale of Old-Spelling Editions of the Plays of Shakespeare and his Contemporaries: A Rejoinder', *ibid.* pp. 69–76.

problems be solved, even at the cost of a break with tradition, so that the different segments of the reading public can find the kind of edition they need.

The New Shakespeare *Lear* has unusual interest, because it is G. I. Duthie's second independent edition of the play in the space of about ten years.[1] One needs only to read the sections devoted to the copy for Q1 and F and the relative authority of the two texts to realize how much more is known of such matters now than in 1949. It is significant that Duthie has abandoned his earlier hypothesis that Q1 is based on a communal act of memory by the King's Men while on tour without their prompt-book in favour of one that makes a surreptitious transcript of Shakespeare's foul papers the source of Q—a transcript, however, involving one or more persons who used dictation for at least a part of the transcript and whose familiarity with the text led them to contaminate it by their faulty recollections.

Another difference between the editions is that now Duthie takes into account the evidence produced—but not understood—by P. A. Daniel in 1885 that F, though a reprint of an edited copy of Q1, is also partly derived from Q2. Miss Doran gave additional proof of this in 1931, and five years ago A. S. Cairncross revived interest in the subject and listed the pages of Q2 which, after editing, seemed certainly to have served as printer's copy.[2] The suggestion by Cairncross that in Jaggard's shop a scribe collated a batch of pages of Q1 with the prompt-book and handed them to a compositor to use while he collated a second batch of pages that happened to belong to the second edition instead of the first, Duthie is very sceptical about—and quite properly so, for I cannot believe that the King's Men permitted their prompt-book to get into a printer's shop, and such a process as Cairncross describes would make it impossible to count copy as we know Jaggard did in the Folio. Duthie takes into account the discovery by Philip Williams that a long passage of F text from about III, iv, 129 to IV, vi, 247 (most of signature rr 3ᵛ to rr 6ᵛ) differs from the rest of the play in using roman type for certain proper names. Williams interpreted this as meaning that copy for this passage in F must be based on a manuscript, for Jaggard's compositor *B* (who had also set all the text of Q2 *Lear*) would hardly depart from his copy so consistently at this one place and then return to its conventions throughout the rest of the play.[3] Duthie recognizes the weight of the evidence and frankly admits that he cannot decide whether Jaggard used edited pages of Q1 and Q2 or manuscript copy or a mixture of the three.

His indecision might have been less had he not ignored the argument in 1957 by Charlton Hinman that the work on F *Lear* was shared by *B* with a hitherto unidentified compositor *E*. To this man, whose initial clumsy work on the Folio had restricted his role chiefly to setting from clean printed copy—such as *Titus Andronicus* Q3—are attributed eleven full pages of *Lear* and parts of others.[4] The distribution of work between *B* and *E* differs so radically from the

[1] G. I. Duthie and J. D. Wilson (eds.), *King Lear* (New Shakespeare. Cambridge University Press, 1960). Duthie is mainly responsible for the bibliographical and textual work.

[2] These are B4ʳˑᵛ, C1ᵛ, C2ᵛ, D4ʳˑᵛ, E1ᵛ–3ᵛ, E4ᵛ, F1ʳ–F2ᵛ, G1ʳ, I3ʳ, K1ʳ, K2ʳˑᵛ, K4ʳ, L1ᵛ, L2ᵛ. He allows for the possibility that there may have been others.

[3] We need not concern ourselves here with Williams' conjecture that in 1622 the badly worn prompt-book consisted of 'a conflation of "good" pages from Q1 supplemented by inserted manuscript leaves to replace corrupt passages of Q1' and that Jaggard was given a transcript of this conflated text. See *Shakespeare Quarterly*, IV (1953), 451–60.

[4] These are qq 2ᵛ, 3, 4ᵛ, 5ᵛ, 6, 6ᵛ; rr 1, 1ᵛ (part), 2, 3 (the greater part); ss 1ᵛ, 2, 2ᵛ.

pattern of *A* and *B* that Hinman inquires whether the copy for certain pages was too hard for *E*—
'or at least different enough to make advisable the anomalous exchanges that have been noticed'.
It is not a little interesting that the Folio pages (rr 3ᵛ–6ᵛ) Williams believed to have been derived
from manuscript are among those Hinman thinks might have been taken away from *E*, who
had proved incompetent to deal with manuscript, and given to *B*.

Belief that Shakespeare's foul sheets underlie Q1 gives that text higher authority than it has
been accorded by many editors. It may be expected that the next editor of the play will attempt
to continue the process of deciding what pages of Q1 or Q2 served, after editing, as copy for F
and what passages in F derive from manuscript, so that the collational pattern can be matched
with that of the compositors.

In the New Shakespeare *Cymbeline*, J. C. Maxwell carries the principal burden.[1] He accepts
Miss Alice Walker's account of the text, 'the actual copy was a scribe's transcript of difficult foul
papers which had preceded the prompt-book'. If this is meant to imply a scribal copy made
immediately after the composition of the play and intermediate in time between the foul sheets
and the prompt-book, I should be inclined to disagree, if only for the reason that no similar
manuscript is known to us. It appears more probable that it is an *ad hoc* transcript of the foul
papers made expressly to serve as printer's copy. And I suggest that the foul papers had been
worked over by the book-keeper at least to the extent of shortening and simplifying the stage
directions in the first part of the play. Maxwell rightly accepts as Shakespearian the vision in
v, iv, despite Dover Wilson's insistence that Shakespeare could not have written 'the jingling
twaddle of the apparition' (the phrase is quoted from Granville-Barker). But I do not understand why he perpetuates the lineation of F, when the capitalization shows clearly that the
compositor has lined the fourteeners as he did only because they were too long for his measure.

The Bibliographical Way[2] is an eloquent apologia for critical bibliography by F. T. Bowers,
who quite naturally draws many of his illustrations from the texts of Dekker's plays. Keeping
up with Shakespeare is now so strenuous an undertaking that there is danger of neglecting what
may be learned from the critical editions of his contemporaries. Bowers has found and solved a
number of bibliographical problems in Dekker that have no known counterparts in Shakespeare,
but it is foolhardy not to become familiar with the methods by which the problems were solved.
In describing that hazardous segment of the bibliographical way where certainty is impossible,
so that a choice has to be made between a plausible bibliographical explanation and an equally
plausible literary or historical explanation, Bowers has selected the famous 'clock' passage in
Richard III, IV, ii as an illustration. Some eighteen or twenty lines present in the quartos are
absent from the more authoritative Folio text. Editors have conjectured that they were omitted
out of respect to James I or fear of Buckingham. Bowers believes that compositor *A* failed to
include them because a miscalculation had occurred in counting the copy. In Qq 3 and 6, which
were used as printer's copy for F, the passage occurs at the foot of one page and the head of the
next. It could not have been overlooked by eye-skip or because of mutilation. In F, it should
come near the foot of the second column of page s 3ᵛ. This page was set by compositor *A*. The
following page, s 4, was set by *B*. Bowers assumes that *A* and *B* worked simultaneously on these
two pages of the inner forme of the inside sheet of quire s. He argues that as *A* neared the end

[1] J. C. Maxwell (ed.), *Cymbeline* (The New Shakespeare. Cambridge University Press, 1960).
[2] Fredson Bowers, *The Bibliographical Way* (Lawrence: The University of Kansas Libraries, 1959).

of the second column of s 3ᵛ he discovered he had more text than could be put on the page. His last line had to be 'The most arch deed of pittious massacre' (IV, iii, 2), because B had begun the following page with the next line, 'That euer yet this land was guilty of;'. A's only course was to omit a block of text, the 'clock' passage. This seems a plausible explanation, but is it necessarily the correct one? Reference to the Folio shows that there are at least a dozen white lines on the page that might have been used, and at least two places where a line might have been saved by combining short speeches. Setting three long lines with turnovers would have saved yet more space. There are other pages in F where rules are omitted from scene heading and long lines printed with turnovers.[1] Is it likely that A would have left out a long passage of text rather than remove a few leads and close up the lines of type so that the passage might be included?[2] He might even have asked B, whose type was still on the composing table, to remove a few leads from his columns and fit in an equal number of lines of text. Such minor adjustments should have been easy for two men working together on so large a book as F. The bibliographical probability in this case is no more impressive than the literary or historical.

A more extended and detailed apologia for biblio-textual study of Shakespeare is found in Bowers' *Textual and Literary Criticism*.[3] The first lecture states and illustrates the fact that editors, publishers, and critics have been shockingly indifferent to the purity of text of the poetry and fiction of the last two hundred and fifty years. Not even the foremost authors of this present decade can be trusted to recognize their own revisions in works that have gone through several editions (cf. the anecdote of T. S. Eliot, pp. 32–3).

The second lecture, an apparent digression from Elizabethan studies into American literature, demonstrates that the minute study of the physical characteristics of a group of manuscripts can give new information about the date of composition of certain poems in *Leaves of Grass* (1860) and at the same time enable critics to think Whitman's thoughts after him as his ideas ripened and his plans for the volume matured. It becomes possible to form a new estimate of the poet's method of composition and revision. The humble means to this great end consist in part of fitting together in their original patterns the slips of paper of various colours and textures that in their present form, as assembled by Whitman in the course of revision, are interspersed with scraps of galley proof and lines of manuscript—a glorified literary jigsaw puzzle. There is no such wealth of material for the direct study of the composition of *Hamlet* or the contemplation of how Shakespeare's mind worked. Instead, it is necessary to adopt Polonius' method of indirection and examine compositorial spellings and such vermiculate data.

The significance of the apparent digression is that the labours of the biblio-textual scholar are not to be treated with lofty disdain, as is the fashion in some circles. Chance, patience, perspicacity may at any time yield surprising results. The continuous effort to establish the text of

[1] Cf. *Tempest*, p. 1, column B; *Merry Wives*, p. 49, column B.

[2] It may be argued that A did indeed compress the lines of type so that he might squeeze in as much text as possible, for there are no rules above and below the stage direction '*Enter Tyrrel*' that begins Scene Three in modern texts. But there was never any intention of marking a new scene at this point in F. 'Scena Tertia' begins column 2 of page 54, which—to use Bowers' own time scheme—was set by compositor B long before A reached the bottom of his second column.

[3] (Cambridge University Press, 1959.) The Sandars Lectures in Bibliography for 1957–8 at Cambridge University and a paper read before the Bibliographical Society in 1958. See especially the preface and chapters, I, III, and IV. Chapter II treats of the textual problems of Whitman's *Leaves of Grass* (1860).

Shakespeare and make it readily available for every reader is of prime importance, if only for the reason that scholars should not view with indifference or complacence even a slight taint of illegitimacy in the poet's brain children.

In chapter III, Bowers enumerates the groups of variants that require scrutiny and, after naming and appraising the principal editions of Shakespeare now in circulation, illustrates how a modern editor attempts to discover the manner in which his text was transmitted and then to recover the author's words. Studies of this sort take time, for what seems valid for Shakespeare must be tested by similar studies of other playwrights. Of one thing we may be sure: the definitive text of Shakespeare will not be produced this year or next.

The advocates of textual-bibliographical studies are not without their critics. In reviewing Bowers' *Textual and Literary Criticism*, D. F. McKenzie comments at length[1] on 'the author's general assumptions' in the lecture on textual criticism of Shakespeare. The 'present achievement [of "the newer bibliography"]' is slight and painfully gained compared with its mooted possibilities'. Furthermore, 'its very bases appear to many, if not actually suspect, at least a little uncertain, at least in the present state of our knowledge'. 'It cannot', he continues, 'be too frequently stressed how difficult the task of isolating a compositor's work may be....Determination tests, moreover, have too often had indeterminate results: if Folio compositor *A* is now partly *C*, and Folio compositor *B* is like a twin brother to *E*, may the general reader not view with suspicion any compositor-determination study based on evidence less exhaustive than Dr Hinman's?' McKenzie's caution is not unprecedented. When Greg and Neidig discovered the truth about the falsely dated Shakespeare quartos of 1619, they were not given universal assent. And when McKerrow modestly offered his *Introduction to Bibliography* there were literary students who dismissed it lightly. Some of the initial hypotheses of Pollard and Greg have had to be abandoned, and even McKerrow has proved to be occasionally wrong. But what a new world of textual and literary studies there is today because of Pollard and Greg and McKerrow. Bibliographical studies are advancing today as the science of chemistry once did. The spade-work may be dull and painful—it is! For one success, there may be many partial and some total failures; for one Hinman, there may be a dozen journeyman bibliographers. But the movement is irresistible. 'Prate not of most or least, Painful or easy!' Not every bombarded atom yields the expected isotope.

If the spelling of an edition of Shakespeare is controversial, how much more so may be the punctuation. From an early date, compositors have exercised considerable independence in the pointing of texts. Commentators write of dramatic punctuation as opposed to other systems, but, for the very good reason that no dramatic manuscript before 1700 that served as printer's copy is in existence, we do not actually know what Shakespeare's habits of punctuation were or what changes compositors introduced. Using the indirect, Polonian approach, D. F. McKenzie examines the work of Jaggard's compositor *B*, who in 1619 set *The Merchant of Venice* from the first Quarto of 1600.[2] He tabulates and classifies the 3200-odd changes in punctuation made by *B* and finds it possible to generalize cautiously.[3] *B*'s 'general tendency was clearly to punctuate heavily', for the most part by the insertion of commas, particularly at the ends of lines. The

---

[1] *The Library*, 5th series, XIV (1959), 208–13.

[2] 'Shakespearian Punctuation—A New Beginning', *Review of English Studies*, X (1959), 361–70.

[3] Obviously McKenzie knows at first hand the drudgery of some kinds of bibliographical and textual study.

modern editor must take this fact into account. He will not be able to work confidently, how-ever, until similar studies have been made of other books from Jaggard's shop and especially those set by *B*. Nor may it be safely assumed that *B*'s habits were unchanging. Philip Williams observed several years ago that when *B* set Q2 *Lear* from Q1 he exhibited traits that are markedly different from those to be found in his work on *Lear* in the First Folio.

As if the textual problems of *Hamlet* were not sufficiently baffling, Harold Jenkins now attacks the verbal accuracy of F, one of the substantive texts, charging it with theatrical con-tamination.[1] Sixty-five times when Q2 and F differ in verbal detail, he is confident that the later text has been corrupted by the insertion of non-Shakespearian words. Most of these are repetitions that originated with the actors, though a few such as '*Ham. within.* Mother, mother, mother' in the Closet Scene clarify the obvious. Others are as banal as F's 'O, o, o, o', tacked on to Hamlet's dying words, 'The rest is silence'. These corruptions are charged to the actors, actors whose memories were faulty or who were willing to delay some necessary business of the play while they re-enacted an effective piece of stage business. Jenkins is sure that the corruption is not limited to the sixty-five readings he lists and discusses. Nor, indeed, is it found only in *Hamlet*. He cites examples in *Othello* and *Richard II*, as others have done; and the variants of Q1 *Richard III* lend weight to his arguments. There can be no doubt that actors seldom read their lines with perfect accuracy. Doubters should read the text while playing Shakespeare records *based on performance*. There are the same repetitions, insertions of interjections, and paraphrases that Jenkins writes about. Even the best editions retain far too many of these objectionable words, though they are known to be corruptions. They are more apt to purify the text in passages of blank verse than in speeches written in prose, possibly because metre renders the excrescences more conspicuous. Sometimes editors justify a suspected reading with half-hearted apologies; sometimes they retain one because of the power of tradition. Audiences accustomed to F's hypermetrical

> For *Hecuba.*
> What's *Hecuba* to him, or he to *Hecuba*?

would be as much put out by Q's

> For *Hecuba.*
> What's Hecuba to him, or he to her?

as they, and editors, are reluctant to accept Juliet's 'A rose by any other word [F: name] would smell as sweet'.

What Jenkins is asserting is that the F text of *Hamlet*, and of other plays too, is not as Shake-speare wrote it. Somehow, in the preparation of the prompt-book, or in the transcription (at sometime for some reason or other) of the prompt-book, many locutions invented by the actors have got into the text. He is well aware of the seriousness of his charge. As yet, he declines the opportunity to explain how or when the debasement occurred.

Whatever liberties the Elizabethan compositor took with the spelling of words in general, he appears to have recognized that poets often used clipped forms of words for metrical reasons and frequently adapted the spelling of words to produce visual rhymes. This is the thesis of

---

[1] 'Playhouse Interpolations in the Folio Text of *Hamlet*', *Studies in Bibliography*, XIII (1960), 31–47.

H. T. Price,[1] who shows that in setting the text of Harington's translation of *Orlando Furioso*, Richard Field's compositors[2] tended to impose their habitual spellings in the prose and also in the poetry, but were generally careful to follow the poet in the use of clipped forms where the metre required them and in the modification of spellings that produce visual rhymes. Price notes in passing that unusual word forms in the manuscript often survive in print, where normalization would be expected. This gives encouragement to the search for Shakespearian spellings in works printed from his manuscripts. In *Seneca his tenne tragedies* (1581), set partly from manuscript and partly from earlier editions, there is general respect for metrical spellings; this is true also of Spenser's *Faerie Queene* (1590) and *Colin Clouts Come home againe* (1595). So when Price finds metrical spellings in *Titus Andronicus* (1594), he is reasonably sure they originated in the manuscript copy. He warns against the expansion of metrical spellings in modern editions.

The authorship of *Henry VIII* continues to be debated. R. A. Law, a believer in joint authorship, enlarges his earlier argument that Fletcher uses his source material mechanically, with little attempt to characterize speakers and heavy reliance on rhetoric and spectacle, while Shakespeare reworks the sources boldly, adapting the dialogue so as to bring out the character of each speaker and produce strong dramatic effects.[3] Law also cites passages to illustrate Lamb's dictum that in his imagery Fletcher 'lays line upon line making up one after another, adding image to image so deliberately that we see where they join. Shakespeare mingles everything, embarrasses sentences and metaphors; before one has burst its shell, another is hatched and clamours for this disclosure.'[4] Law's chief contribution to the discussion of authorships is his observation that the scenes attributed to Fletcher are characterized by 'a trick of style [that] may be briefly defined as the ending of a feminine line with a verb followed by an unstressed pronoun. For example, "I knew him, and I know him; so I *leave him*".' In 1512 blank verse lines, the construction occurs 125 times or at the rate of 8·3 per cent. This compares with 9·4 per cent in the so-called Fletcherian portion of *The Two Noble Kinsmen* and an average of 10 per cent in *Bonduca*, *Valentinian*, and *The Wild-Goose Chase*. Shakespeare uses the construction occasionally in his later plays, but much less frequently. The average computed by Law for *Cymbeline*, *A Winter's Tale*, and *The Tempest* is approximately 3·3 per cent; for Shakespearian portions of *The Two Noble Kinsmen*, 2·5 per cent; and in *Henry VIII*, 2·8 per cent.[5] Evidence of this sort is hard to controvert.

Shakespeare's prologues and epilogues are the subject of an exploratory study[6] by Clifford

[1] 'Author, Compositor, and Metre: Copy-Spelling in *Titus Andronicus* and Other Elizabethan Printings', *Papers of the Bibliographical Society of America*, LIII (1959), 160–87.

[2] Price had no need to ascertain the number of compositors or tabulate their preferential spellings, because he found no evidence of difference among them in their attitude towards metrical spellings and rhyme words.

[3] 'The Double Authorship of *Henry VIII*', *Studies in Philology*, LVI (1959), 471–88. See also his 'Holinshed and Henry VIII', *Texas Studies in English*, XXVI (1957), 3–10.

[4] Charles Lamb, *Specimens of English Dramatic Poets* (London, 1854), p. 356. Law points out that Lamb was making a general observation about the styles of the two playwrights, not dealing directly with *Henry VIII*; he credits G. C. Macauley (*Cambridge History of English Literature* (1907–16), VI, 133) and Wolfgang Clemen (*The Development of Shakespeare's Imagery* (1951), pp. 77–8) with earlier citation of the passage.

[5] The statistics are based on modernized texts that Law identifies; unedited texts might yield slightly different results.

[6] 'Shakespeare's Prologues and Epilogues', in *Studies in Honor of T. W. Baldwin* (University of Illinois Press, 1958), pp. 150–64.

Leech. The conclusions, though necessarily tentative, are helpful in the interpretation of *2 Henry IV* and *Twelfth Night*, for example. *Troilus and Cressida* may be more truly understood in the light of its prologue and epilogue; but Leech fails to warn readers that the preservation of the prologue of this play is a bibliographical accident. In its absence, there would be firmer ground for a different attitude towards the play. And who knows how many other helpful prologues and epilogues may have failed of preservation, either because F reprints Q or because the editor of F was indifferent to such paraphernalia?

The identification of the quarto of *Richard III* that was collated with a playhouse manuscript to serve as copy for F is again put in doubt by F. T. Bowers,[1] whose study of the problem since reviewing J. K. Walton's monograph[2] convinces him that both Q3 and Q6 were used. He makes a nice bibliographical point about Q3, Q6 and F variants in IV, iv, 536 and predicts that the ultimate solution will be gained by a study of the accidentals rather than the substantive variants in the three editions.

The translation of a dramatic text from manuscript to type was often accompanied by faulty placing of stage directions and speech tags. One such error is pointed out by Harold Jenkins in *Hamlet* IV, v, 152–3.[3] The passage should be printed:

> *King.* Why now you speake
> . . . .
> As day dooes to your eye.
>   *A noyse within.*
> Let her come in.
>   *Laer.* How now, what noyse is that?
>   *Enter Ophelia.*

An even more common error in setting type is to misread secretarial *e* as *d*. Jenkins restores Shakespeare dramatically at *Hamlet* IV, vii, 58 by reviving Marshall's emendation (*A Study of Hamlet*, 1875), for surely the vengeful Laertes cries out, when he learns of Hamlet's return to Denmark:

> but let him come,
> It warms the very sickness in my hart
> That I shall liue and tell him to his teeth
> Thus diest thou. [*not* didst]

Although Laertes is thinking of a sword thrust that will finish off Hamlet as the Prince's sword had pierced Polonius, the literal error is confirmed by Q's version of the last line, 'That I shall liue to tell him, thus he dies'.

'The careful analyst will occasionally wish to identify the first formes in a book under investigation; often, perhaps, to check someone else's assumption that the inner forme was regularly printed first, or to verify a plausible interpretation of skeletons or press-figures.' So begins a modest note by Kenneth Povey.[4] If one or more unpressed copies be available, it is possible to

---

[1] 'The Copy for the Folio *Richard III*', *Shakespeare Quarterly*, X (1959), 541–4.

[2] Bowers' review of *The Copy for the Folio Text of Richard III* is in *Shakespeare Quarterly*, X (1959), 91–6.

[3] 'Two Readings in "Hamlet"', *Modern Language Review*, LIV (1959), 391–5. He cites IV, v, where a similar mistake occurs at Ophelia's first entrance. The Queen, as the person of highest rank, should command: 'Let her come in.'

[4] 'The Optical Identification of First Formes', *Studies in Bibliography*, XIII (1960), 189–90.

examine the pages under the illumination of a beam of light directed parallel to the surface of the paper and discern on the first formes small hillocks of ink produced by the indentation of perfecting types of the second formes. When the condition of a book permits, one may thus determine priority of formes, distinguish between concurrent and consecutive perfecting, and discover whether a printer used common imposition in half-sheets or worked two half-sheets together.[1]

Another exercise in methodology is found in the study of the compositors in the shop of Valentine Simmes, who set *Henry IV, Much Ado, The First Part of the Contention* (1600), and *The Shoemakers' Holiday* (1600).[2] One man, *A*, had strong preferences in the centring of stage directions, the use of roman and italic types, etc.; he is readily proved to have worked alone on *2 Henry IV* and *Much Ado* and to have set most of *The Contention*. In Dekker's play, he had some assistance, but not necessarily from *B*, who had helped with *The Contention*. The men handled punctuation with great independence, as may be observed in their treatment of the printed copy used for *The Contention*.

In a closely reasoned essay, Robert K. Turner, Jr., uses the patterned shortages of certain types to trace the progress of a play through the shop of Nicholas Okes, who in 1622 printed *Othello*.[3] Corroborative and supplementary evidence is supplied by the patterns of the running-titles and the preferential spellings of three compositors who set the type. The results are valuable for the play under scrutiny but have wider significance as an illustration of techniques.

Argument about the dying Falstaff's 'green fields' promises to continue until the disputants themselves have walked through the valley of the shadow. S. F. Johnson puts in the record[4] a misreading in the reverse direction that he has noted in Ford's *Love's Sacrifice* II, i. According to the 1633 Quarto, a man is invited to dinner 'To grace our talke with your grave discourse'. Since 1811, all editors have substituted *table* for *talke*, and so Johnson wishes to amend the Hostess's line to read, 'and a' talked of green fields'.

Equally persistent is the controversy about Hamlet's *solid* or *sallied* (=*sullied*) flesh. Samuel A. Weiss traces certain cluster images in *2 Henry IV, As You Like It, Troilus,* and *Hamlet,* and finds the idea of the melting of a solid in all four plays closely associated in the minds of disillusioned characters with disease, food, gardens, storms and fortune, clothing, beds, and books.[5] For him, line I, ii, 129 means that Hamlet wishes the end of his existence, but his too, too *solid* flesh will not melt.

An interesting emendation is introduced by John E. Hankins at III, ii, 49 of *Romeo and Juliet*.[6] For A2's 'Or those eyes shut, that makes thee answer I', he reads, 'Or those eyes' shot that makes the answer "I"'. His emendation accords with the imagery of the passage and with the Elizabethan theory of vision. The text of this edition is conservative, with all important

[1] Information is given for the construction of a home-made lamp, and an editorial note mentions the prospect of a commercial product.

[2] W. Craig Ferguson, 'The Compositors of *Henry IV, Part 2, Much Ado About Nothing, The Shoemakers' Holiday,* and *The First Part of the Contention*', *Studies in Bibliography*, XIII (1960), 19–30.

[3] 'The Printing of Beaumont and Fletcher's *The Maid's Tragedy* Q1 (1619)', *Studies in Bibliography*, XIII (1960), 199–220.

[4] '"A Table of Green Fields" Once More', *Shakespeare Quarterly*, X (1959), 450–1.

[5] '"Solid", "Sullied" and Mutability: A Study in Imagery', *Shakespeare Quarterly*, X (1959), 219–27.

[6] (Pelican Shakespeare. Baltimore, 1960.)

departures from Q2 listed. In his sensitive introduction, Hankins dates *Romeo* later than *A Midsummer Night's Dream* in defiance of the general belief that the Pyramus–Thisbe play is a gentle satire on the story of Romeo and his Juliet.

A list of London printers' apprentices, 1605–40, would seem to offer as little prospect of excitement as a page in a dictionary.[1] Is it being too imaginative to find in the entry of 11 April 1622 by which John Leason, son to John Leason of Hersley, Hants, yeoman, was bound to William Jaggard, the identity of the hypothetical prentice whose inexpert workmanship caused some of the textual problems in the First Folio?[2]

Two more titles have been added to the Folger General Reader's Shakespeare: *Julius Caesar* and *Romeo and Juliet*.[3] In the format usual in this series, the plays have conservative texts. By mischance, Q2 of *Romeo* is said to be derived from the playhouse copy rather than the author's foul sheets. Readings adopted from Q1 are given in a table at the end.

With the three parts of *Henry VI* in one volume and the narrative poems in another, G. B. Harrison brings to completion his Penguin Shakespeare.[4] He declines to commit himself on the relations between the F texts of *2* and *3 Henry VI* and *The First Part of the Contention* (1594) and *The True Tragedie* (1595). Then, using three speeches by Talbot in *Part One*, he points out the difficulty of attributing this whole play to one man and concludes that Shakespeare did not work alone. The paragraphs introducing *Venus* and *Lucrece* might profitably have been enriched by linking the poems to the classical epyllion and mentioning the characteristics of the genre.

[1] D. F. McKenzie, 'A List of Printers' Apprentices, 1605–1640', *Studies in Bibliography*, XIII (1960), 109–41.

[2] See C. K. Hinman, 'The Prentice Hand in the Tragedies of the Shakespeare First Folio: Compositor *E*', *Studies in Bibliography*, IX (1957), 3–20.

[3] Louis B. Wright and Virginia A. LaMar (eds.), *The Tragedy of Julius Caesar* (PL 66), (New York: Pocket Library, 1958); *The Tragedy of Romeo and Juliet* (W 121), (New York: Washington Square Press, 1959).

[4] G. B. Harrison (ed.), *Henry VI, Parts One to Three* (Harmondsworth: Penguin Books, 1959); *The Narrative Poems* (1959).

BOOKS RECEIVED

[Inclusion of a book in this list does not preclude its review in a subsequent volume.]

BENNET, J. U. (ed.) *Renaissance Studies in Honor of K. J. Holzknecht* (New York University Press, 1959).

EVANS, B. *Shakespeare's Comedies* (Oxford University Press, 1960).

GUIDI, A. *L'Ultimo Shakespeare* (Padua: Guidi di cultura contemporanea, 1958).

HARVEY, J. *Macbeth*: Notes on English Literature series (Oxford: Blackwell, 1960).

HOLMES, M. *Shakespeare's Public* (London: John Murray, 1960).

HOPKINS, V. C. *Prodigal Puritan: a life of Delia Bacon* (Harvard University Press: London, Oxford University Press, 1959).

HOTSON, L. *Shakespeare's Wooden O* (London: Rupert Hart-Davis, 1959).

KNIGHTS, L. C. *Some Shakespearean Themes* (London: Chatto and Windus, 1959).

KNORR, F. *Shakespeares Die Beiden Veroneser* (Coburg: Rosenwirth, 1959).

LAWLOR, J. *The Tragic Sense in Shakespeare* (London: Chatto and Windus, 1960).

MUIR, K. *Shakespeare as Collaborator* (London: Methuen, 1960).

ROSEN, W. *Shakespeare and the Craft of Tragedy* (Harvard University Press: London, Oxford University Press, 1960).

SEHRT, E. *Der dramatische Auftakt in der elisabethanischen Tragödie* (Göttingen: Vandenhoeck and Ruprecht, 1960).

SHAKESPEARE, WILLIAM
(The New Shakespeare)
 Coriolanus, edited by J. Dover Wilson (Cambridge University Press, 1960).
 Cymbeline, edited by J. Dover Wilson and J. C. Maxwell (Cambridge University Press, 1960).
 King Lear, edited by J. Dover Wilson and G. I. Duthie (Cambridge University Press, 1960).
(The Arden Shakespeare)
 The Poems, edited by F. T. Prince (London: Methuen, 1960).
(Pelican Shakespeare)
 Romeo and Juliet, edited by J. E. Hankins (Baltimore: Penguin Books, 1960).
(Yale Shakespeare)
 The Merchant of Venice, edited by A. D. Richardson III (Yale University Press: London, Oxford University Press, 1960).

SPENCER, T. J. B. *The Tyranny of Shakespeare* (British Academy Annual Shakespeare Lecture: London, Oxford University Press, 1960).

VYVYAN, J. *Shakespeare and the Rose of Love* (London: Chatto and Windus, 1960).

INDEX

INDEX

Bowers, Fredson (*cont.*)
  Principles of Bibliographical Description, 6
  (ed.) *Studies in Bibliography*, 6
  Textual and Literary Criticism, 6, 157; reviewed, 160–1
  The Bibliographical Way, reviewed, 159–60
  (ed.) *The Dramatic Works of Thomas Dekker*, 9
Brabander, Gerard den, 122
Bradbrook, M. C., 4
  Growth and Structure of Elizabethan Comedy, 3
  Themes and Conventions of Elizabethan Tragedy, 3, 55 n.
Bradley, A. C., 66, 67, 72, 73, 74
  Shakespearean Tragedy, 75 n.
Brandimarte, Anna, 121
Brewster, Paul G., 156
Briggs, K. M., *The Anatomy of Puck*, 24 n., reviewed, 155
Britten, Benjamin, 152
Brooke, Arthur, *Romeus and Juliet*, 44 n.
Brooke, C. F. Tucker, 8
  Life of Marlowe, 9
  (ed.) *The Shakespeare Apocrypha*, 7
Brooke, Rupert, *John Webster and the Elizabethan Drama*, 11
Broomfield, David, 127
Brown, Arthur, 157 and n.
Brown, J. R., 14 n., 152, 157 and n.
Buckingham, Duke of, *see* Villiers, George
Bullen, A. H., 13, 87
Bullough, G., (ed.) *Poems and Dramas of Fulke Greville*, 75
Bunim, Samuel, 120
Burbage, Richard, 76, 151
Burgersdyk, L. A. J., 117, 122
Burian, Orhan, 124
Burns, Robert, 77
Byrne, Muriel St Clare, 151
Byron, Lord George, 86, 156

Cairncross, A. S., 158
Calder-Marshall, Arthur, *Havelock Ellis*, 89 n.
Calderón, 144
Campbell, Douglas, 117
Campbell, L. B., 55 n.
Campbell, Mrs Patrick, 129, 137 n.
Campion, Edmund, 26
Campion, Thomas, 146
Canada, Report on Shakespeare in, 117
Canova, Mahin, 124
Caravaggio, 156
Carlyle, Thomas, 85, 153
  The Nibelungen Lied, 88 n.
Case, R. H., 8
Cass, Deborah, 117
Castiglione, Baldassare, 93
Caxton, 153
Cecil, Lord David, *Poets and Story-Tellers*, 11
Çelenk, Ali C., 124
Cellini, Benvenuto, 121

Chambers, Sir E. K., 7, 106
  The Elizabethan Stage, 1, 13
Chapman, George, 7, 8, 11, 12, 13, 31, 82, 87
  Homer, 80
Charlemagne, 152
Charlton, H. B., 8
Charney, M., 142
Chaucer, 97, 99, 100, 142, 154
Chelli, Maurice
  Etude sur la Collaboration de Massinger avec Fletcher et son Groupe, 12
  Le Drame de Massinger, 12
Cheney, David R., 141
Chetsingh, Rajan, 120
Chettle, Henry, 26, 97
  Kind-Heart's Dream, 26
  See also Mundy, Anthony
Chetwood, William Rufus, 81
Christensen, Pelle, 122
Chwalewik, Witold, 122
Cibber, Colley, 78
  Apology for the Life of Colley Cibber, 88 n.
Clark, A. M., *Thomas Heywood*, 12
Clarke, C. C., 145 n.
Claudel, Paul, *L'Echange*, 119
Claudian, 154
Clayton, Mr —, 114
Clemen, Wolfgang, 147–8
  The Development of Shakespeare's Imagery, 163 n.
Coleridge, Hartley, 87
Coleridge, Samuel, 79, 83, 84, 85, 153
  Table Talk, 88 n.
Collier, J. P., *Five Old Plays*, 83
Collinder, Björn, 123
Collins, William, 78
Condell, Henry, 90, 97
Congia, Vittorio, 121
Congreve, William, 78
Contention betwixt the two famous houses of Yorke and Lancaster, The First Part of, 165, 166
Copeau, Jacques, 119
Corin, Fernand, 152
Court, Mrs —, 112
Cowley, William, *Naufragium Joculare*, 61
Craig, Edward Gordon, 118
Craig, Hardin, 11, 94
Craik, T. W., *The Tudor Interlude*, 4
Creizenach, W., *The English Drama in the Age of Shake-speare*, 1
Croft, Michael, 126
Cromwell, O., *Thomas Heywood*, 12
Cruickshank, A. H., *Philip Massinger*, 12
Culbert, T., 145 n.
Cunliffe, J. W., *Early English Classical Tragedies*, 7
Cunningham, D., 11
Cunningham, F., 13, 87

INDEX

Harrison, G. B., 157 n., 166 and n.
Hart family, 112
Hatcher, O. L., *John Fletcher*, 12
Hathaway, Anne, 111, 112, 113
Hathway, Richard, *see* Mundy, Anthony
Hauser, Frank, 127
Hawkes, T., 141, 143
Hawkins, Thomas, *The Origin of the English Drama*, 81
Hawthorne, Nathaniel, 153
Hayter, Richard, 126
Hazlitt, W., 56, 64, 84
 Lectures on the Dramatic Literature of the Age of Elizabeth, 84
Heffner, R. L., Jr., 4
Hegenbarth, Josef, 156
Helsztyński, Stanisław, 122
Heminges, John, 90, 97
Henderson, T. F., 88 n.
Henley, W. E., 88 n.
Henrikson, Anders, 123
Henry IV, King of France, 102
Henslowe, Philip, 25, 31
 Diary, 5, 31
Hepton, Bernard, 126
Herbert, T. W., 152
Herford, C. H. and Simpson, P., (edd.) *The Works of Ben Jonson*, 8, 44 n.
Herrick, M. T., *Comic Theory in the Sixteenth Century*, 3
Hertford, Lord (of Ragley), 115
Heywood, John, *Play of Love*, 22
Heywood, Thomas, 12, 13, 56–65 passim, 153
 A Woman Killed with Kindness, 56, 57, 65
 The Captives, 56, 64
 The English Traveller, 56–65
 The Rape of Lucrece, 9
Higgins, Michael, 11
Hilpert, H., 123
Hinman, Charlton, 6, 158, 159, 161, 166 n.
Histriomastix, 28, 31, 33 n.
Hitchens, Mr (or Higgins), 110
Hjelm, Keve, 123
Hockey, Dorothy C., 143, 147
Hodges, C. W., 150
 The Globe Restored, 13
Hoffman, C., *The Man who was Shakespeare*, 10
Hofmannsthal, Hugo von, 156
Holaday, A., 9
Holinshed, Raphael, 33, 40, 153
Holmes, Martin, 154
 Shakespeare's Public reviewed, 151
Holzknecht, K. J., *Studies in the English Renaissance Drama in memory of K. J. Holzknecht* reviewed, 140, 141, 145
Honigmann, E. A. J., 153
Hooker, Richard, 143

Hopkins, Vivian C., *Prodigal Puritan: A life of Delia Bacon* reviewed, 153
Horsman, A. E., 14 n.
Hosley, Richard, 150
Hotson, L., 13, 33 n., 91
 The Assassination of Christopher Marlowe, 9
 The First Night of Twelfth Night, 13
 Shakespeare's Wooden O, 13; reviewed, 149–50
Hovenden, Valery, 127
Howard, Henry (Earl of Surrey), 146
Howe, P. P., 88 n.
Hoy, Cyrus, 6, 8, 12
Hrušínský, Rudolf, 118
Hugo, F. M. V., 123
Huizinga, Johan, 16
Hume, David, *History of Great Britain*, 80, 88 n.
Hungary, Report on Shakespeare in, 120
Hunt, Leigh, 83
 Imagination and Fancy, 88 n.
Hunter, G. K., 146
Hurd, Richard, 99
Hurry, Leslie, 130
Hynes, Sam, 145

Ilsever, Üner, 123
India, Report on Shakespeare in, 120
Ingram, J. H., *Christopher Marlowe and his Associates*, 9
Institucion of a Gentleman (1555), 90
Irving, Henry, 151
Irving, Washington, 111
Israel, Report on Shakespeare in, 120
Italy, Report on Shakespeare in, 121

Jack, Ian, 11
Jackson, Peter, 126
Jacquemont, Maurice, 119
Jacquot, J., *George Chapman*, 12
Jaggard, Isaac, 158 and n., 161, 162
Jaggard, William, 166
James I, King, 27, 80, 85, 155–6, 159
Jancsó, Adrienne, 120
Japan, Report on Shakespeare in, 121
Jarvis, William, 120
Jeffrey, Francis, 83
Jenkins, Harold, 162, 164
Jew, The, 32
Johnson, R. Brimley, (ed.) *Letters of Mary Russell Mitford*, 88 n.
Johnson, Samuel, 49, 55 n., 78, 80, 142
 Dictionary, 80
 Shakespeare, 55 n., 81
Johnson, S. F., 165
Johnston, Margaret, 144
Jones, Eric, 128
Jones-Davies, M. T., *Un Peintre de la Vie Londonienne: Thomas Dekker*, 12

173

INDEX

Jonson, Ben, 4, 8, 10, 14 n., 27, 29, 31, 44 n., 76, 77, 80, 81, 82, 84, 87, 90, 97, 101 n., 105, 146, 154
    Bartholomew Fair, 14 n.
    Chloridia, 11
    Epicoene, 79
    Masque of Gipsies, 8
    The Case is Altered, 33 n.
    Timber, 43
Jorgensen, Paul, 144
Joseph, B. L.
    Elizabethan Acting, 12
    The Tragic Actor reviewed, 151

Kállai, F., 120
Kamarás, Gy., 120
Karaali, Oguz, 124
Kaufmann, H. A., 153
Käutner, Helmuth, 120
Kean, Edmund, 151
Keats, John, 83
Kelway, Anne, 103
Kemp, Will, 76
Kennedy, C. W., 11
Kenter, Yildiz, 123
Kenya, Report on Shakespeare in, 121
Kernodle, George R., 150
Kéry, L., 120
Kiasashvili, Nico, 148
Killigrew, Thomas, 78
King Leir, 32
King, Walter N., 147
Kite, Mr —, 111
Klein, David, 13
Kleist, Heinrich von, 156
Knight, G. Wilson, 47, 138, 156 n.
    The Wheel of Fire, 55 n.
Knights, L. C.
    Drama and Society in the Age of Jonson, 2
    Some Shakespearean Themes reviewed, 138
Knorr, Friedrich, 147
Knowland, A. S., 141
Kocher, P. H., *Christopher Marlowe*, 10
Kolstad, Lasse, 122
Koźmian, Stanisław, 122
Kraus, Jaroslav, 118
Kraus, Karl, 116
Kreider, P. V., *Elizabethan Comic Character Conventions in the Comedies of George Chapman*, 11
Kubiak, Zygmunt, 122
Kuruç, Bozhurt, 124
Kyd, Thomas, 34, 89 n.
    The Spanish Tragedy, 8, 10, 50, 82, 105

Lactantius, 143
Lafforgue, René, 119
La Mar, Virginia A., 166 n.

Lamb, Charles, 57, 82, 83, 84, 163
    Extracts from the Garrick Plays, 84
    Letters, 88 n.
    Specimens of English Dramatic Poets, 82, 83, 163 n.
Lange, Bob de, 122
Langham, Michael, 117, 135, 136, 137
Laseur, Cees, 122
Laurie, John, 116
Law, R. A., 163 and n.
Lea, K. M., *Italian Popular Comedy*, 3
Leason, John, 166
Leason, John of Hersley, 166
Leavis, F. R., 144
    (ed.) *Determinations*, 11
Leech, Clifford, 8, 163–4
    John Ford and the Drama of his Time, 12
    John Webster, 11, 55 n.
Leishman, J. B., 145
Lerner, Laurence, 154
Lever, J. W., 155–6
Lever, K., 10
Levin, H.
    The Overreacher, 10
    The Question of Hamlet reviewed, 140
Leviush, Zalman, 121
Library
    British Museum, 81
Lloyd, Michael, 142, 154
Locrine, 10
Lodge, Thomas, 7, 23, 29
Lomax, Harry, 127
Longus, 148
Lordi, Robert J., 153
Lowes, J. L., 153
Lucas, E. V., 88 n.
Lucas, F. L., (ed.) *The Complete Works of John Webster*, 8, 65 n. 5
Lucy, Sir Thomas (and family), 112, 113
Lukács, M., 120
Lukavský, Radovan, 118
Luthi, Max, 156 n.
Lutz, Ton, 122
Lyly, John, 7, 15–24 passim, 82
    Campaspe, 17, 20, 21
    Endimion, 16, 20, 23, 24 n.
    Gallathea, 17, 18, 24, 24 n.
    Love's Metamorphosis, 18
    Sapho and Phao, 16, 18, 20, 21, 24 n.
    The Woman in the Moon, 18

McArthur, H., 145 n.
Macauley, G. C., 163 n.
McClure, Norman E., *The Letters and Epigrams of Sir John Harington*, 109 n.
McCullen, J. T., 10
McElwee, W. L., 127

INDEX

Nashe, Thomas, 28, 31, 146, 153
   Have with You to Saffron Walden, 33 n.
Nathan, Norman, 143
Navon, Arie, 121
Neidig, W. J., 161
Nelson, Ralph, 125
Németh, Antal, 120
Netherlands, Report on Shakespeare in, 121
Neville, John, 134
Nicoll, Allardyce, 150
   (ed.) *Shakespeare Survey I*, 1, 12, 13
   (ed.) *Works of Cyril Tourneur*, 8
Nógrádi, R., 120
Norton, Thomas, *see* Sackville, Thomas
Norway, Report on Shakespeare in, 122
Nowottny, Winifred M. T., 142

Obertello, A., 148 n.
O'Brien, Gordon W., 141
Okes, Nicholas, 165
Oliphant, E. H. C., *The Plays of Beaumont and Fletcher*, 12
Oliver, H. J., 142
   The Problem of John Ford, 12
Orange, Prince of, *see* William, Prince of Orange
Orbay, Ergin, 124
Ornest, Ota, 118
Ornstein, Robert, 141
Ost, Geoffrey, 126
O'Toole, Peter, 135, 136
Overholzer, Winfred, 156
Ovid, 92, 154
   Metamorphoses, 36, 91, 92
Oxford, Earl of, *see* Vere, Edward de
Ozawa, Bitaro, 121
Ozu, Jiro, 121

Pafford, J. H. P., 151, 152
Page, Anthony, 126
Painter, William, *The Palace of Pleasure*, 53
Palme, Ulf, 123
Palmer, J., *Ben Jonson*, 10
Paridon, Egbert van, 122
Parker, Mr —, 113
Parrott, T. M.
   (ed.) *The Comedies of George Chapman*, 8
   (ed.) *The Tragedies of George Chapman*, 8
   The Parrott Presentation Volume, 11
Partridge, E. B., *The Broken Compass*, 11
Pasqualigo, Luigi, 25, 28
   Il Fedele, 27
Paszkowski, Józef, 122
Patterson, F. A., 100 n.
Pattison, Mark, 98
Paul, St, 143
Peacham, Henry, 107
Pearce, T. M., 142

Pearson, John, 13
Pecci-Blunt, Anna Laetitia, 121
Peele, George, 7, 44 n., 82
Peraldus, Guillaume, 142
Percy, Bishop Thomas, *Reliques of Ancient English Poetry*, 81
Pérez, Antonio, 102, 108 n.
Perkinson, R. H., 11
Petit, Jacques, 102, 103, 104, 107, 108, 109 n.
Philip II, King, 102
Philips, Edward, 101 n.
Piachaud, R.-L., 123
Pindar, 145
Pitoëff, Georges, 119
Pleskot, Jaromir, 118
Plautus
   Mostellaria, 57–9, 61, 64
   Gunaikeion, 59, 64
Plummer, Christopher, 117
Plutarch, 33, 153, 154
Pokorny, Jaroslav, *Shakespeares Zeit und das Theater* reviewed, 155
Poland, Report on Shakespeare in, 122
Pollard, A. W., 7, 161
   Shakespeare's Fight with the Pirates, 5
   Shakespeare Folios and Quartos, 5
Pope, Alexander, 78, 80, 81
   Imitations of Horace, 88 n.
Porath, Orna, 121
Porter, Eric, 132
Porter, Henry, 23
   Two Angry Women of Abington, 88 n.
Pound, Ezra, 156
Povey, Kenneth, 164
Presson, R. K., 154
Price, H. T., 163
Prior, Camille, 127
Proske, Max, 156 n.
Pruvost, René, 153, 155
Prynne, Henry, *Histrio-mastix*, 98
Puttenham, George, 80

Quiney, Adrian, 114
Quiney, Judith, 113–14
Quinn, Michael, 146

Rain, Douglas, 117
Raksányi, G., 120
Raleigh, W., (ed.) *Johnson on Shakespeare*, 88 n.
Raleigh, Sir Walter, *History of the World*, 80
Randolph, Thomas, 13
Randone, Salvo, 121
Raysor, T. M., 88 n.
Ré, Michel de, 119
Reed, A. W., *Early Tudor Drama*, 2
Reed, Robert R., 155

INDEX

INDEX

INDEX

INDEX